Boatwords

Boatwords

OVER 1500 BOATING WORDS AND TERMS EXPLAINED

Denny Desoutter

WATERLINE

Published by Waterline Books
an imprint of Airlife Publishing Ltd
101 Longden Rd, Shrewsbury, England

ISBN 1 85310 299 7

A Sheerstrake production.

A CIP catalogue record of this book is
available from the British Library.

Introduction

When you take up a pastime you need to know the words.Not just the bald, scant definitions, but also something of the way people use them in real life.

Anyone may guess that a man who owns a yacht is a yachtsman, but you might not know that a yachtsman always talks about 'my boat', and never about my 'yacht'. And when you are buying a boat you should be able to cope with a salesman who talks about 'slack bilges', who assures you that 'she's certainly not been pinched', or that she has lovely 'buttock lines'.

On the other hand, a practical boating dictionary has no place for words which were useful enough for Drake or Nelson, but which refer to fittings, gear and techniques which are now things of the past. We need useful, real-life words. In times past the 'well' in a ship was a long wooden duct running from the deck right down to the bilges. If a modern owner has a well it is either a small cockpit or an open box through which an outboard can be shipped.

Some old words have gradually changed their meanings to fit new concepts, but there are also some new words. One has as much need nowadays to know about gel coats as about mast coats.

My aim has been to concoct a useful dictionary, but not a dull one, so I have allowed myself to break away from the cold, constrained manner of the professional lexicographer. In short, I have taken a rather personal approach and have followed few rules, other than to try and offer help with the uncertain language of boating - and perhaps a little pleasure too.

Denny D

Note

Abbreviations Some abbreviations have been included, but not those which are used on charts, since they belong with conventional signs and similar matter peculiar to hydrography.

Cross-reference To make cross-reference between entries comprehensive without being obtrusive, key words which are used in an entry which feature as entries in their own right are distinguished by an initial capital. (E.g. **Afterbody** The after part of the hull, in fact all that part which is Abaft {see Abaft} the midship Section {see Section}.) Nevertheless, it has not been thought conductive to easy reading to mark every word listed in the book in that way. Thus the absence of a capital initial is by no means an indication that the word itself is absent.

A

A As a single letter in the International Code of Signals the letter A means, '*I have a diver down; keep well clear at low speed*'. It is a signal which should be flown by any boat tending skin-divers, and one which should be heeded by all passing skippers. Like most other single-letter signals, this one may be made by light, sound or any other means. In speech the word to use is Alpha. In Morse code the letter A is ● —. A series of As is transmitted by a station to attract attention to the message which is to follow.

Aback A sail is aback when it is sheeted towards the windward side of the boat. A headsail is sheeted aback when a boat is Hove-to, so that the wind pressure on it counterbalances the forward pressure on the mainsail and the boat is brought nearly to rest. (See sketch under Heave-to.) A headsail may also be held aback in order to help blow the head of the boat round on to a fresh Tack. In a small boat, such as a dinghy or day-sailer, the mainsail can be pushed aback (or Backed) so that the wind pressures is on the forward surface of the sail and the boat is thrust sternward. (And see Aft and After.)

Abaft Behind. A position abaft the mast is behind the mast – nearer the stern. The opposite used to be afore, but many people would nowadays think Afore affected, and would prefer to say Forward of the mast, or Forward if that comes more naturally. In references to navigation lights, collisions and other important occasions the word is commonly used in the phrase 'Abaft the beam'. That defines the area from half-way along the vessel to right astern. It is as if looking over one's shoulder. The mid-point in this sector, on each side, is the vessel's Quarter, though it is common to refer to the whole sector as the quarter. Thus one may say, 'There's a ship coming up on our starboard quarter...' And if things continue to extremes, your lawyer may subsequently write, 'and she struck my client's vessel abaft the beam...'

Abeam A position at a right angle to the fore and aft line of the vessel, and not on the ship herself. A lighthouse, for example, comes abeam when it is at a right angle to the centre line of the boat. For navigational purposes the right angle is important – a landmark may seem to be abeam over quite a wide arc. To make sure, it is best to compare the compass bearing of the object with the heading of the boat.. Alternatively it may be possible to sight along some part of the boat herself (such as a bulkhead) in order to establish the correct line. (And see Athwart.)

About To go about is to Tack the vessel through the wind. That is, to turn a sailing boat towards the wind, till the wind is dead ahead and to continue until the wind is on her other side. That done, she is about. When it is to be done the preparatory command, 'Ready about' can be given so the crew (if any) knows what to expect. This is followed by 'Lee-oh' as the helm is put down to leeward to start turning the boat.

A-bracket A metal bracket which supports a propeller shaft beneath the hull, just ahead of the propeller. In form it is more like a V than an inverted A. A single-legged bracket doing the same job is called a P-bracket, and looks more like this **b.**

ABS The common name of the plastics material acrylo-butadene-styrene, which can be moulded without reinforcement to make small craft such as dinghies or canoes.

Accelerator An additive to polyester resin to speed its cure at normal temperature. Otherwise the resin could be cured by heating from an external source. Many resins are supplied with the accelerator ready-mixed, but if it is separate, care must be taken not to mix the accelerator and the Catalyst together as an explosive reaction may result. (Please see Polyester resin.)

Accommodation (s) The habitable part of a boat. But the accommodation ladder is not the ladder leading to it ! The Accommodation ladder is over the ship's side and brings you on board from a dinghy. (And see Companion way.)

Admiralty warrant The authority by which members of some British yacht clubs may fly the Blue Ensign instead of the Red. Permission is granted to an individual upon application, and the blue may be flown from his vessel only when he is aboard or in effective command. If you are interested in this sort of thing get full details from your club – though you may have to join another if yours is not one of the elect...

Adrift As in ordinary language, something that is drifting on the water, such as a boat whose mooring has broken. But also used of fixtures or fittings which have become unfixed or unfitted, as in 'The tiller's adrift' which is another way of saying 'It came to pieces in me 'and'.

Afore Forward of, ahead of (but only as between things on board the vessel). Seldom used.

After After what I said above need I say more?

Afterbody The after part of the hull, in fact all that part which lies Abaft the midship Section.

Aground When the boat is resting on the bottom in a place where she would otherwise be afloat. Resting on the grass in the boatyard she is Ashore and she would also be ashore if driven high up on the beach by the wind and tide to a position where should would not naturally be re-floated. When a boat is deliberately put aground she is Grounded. She may 'take the ground' regularly on a drying mooring, and in that case you would say 'She's aground', when her weight begins to be supported on the bottom, and 'She's dried out' when all the water has receded.

Ahead Ahead. (And the same may be said of up, down, afternoon, and supper time. Let's not bother any more with obvious words.)

Ahoy! Wotcher! (UK) Hi there! (USA)

Ahull Lying to the wind with no sail set. A heavy-weather tactic, adopted only when the wind is so strong that no canvas will stand and heaving-to becomes impracticable. (Or when all the canvas is blown to tatters anyway.) In severe gales or storms the Windage of the spars and rigging will press the boat over and steady her. She may lie broadside or, with helm lashed down, may sail 'Under bare poles' with the wind on her Quarter.

Airtank Just what it says – a hollow box or tank, made of wood, metal or other, containing nothing but air and completely watertight. Some lifeboats have a great many such tanks, carefully shaped so as to pack into any available space, providing a reserve of buoyancy. The use of many separate tanks means that even if the hull is holed only one or two local tanks might be damaged, with little loss of buoyancy.

Aldis lamp A signalling lamp. Its beam is very narrow and concentrated, and thus visible at a great range – so long as it is aimed correctly. The pencil-wide beam is aimed by a telescopic sight on the top of the lamp.

A-lee On the opposite side to that from which the wind is coming. The helm is a-lee when it is put down to Leeward. When put to Windward it is put Up because the heeling of the boat makes one side up, t'other down. A-lee is not often used, and though one might say, "That's Fred's boat a-lee, isn't it?, most people use 'To leeward' instead. (And leeward is pronounced loo-erd.)

All fours A vessel is moored all fours when she is held by four lines, two from the Bows and two from the Quarters, as she would be in a mud-berth, for example.

All standing With all sail set. To 'Gybe all standing' is to gybe without taking any precautions to relieve the shock – just slam-bang. To 'Turn in all standing' is to sleep in your clothes, perhaps before an early start, perhaps because you expect to be up and down during the night, or because you've forgotten your pyjamas.

Almanac An annual tabulation of astronomical information, especially as required for celestial navigation. There are a variety of almanacs for various purposes, ranging from *Old Moore's* to the *Air Almanac* which is intended for aeronautical navigation. For boat-owners and skippers *Reed's* or *The Silk Cut* are the primary references, though oddly enough most of us are less concerned with the almanacal information than with its other content. In fact both contain much more than the astronomical ephemera, since they are packed with advice on seamanship, first aid, radio communications, and so forth. They also list lights, buoys and other marks. I cannot mention all the content here, but I am of the opinion that every sea-going boat should have a copy of one on board. Even an out-of-date copy of either has much practical value. *Practical Boat Owner's* cruising almanac is simplified, inexpensive, and benefits from monthly up-dating in the magazine itself.

Aloft A position somewhere above the deck, and usually well above. In other words well up the mast or rigging. If you are aloft in a bosun's chair, those on deck are alow, but it would be something of an affectation to use the word nowadays; Below would be more customary, even though it has the specific meaning of below decks. Aloft is also an adverb, as in 'a good sailor always looks aloft'.

Alongside By the side of the ship, or by the side of a quay or dock. Your dinghy may be alongside your boat, or you may put your boat alongside a quay. When berthing next to another boat one normally asks 'May we come alongside?', if there is anybody to ask.

8

Alternating (light) A navigational beacon or mark whose light shows changing or alternating colours.

AMRINA Associate Member of the Royal Institute of Naval Architects.

Anchor Various types of anchor are shown overleaf. Weight for weight, the Bruce, the CQR and the Danforth have by far the best holding power. The principal anchor of a boat, dropped from the bows, is called the Bower anchor. The Kedge is a lighter, subsidiary anchor, used for a lunchtime stop or taken out in the dinghy to haul off when you have run aground. This is then called Kedging, or Kedging off.

Anchor buoy A buoy supporting the Anchor Tripping Line, see below.

Anchor Light An all-round white light which must be shown by any vessel lying at anchor between the hours of sunset and sunrise. Normally in the fore-part of the vessel, though you may show two such lights (Rule 30).

Anchor rode The anchor cable.

Anchor tripping line A line made fast to the Crown of the anchor, and supported in the water by a buoy at its upper end. The line may be used to unhook the anchor and pull it out head-first if it gets foul of a rock or an old mooring cable on the bottom. Many skippers think the cure is worse that the disease, involving the chance that the line will get foul of a passing boat's propeller – or even your own.

Anemometer An instrument for measuring wind-speed.

Angle of incidence The angle at which air flow meets a sail, or water flow meets a keel or rudder. The term is general to physics, and relates to the angle at which light falls on a mirror, or at which radio waves meet a radar reflector. In aerodynamics, the expression "angle of attack" is sometimes used with the same meaning, notably in the US of A.

Anode, Sacrificial Please see Galvanic corrosion.

Answer The response of a boat to her helm. "She doesn't answer' is the anguished cry of the helmsman whose rudder has dropped off or whose boat is aground.

Anchor types and parts

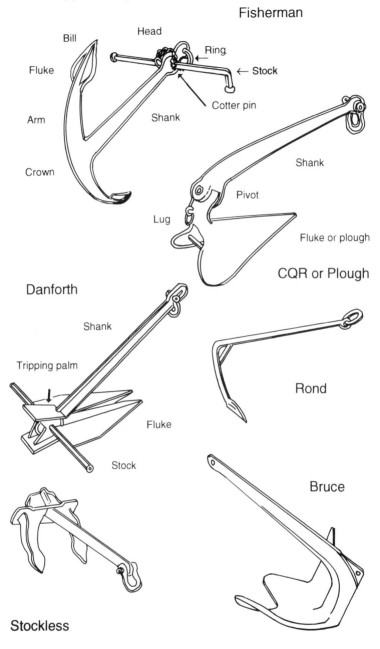

Fisherman

Bill
Head
Fluke
Ring
Arm
← Stock
Shank
Cotter pin
Crown
Shank

Pivot

Lug

Fluke or plough

Danforth

CQR or Plough

Shank

Tripping palm

Rond

Fluke

Stock

Bruce

Stockless

10

Anti-cyclone Please see Cyclone.

Anti-fouling net Used to prevent spinnaker foul-ups, it takes the form of a series of light ropes or tapes arranged in the form of an open network with very large mesh. It is hauled up the forestay and fills the gap between forestay and mast like a sort of skeletal staysail, and so prevents the spinnaker from passing behind the forestay. To appreciate the need for an anti-fouling net (or Lazy jacks) you really need to see the horrid sight of a spinnaker which has wound itself tightly round a forestay, defying all attempts to clear it or lower it.

Anti-fouling paint A paint for the under-water parts of a hull, formulated to prevent the growth of living organisms such as weed or barnacles. The paint contains poisons of various kinds – such as compounds of copper, tin, arsenic or the like – and these compounds leach out slowly to the surface. At the surface they should kill any microscopic young forms of life before they can gain a foothold. Fouling growths do not feed off the material of the hull, they merely use it for an anchorage, and if they are not killed before they hitch on, they quickly grow big enough to draw their nourishment from water well clear of the poison at the paint surface. Scrubbing will remove young growth and may release extra supplies of poison to hold new invaders at bay. For practical purposes it is important to know that there are two types of anti-fouling paint – those that must be immersed in water within a few hours of application (Soft), and those which may be applied and left for a matter of weeks before launching (Hard).

Apparent wind The wind direction and strength as measured from the boat herself. This is a compound of the natural, or True wind and the wind due to the boat's own movement over the face of the earth. The boat's movement is the sum of her movement through the water and the movement of the water over the bottom. In a flat calm, a boat moving forward with the tide or under engine has an apparent head-wind. If a natural beam wind then springs up it will appear to 'draw ahead' of its true direction by reason of the boat's self-made head-wind.

Appendage An underwater surface which protrudes from a hull. That's to say any sort of keel, rudder, or skeg.

Apron A timber in the form of a broad, thick plank which is fitted immediately abaft the stem to form landings for the plank ends. More recently it has come to be used for the raked forward face of a catamaran's bridge-deck. It is also a thing worn by the galley slave to keep splashes off her clothes, and by the leadsman when taking soundings by lead-line, which is very wet work.

AR Aspect ratio.

Archboard Please see Transom.

Arming Tallow or other stiff grease which is pressed into the saucer-like depression at the bottom of a sounding Lead. Its purpose is to pick up a sample of the bottom as an indication of position. The nature of the bottom is marked on charts with abbreviations such as, S sand, M mud, Sh shells, R rock, and Co coral (though most of us will be well off course if we come across the last-named). See Admiralty Chart 5011, now in booklet form, for full details of chart symbols and abbreviations.

Armstrong's patent Jocular term for a windlass or the like, whose power source is the strong arms of the crew.

Asleep A sail is asleep when it has no wind in it and, though set, is doing no work. It may be asleep as the boat goes about, in the interval between drawing on one tack and drawing on the next. This is a good moment to shorten the sheet, while there is no load to pull.

Aspect ratio The aspect ratio of a sail is its length in relation to its breadth, or its height in relation to its fore and aft dimension. A tall, narrow Bermudan sail has a high aspect ratio, a gaff sail has a low AR. A high-aspect-ratio sail shows greatest efficiency when on the wind (i.e. close-hauled) but a low-AR sail is better off the wind, when running free (as in the Trade Winds). The actual numerical value of AR is found by dividing the length of the luff by the mean chord – that's to say, the fore and aft dimension half-way up the triangle. If the latter dimension is not easily found, you may find it more convenient to square the luff length and divide by the sail area. The simplest answer of all is to divide the luff length by half the length of the foot of the sail – the result will be accurate enough for any ordinary purpose.

Astern A position somewhere aft of the boat. Motor cars reverse, but boats 'Go astern' under the power of their engines. When the engine is no longer actually pulling her astern and she is moving under her own momentum she is said to be 'Carrying stern way'. Likewise she would be 'Making stern way' if nudged backward by the wind. (Some people claim that a ship is 'under weigh' when moving ahead , but they don't use 'Weigh' when she's going astern. Draw your own conclusions.)

Astro Short for astro-navigation, which itself is short for Celestial navigation.

Athwart Across in ordinary language. Athwartships means across the boat herself, as opposed to fore and aft. Note that the seat running across a dinghy is called a Thwart.

Autopilot This is the word I myself prefer for automatic steering gear, because it is more compact and is already well established in aviation. Automatic steering gears take two principal forms, those which are wind-powered and those which are battery-powered. The wind-powered steer in relation to the wind direction, and therefore the boat's track changes when the wind shifts. Electric autopilots normally steer a compass course, which is preferable for nearly all purposes, but when a boat is under sail there is a drain on the batteries.

Aux. Auxiliary engine.

Aweigh An object is aweigh when it is hanging by a rope or chain. Normally the term is used only of the anchor, which becomes aweigh when it is hanging free, either ready to drop, or ready to lift because it has just broken out of the ground. Lifting a dinghy from the deck with tackle you could say 'Dinghy's aweigh' as soon as she is lifted clear, but the risk of confusion with 'away' is only too obvious. I don't think many people even say 'Anchor's aweigh' in real life: they are more likely to shout 'It's free', or something equally meaningful and understandable.

Azimuth The azimuth of a heavenly body is its bearing in relation to True North, as observed by you. The use of the word in this way is navigators' jargon, and as such is correct. The azimuth of the body concerned is properly speaking an arc extending from a point vertically above your head (the Zenith) and running down to cut the horizon – like a big slice through the celestial globe. The bearing is measured between True North and the point where the azimuth cuts the horizon, hence the abbreviation azimuth as used in everyday seamen's parlance.

B

B The single-letter signal means, 'I am taking in, or discharging or carrying dangerous goods'. The flag is a plain red swallow-tail and you will see it on vessels carrying petroleum or explosives. In the phonetic alphabet the word is Bravo. The Morse code is – ●●● , but note that while most single-letter signals may be made by any means, a long and three shorts on a ship's siren means she is being towed. You should hear it immediately after the long and two shorts (letter D) sounded by the vessel which is towing her.

B (abbr.) Beam (But on a chart it means Black.)

Back, to (1) The wind backs when it shifts anti-clockwise – for example, when it shifts from North to West. When it shifts clockwise it is said to Veer.

Back, to (2) A sail is backed by sheeting it to windward, or by pushing the boom up to windward when it is a boomed sail. (And see Aback.)

Back splice A back splice is used to finish the end of a rope so that the strands will not become unlaid. The strands are separated for a suitable length, formed into a Crown knot, and then tucked back into the rope against the Lay. (See sketch under Splice.)

Backstay A wire stay running back from the mast to the after end of the boat, and so preventing the mast from falling forward. Like Forestay, backstay's meaning is clear enough, but confusion can arise from the use of other words, such as preventer, or Runner. Preventer is not much used nowadays but at one time was quite often used for 'Preventer backstay', a stay brought into use to prevent topmasts of gaff-rigged vessels in particular from falling forward. 'Preventer' can also be properly applied to any rope or wire which is rigged to prevent something shifting. The word Runner is really a short form of Running backstay, by which is meant one which can be slackened or tautened as required. With Bermudan rig there is no need to slack off the backstay, but with gaff or gunter rig a standing stay would foul the gaff or yard as it swings across from one tack to the next. Thus the runners have to be set up on the windward side on each tack, and eased on the leeward side. That may be done with tackles, winches or with the Highfield lever.

Back water, to In rowing, to use the oars in reverse, so as to slow the boat or drive her astern.

Backwind, to A sail backwinds another sail when it turns the wind on to its leeward side. With the type of boat that most of us sail, it is the Staysail (or Jib if you prefer) which may backwind the mainsail when both are close-hauled. When it happens, the luff of the main goes floppy and fluttery as the wind coming off the staysail strikes it on the 'wrong' side.

Badge Bow badges are like cap badges, only bigger. Of carved wood, and handsomely painted (usually to represent the Burgee of the owner's yacht club), they are fitted one to each bow of his yacht's Tender instead of to his hat. Very fine they look too, and a very justifiable piece of one-upmanship. 'Quarter badges', on the other hand, are at the other end of the boat and are very rarely decorated. Even so they may be decorative, though their function is to protect the after end of the hull, especially the corners of the transom which tend to suffer in harbour manoeuvres.

Baffling Writers sometimes talk about baffling winds in harbour mouths and cliffy narrows. The term simply means unsteady and shifting. Just what you would expect in fact – I wonder why I mentioned it, but you have to fill a book somehow....

Baggywrinkle Sometimes called Bags o' wrinkle, are bunches of old rope yarns made up in the same sort of way that women make soft balls for infants from ends of wool. Baggywrinkle is lashed to shrouds or backstays to pad the mainsail at those points where the sail would chafe.

Bail Both noun and verb. Though most commonly used as a verb nowadays, the verb is derived from the noun which is the bucket or scoop with which bailing is done. Most people nowadays say Bailer when they mean the noun, though that might better have been reserved to the person who is doing it. Need I say that 'to bail' is to remove water from a boat with a Bail.Incidentally, and for those who are amused by such things, the French sailorman's word for a bucket is une baille. A small open boat and her bailer should be inseparable. Tie boat to bail with a suitable cord. (See also self-bailer)

Balance This is the quality of a boat under sail which relates to her tendency to sail a straight course unaided. Most sailing boats are unbalanced or out of balance at some time or other: that's to say, if the helm is left free the boat will no longer hold her course. Normally it is considered desirable for a sailing boat to be slightly out of balance, so that she is always trying to luff up towards the wind, but being restrained by the pressure of the helm (Weather helm). A well-balanced boat is one which requires only a small helm angle to keep her on course. That implies only a small tiller load too, but the two are not necessarily linked, since a Balanced rudder may require only slight muscular effort even at large angles. Much effort and argument have been expended in the search for hull forms which will show good balance, the problem being to design a shape which behaves well when heeled. A sailing boat's waterline plan is symmetrical when she is upright in the water, but when she sails she heels, and the waterline then becomes distorted, showing a bulge to the leeward side. Among the most famous, and many would say most successful, techniques for designing a balanced hull was Admiral Turner's Metacentric Shelf theory. But it is evident that the rig also has its influence on balance, as is evidenced by the situation of a boat running before the wind with mainsail squared out. That is a notably unbalanced condition, yet the hull is upright. Except when running under a spinnaker, the sail thrust of a modern yacht is always to leeward of the centreline of the hull. Closehauled and heeling to an angle of twenty degrees, the sail thrust is about as far off the centreline as it is when running with the mainsail squared off. Thus the designer's true task is to balance the aerodynamic and hydrodynamic forces against each other. The wind force also has a component, acting to leeward - in effect tending to drive the boat sideways - while the keel provides a resisting force in the opposite direction. These two can form a couple whose tendency is to turn the boat's head away from the wind - thus counteracting hull and sail forces which tend to turn her to windward. (Please see Centre of effort, and Metacentre.)

Balance lug A four-sided sail (illustrated), commonly used on small sailing dinghies, having a boom at the foot and a yard at the top. The 'balance' comes from the fact that the forward part of the sail (and its spars) projects ahead of the mast. The halyard is attached about one-third of the yard's length form its forward end, and the Downhaul or Tack is attached to the boom at about a quarter of its length. Sail and spars remain always on the same side of the mast. The yard is held close to the masthead by the halyard, but the boom may sag away more than seems desirable unless a Grommet or lashing is used to hold it in, though by tradition the boom is held only by the downward pull of the tack tackle. The balance lug has its devoted enthusiasts (I am one of them) because it is so handy. No jib is used with the sail, which is excellent for both running and beating - the sail area forward of the mast keeps the after end of the yard up to windward and virtually eliminates twist. For a working dinghy, whose rig must go up or down quickly, it is ideal, though the yard and boom may come down too quickly for comfort if you don't rig a double Topping lift or Lazy jacks to keep the gear above your head. (Please see Lugsail.)

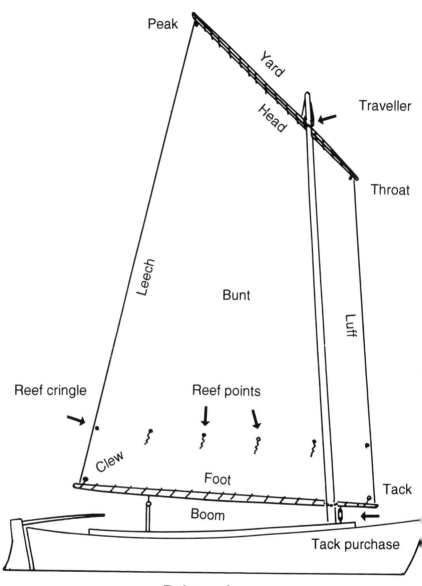

Peak

Yard

Traveller

Head

Throat

Leech

Bunt

Luff

Reef cringle

Reef points

Clew

Foot

Tack

Boom

Tack purchase

Balance lug

Balance reef. Only those with a gaff mainsail will find this reefing mode of any value. It reduces the four-sided sail to a three-sided one by means of a reef band, with points, extending from the throat of the gaff to the clew at the boom-end. Thus, when reefed in heavy weather, the whole of the lower, front corner of the sail is furled up, and the gaff may lie almost vertically against the mast, rather like a gunter yard.

Balanced rudder This is a rudder which has some of its area ahead of its pivotal axis; about fifteen per cent or one-sixth is very often satisfactory, and will usually achieve the purpose of taking a large part of the load off the tiller. This proportion is sufficient, since the centre of pressure of a rudder (like that of a sail) is about twenty to twenty-five per cent back from the leading edge, and it is desirable to have this centre aft of the pivot axis so that there is still some load in the tiller for the helmsman to feel.

Balanced rudder

Ballast Weight carried low in the vessel to aid stability. In most modern craft the ballast is integral with the boat, and consists of lead or iron bolted to the keel, or perhaps filling a hollow keel moulded in resinglass. Such a keel is known as the Ballast keel to distinguish it fromthe structural Keel. In the past, ballast was often of stones, and was simply laid in the bottom of the boat, and some modern craft still follow the same principle, which is appropriate to beamy boats of shallow draft.

But in less beamy boats the aim is to get the ballast as low as possible so as to maximise its effectiveness as a righting force. If the draught is fixed at some convenient limit, then the more dense the ballast material the lower it can be, and the less the weight that will be needed. That in turn is valuable, since a lighter boat may often be a faster boat. Lead, being very dense, makes excellent ballast, and has the advantage that it does not rust. Iron is not quite so dense, and thus not so good, concrete is even less dense, and although it is cheap and convenient it must be made heavier by embodying scrap iron in the mix. The result can be a good balance between effectiveness and economy. Water, because of its relatively low density, is of little value for ballast in sailing craft though, like any other heavy items, it should be stowed as low as possible in the boat. On the other hand water is useful as Trimming ballast in fast power boats because it can be collected or discarded with great ease. Tanks may, for example, be fitted in the bows of a power boat where they may be filled with water if she is running with the stem too high and her stern tucked down and dragging. Forward-facing scoops may be enough to fill such tanks.

Ballast ratio   The weight of a boat's ballast as a percentage of her design displacement. The figure provides a useful comparison between boats of the same hull form, but not where hull forms are different.

Balloon   A term applied to a light-weather sail which is cut full and rounded. At one time balloon jibs and balloon topsails were quite common, but nowadays the spinnaker is the real balloon sail, and the word balloon is dropped, since Spinnaker alone normally implies a balloon-shaped sail.

Bank (1)   By seamen and hydrographers, this word is used for a locality where the sea bottom is raised, so that the water is shallower than it is roundabout, yet still deep enough for navigation. The Grand Banks, south and east of Newfoundland, are one famous example. Nonetheless, skippers should be aware that some shoals which bear the name 'bank', do in fact dry at low water.

Bank (2)   Yes, everyone knows what the word means when a river bank is mentioned, but just in case, please allow me to remind you that the right bank of a river is the one on your right when going downstream. BUT the right bank of an estuary or sea creek, or channel is the one on your right when going in the direction of the flood stream. A good way to work up a thirst is to start an argument over the point at which the change-over takes effect. Just don't ask me...

Bar   A shallow region just outside the mouth of a river or creek, formed by silt deposited by the ebbing tide. The very last lap of a sea passage, the crossing of the harbour bar, may very often the most dangerous period of all. That is especially the case when the tide is ebbing and the wind is onshore - very rough and dangerous seas are then likely to form, and even break, on the bar.

Barber hauler A line, additional to the sheet, which is attached to the clew of a headsail. It is used to adjust the flatness or fullness of the sail by deflecting the sheet downward, outward or inward.

Bare boat charter Not so bare as it sounds. The term, originating from the western side of the Atlantic, means that the boat is offered for charter, fully equipped, but without crew or consumable stores.

Bare poles With no sail set. In storm winds a boat may run at two or three knots simply under the pressure of the wind upon her mast, rigging and superstructure.

Barnacles Shell-fish which attach themselves to the bottom of your boat in large numbers and cut your speed by a quarter. Usually they form hard, conical cup-shaped shells, glued firmly by their broad base to any solid under-water object. Another barnacle species, the goose-necked barnacle, has a long flexible stalk, one end of which is attached to your boat, while the other carries the shell. Neither kind harms the structure of the hull, but either creates a tremendous drag when present in large numbers - and they do seem very sociable. Apart from beaching and scraping or scrubbing them off, they are kept at bay by Anti-fouling paints which kill them while in their free-floating larval form, when they are of microscopic size.

Barograph A barometer which draws a continuous graph of the atmospheric pressure changes. A very valuable aid to forecasting, but don't despair if you can't afford one - read your barometer at regular intervals (at least four times a day) and plot the readings by hand. Use graph paper, or make up your own scale. The result will be very revealing.

Barrel Barricos apart, the word has significance on a modern small yacht, since it is the part of a winch or windlass around which you turn the rope. And few small craft are without some sort of winch these days.

← Barrel

Winch barrel

20

Barrico Now outmoded by the unromantic jerrycan. The word is Spanish and means a keg. No doubt our lads picked it up from the Dons in the days of Drake and his cullies, but they can't have been very nimble with their tongues, because in English the word is pronounced Breaker. Breakers in fact seem always to have been water-barricos, never wine or rum barricos. Anyway, it's useful bit of one-upmanship to talk about them nowadays, and you will be marked down as a real sea-dog if you keep your outboard petrol in a two-gallon barrico.

Batten A flexible strip of wood, metal or reinforced resin, which is used to stiffen a sail. The batten is slipped into a batten-pocket, and usually extends only a foot or two forward of the leech of the sail. But many catamarans, and a few monohulls, have fully battened sails which extend all the way from luff to leech. The Chinese lug is a sail which is assembled around full-length battens, often with separate panels of cloth laced between each pair of battens.

Bawley An English East-coast fishing boat now rarely to be found, though a few are preserved as yachts or as diesel-powered workboats. The bawley had modest draft, with a long straight keel, and was beamy with straight stem and raked transom. The deck was surrounded with bulwarks, and the tiller worked through the top of the transom. You, dear reader, are not likely to be offered a bawley nowadays, but many yacht designs have been inspired by the type, and you might be offered something in the bawley tradition. Maurice Griffiths developed many bawleyish yachts, and you could find out a bit more in his book *Dream Ships*.

Beacon A fixed navigational mark, sometimes as a warning of shallows, and sometimes as a reference-point of which you may take a bearing. In the latter case it would be called a Day-mark if unlit. Some beacons carry lights, but many are unlit, and they vary from simple bean-poles stuck in the mud (also known as Withies) to elaborate lattice girders of steel. A radio transmitter, whose purpose is to provide a fixed point on whose transmissions you can take a bearing, is called a Radio (or RDF) beacon.

Beam (1) A thwartships structural member which extends from sheer to sheer and holds the sides of the ship, either apart or together according to circumstances. Beams also support the decks, and may support the side-decks between sheer and cabin sides. A vessel On her beam ends is heeled to ninety degrees, with her beam ends at water level, and is thus in a bad state.

Beam (2) The mid-part of a vessel when used as a reference point. Before the beam means forward of the middle of the ship; Abaft the beam, the other end. On the beam indicates a position out to one side of the vessel (see Abeam) and a Beam wind is one which comes more or less broadside on. Nonetheless, Beam in

21

this sense is never an actual part of the boat herself.

Beam (3)   The maximum breadth of a boat - one of the principal dimensions in her specification.

Beamshelf   In a wooden hull, the ends of the deck-beams are support on a timbers which run the length of the hull on each side. These beamshelves are fitted inside the Frames or Timbers. Their function is purely structural, in no way like any ordinary domestic shelf, except that both may collect dust.

Bear, to   To lie in a certain direction from the observer. 'The harbour mouth bears due North, but it won't be safe to enter until it bears 350 degrees.'

Bear away (and bear up),   To bear away is to turn the vessel's head away from the wind, and that is done by bearing up on the helm. In other words the tiller is moved 'up' towards the windward side of the boat, that being normally the high side. So one bears up to bear away. The opposite manoeuvre, to luff up, is done by 'putting the helm down'. Language is not logical, and I have never heard anyone say 'bear down' as the opposite of 'bear up'. (See Up.)

Bear down, to   Yes, dear reader, one does say 'bear down', but it simply means to sail towards, is always followed by a preposition such as on or upon and has no relation to bearing up.

Bearing   The direction in which an object lies in relation to the observer, and normally stated in relation to the compass, as in the example given under Bear, above. It is important to remember that bearings are always stated from the position of the observer. If the arc of a shore light is given as between North and East the meaning is not that it shines to the North-east quarter, but just the reverse. It is visible to an observer looking anywhere in the arc between North and East. In other words the observer must be in the South-west quarter. In coastal pilotage, bearings are taken of fixed objects with a Bearing compass, normally held in the hand in small craft. Such a bearing yields a Position line leading from the object to the observer. Similarly, a bearing may be taken of a radio beacon with a suitable radio receiver, and a similar position line results.

Beat, to   To sail to windward close-hauled. Some writers have taken the view that to beat is the same as to tack to windward, namely to make a zig-zag track with the wind close-hauled first on one side and the on the other. I believe a beat may be entirely on one tack, and that successive beats on alternate tack are best described by the commonly-used term 'Turning to windward'. (And see Tack.)

Beaufort scale A scale of wind speeds devised by Admiral Sir Francis Beaufort, Hydrographer of the Navy, 1829-55. Although it is customary to talk of a wind of 'Force 4', meaning the Beaufort number, the scale is strictly one of wind speed, and not of wind force.

Becket Originally a short length of rope with an eye in one end, which was used to secure sails or spars. Later, merely the eye or small closed loop itself. Later still, and this is the sense in which we today use it, the eye in the tail of a block. Every block has an eye at its upper end, and that is normally called the Eye, but where there is an additional eye at the tail it is called a becket. (See Bight.)

Bee-block A wooden chock with one or two holes through which a rope is passed. Almost always the chocks fitted to the sides of the boom, at the after end, through which reefing pennants are passed in order to bring the cringle down to the right point when reefed. (Block with two holes looks like letter B, see...)

Before the wind Sailing with the wind astern, Running. Running free. With the wind free.

Belay To make fast a rope or chain to any fixed object, usually a cleat or a bollard. Halyards, mooring ropes, painters and so forth are belayed. The word is also nautical jargon for 'Kindly cease what you're doing'. Yachtsmen who want to give the right atmosphere may use it to correct a slip of the tongue. Instead of 'No I tell a lie', they may say 'Belay that, it was Force 9, not Force 7...'

Belaying pin A stout pin, perhaps better described as a short bar, arranged so that ropes can be belayed to it. Several such pins may be arranged side-by-side in a single timber which then becomes a Pin-rail, or more picturesquely a Fife-rail.

Bell buoy Sounds like a page in a hotel, but at sea is far less chirpy, though equally useful. Simply a navigational buoy with a bell which sounds as the buoy rocks to the seas, so that you can hear it even when fog obscures it. (Please also see Buoy)

Belly The fulness or bulgyness of a sail. Also used as a verb of a sail which swells out full and round, especially when you had wished that it would not so do.

Below In the cabin, and not on deck or in the cockpit. In a boat you don't ask gran to 'go inside' when it starts to rain, you tell her to 'get below '.

Bend, to Both verb and noun, but mainly verb. In ordinary language, to tie. A halyard is bent to a yard, a warp to an anchor, or one rope to another. Although Bend is also a noun as in Sheet-bend, it is not otherwise much used in place of the

23

ordinary knot. In fact, knots are generically known as Bends and Hitches, among which are the Reef knot, the Clove hitch, and of course the Fisherman's bend. Each knot must be called by its proper name, but in general conversation use Bend as the verb and Hitch as the noun. For example, 'Bend on the dinghy painter, old man, use any hitch you like'. (See Knots.)

Bendy rig   Many modern boats have masts which can be made to curve by adjustment of the rigging, and as the mast is bent so the form of the sails changes. For example, if the head of the mast bends aft, the middle must move forward, pulling the cloth of the mainsail with it. Thus the sail is flatter and more suitable for stronger wind that it was when the mast was straighter. A bendy rig is usually chosen by racing owners who want to squeeze the utmost speed from their craft: cruising owners rarely bother.

Beneaped   Aground and forced to remain so because tides are 'Taking off ', or moving away from Springs toward Neaps. Successive high waters are then lower and lower, until neaps itself when they begin to get higher again.

Bermudan rig   Or perhaps Bermudian. Some say it is as wrong to say Bermudan as it would be to say Canadan. Nonetheless, I believe that most people in Britain say Bermudan when they speak of sails, and the kind of sail they mean is a plain triangular mainsail, without gaff or yard. This is the norm for yachts nowadays. The luff of a Bermudan mainsail is held close to the mast, either by slides run-

Bermudan rig

ning in a track, or because the Luff rope itself runs in a groove formed in the after edge of the mast. Modern Bermudan sails tend to be tall and narrow (high Aspect ratio), and require tall masts, which in turn require sophisticated staying. So impressive was the array of wires that the rig when new was dubbed Marconi by allusion to wireless masts, and that term is still sometimes used. Jib-headed is an adjective defining the triangular mainsail, deriving from the time when mainsails normally had gaffs, and a mainsail in the form of a simple triangle (like a jib) was a novelty. The low aspect ratio triangular mainsail is also called the Leg o'mutton, by reason of its shape, but that is a term not much used nowadays. For completeness, this is an opportune moment to mention the Shoulder of mutton, which is very nearly triangular, but has a very short gaff. One is even less likely to come across this term in real life. The Bermudan mainsail features in the illustration for Rigs and for Sail.

Berth (1)   Effectively a shipboard bed, or place where you sleep. (And see Bunk.)

Berth (2)   A position among the crew of a boat. To find a berth aboard a boat is to become a member of her company, whether or not you actually get a sleeping berth.

Berth (3)   A space in dock or harbour which may be occupied by a vessel. Also as a verb - 'May we berth here?' or 'Please berth your boat alongside that barge.' A Mudberth is a hollow in the shore where a boat may lie for the winter.

Berthon boat   A folding dinghy invented by the Rev. E Berthon in 1851. The boat had longitudinal ribs in the form of arcs running from stem to stern, the uppermost pair forming the gunwales. The whole was covered in canvas, and the ribs were arranged to swing down to meet the keel, making a flat package corresponding to a longitudinal section of the developed hull. It is many years since I have seen one, but I live in hopes that they will be revived - with modern materials it would be easy to make a very effective collapsible dinghy after this fashion. (Actually, a 'modern' version has been on the market in France in recent years, but it's too heavy for my taste.)

Bight (1)   An open loop in a rope, wire or chain. Anything, such as a sail, which hangs in a deep U-shaped curve is forming a bight. And see following:

Bight (2)   A bay, and especially a deep U-shaped one.

Bilge   In boatbuilding and design, the bilge is the part of the hull where the bottom turns upward to form the side. On the other hand, in the use of boats the bilge (or Bilges) is the whole space in the bottom of the boat under the cabin and cockpit soles. It becomes the part between the two bilges as first defined above, and is the space where Bilge-water collects, to be pumped out by means of a Bilge-pump. In talking about the shape of a hull, the form of the bilges is very significant. A flat-bottomed boat with vertical sides, like a barge or narrow-boat, would be said to have extremely Hard bilges. 'Firm' would be another term, though ninety-degree bilges are of course rare. The sharper the turn of the bilge, the more acute the angle between bottom and side, the Firmer the bilge is said to be. If the angle is obtuse or shallow, then the bilge is said to be Slack or Soft. (See Chine.)

Bilge keel   A keel fitted near the bilge - that's to say not on the centreline of the hull, but outboard on the bottom. Small dinghies may have shallow bilge-keels (often with handholds in case of capsize) fitted actually at the bilges, but the bilge-keels of cruising boats are farther inboard. Naturally, bilge keels are fitted in pairs, one each side, and thanks to efforts of Maurice Griffiths, Robert Tucker and other designers they have become an accepted form of underwater surface and ballast for cruising yachts. For the same total underwater area as a single-keel they draw less water, and they allow the boat to stand upright when she takes the ground. They often help to minimise rolling, but other things being equal, a boat with two keels must be expected to be marginally slower than one with a single keel. Since the draft is less, the centre of gravity of the ballast masses in the two keels cannot be so low as that of a single keel, so the boat must either carry a greater mass of ballast or have more beam, or firmer sections. Theoretical arguments aside, a bilge-keel cruiser can meet all that an owner is likely to require in stability, weatherliness, manoevrability and so forth. The designer, on the other hand, must take care in providing for the attachment of heavy keels at parts of the hull where there would normally be no strong backbone. Some designers do not ballast the bilge-keels but maintain a shallow ballasted central keel, and use the bilge keels simply to provide underwater area. In such a case the structural problems are simplified, but there must be more underwater drag. (See Twin keels.)

Binnacle   A housing for the steering compass. Usually an upstanding wooden pedestal with the compass housed in the top, but may be less ambitious in the average family boat. (Was Bittacle in bygone times.)

Bitt, to   To make fast a warp, anchor cable, etc., to a cleat, samson post or other fitting on a boat - but not to a bollard ashore. Originally alluded to bitts but now used of cleats etc.

Bitter end   The inboard end of an anchor chain, so called because it must once have been attached to the Bitts, though nowadays it would be fastened to an eye-bolt in the chain locker. At least it should be, otherwise the chain may go out with a run and you may lose the lot. Many small boats carry only a modest amount of chain cable and may need to bend on a warp if anchoring in deep water. At such times it is desirable to be able to free the bitter end quickly.

Bitts Stout posts or vertical timbers, arranged in pairs, sometimes with a cross-bar, to which mooring ropes can be belayed. In past times the two posts located at the inboard end of the bowsprit. As well as serving as mooring bollards, Bitts are also cast in bronze and the like, and bolted to the deck as mooring bollards. Truth to tell, when it comes to these metal fittings I wouldn't know when to call them Bits and when to call them Bollards - but I don't suppose that anyone else is better off... (Bitts is the singular, but like scissors and trousers it takes a plural form in language.)

Black ball A common form of 'shape' as prescribed by the Collision Regulations. May be a hollow metal ball, an inflated plastic one, or two discs slotted so that they can be assembled at right angles. The colour is black, and the standard size is not less than sixty cm diameter (which is minuscule in ship terms), though craft of less than twenty metres length may show smaller balls. A single black ball is hoisted forward to indicate that a ship is at anchor. Two black balls in a vertical line show that she is 'not under command', and three in a vertical line show that she is aground. A black ball at the masthead and one at each yard-arm indicate that a vessel is minesweeping.

Black bands Bands painted on the masts and booms of racing boats to indicate the maximum extensions of the mainsail luff and foot. During a race, neither head, tack nor clew may be set beyond their black band, so no underhand advantage is to be had by stretching a sail beyond its prescribed area.

Blade The flattened or 'palm' end of an oar or paddle. The underwater area of a rudder.

Black bands

27

Blade jib   A high aspect ratio jib for heavy weather - usually made of aramid fibres and used on racing yachts.

Blanket, to   Not surprisingly, this means that something slows the wind as it approaches your boat. The 'something' can be a passing ship, a tall building, or the wicked skipper of a competing yacht who manages to place his boat upwind of yours. You then get his 'dirty wind'.

Blisters   Please see Boatpox.

Block   A pulley in landsman's language. The outer part of the block is the Shell, and the wheel that turns inside is the Sheave. A wooden block has a strop of wire or rope passing round the shell and lodging in a shallow groove called the Score. The strop has an eye at its upper end, and may have a second eye at the tail (or arse), which is then called a Becket. Wooden blocks may be metal-bound for extra strength. Modern shells are made of a variety of reinforced plastics, or simply of metal. The shell in such cases is often nothing more than a fairing over a load-bearing metal skeleton. The opening in the shell through which the rope runs is the Swallow or Throat, and the smaller opening at the tail-end is the Breech. In choosing a block it is important to get the right type of sheave for wire or fibre rope, since they differ.

Block and tackle   Please see Tackle.

Blue Peter   The code flag for letter P, consisting of a rectangular blue flag containing a white rectangle. (See P.)

Bmu   Bermudan.

Board, to   Well, obviously, to go aboard....

Board   As a noun it means a Tack or Leg when turning to windward. Going to windward involves successive boards, to port and starboard. When you are making a board, you are never on starboard or port board, nor on starboard or port beat. 'We beat to windward all the afternoon, making long boards on starboard tack, and short boards on port tack.'

Boat   Ah, here's a tricky one. I wish I could dodge it. Properly, a small open craft - yet the likes of you and me all own 'boats' even though they may be seventy-five feet long (not mine or yours) and with several cabins. Other people may properly call your boat a Yacht, but you would never talk about 'my yacht' because that would mark you down as bogus, perhaps even a bounder. Boats may be sailing dinghies, ten-ton cutters, twin-screw motor yachts, twelve-metres, and (in the

Navy) damn great submarines. Of course we don't own ships, yet in conversation it is quite conventional to use that word of boat. 'When I went down to my boat last week-end the whole ship was reeking of diesel oil ...' Or, of somebody's five-tonner, 'She's a trim little ship she is.' But we all know she's not really a ship.

Boat, to   Please see Ship, to.

Boathook   A long pole with a hook at the end which can be used for picking up a mooring buoy or booming out a jib. There is a similar device which has a spike at the end as well as the hook, and it's a pity that the police don't confiscate all such offensive weapons.

Boatnail   A square-section copper rivet which is driven through a slightly under-sized hole in timber parts, and clenched over a Rove.

Boatpox (Osmosis)   A disease of resinglass hulls taking the form of a rash of pinhead-sized blisters over the underwater surfaces. Each blister contains fluid, and will ultimately burst, taking away a little of the gel coat. As the gel coat provides protection for the underlying laminates of resin and glassfibre, the long-term results of the disease may be serious as well as unsightly. The pox results from a degree of permeability in the gel coat, so that water penetrates into microscopic voids beneath. Once there, the water takes into solution styrene and other left-overs from the polymerisation (curing) process. By the process known as osmosis, further water is then attracted to these pockets of solution, and the resulting pressure is sufficient to raise blisters, and ultimately to burst them. Even well-built boats may suffer from this trouble. As with human diseases, some succumb, others remain untouched. Unfortunately the treatment is expensive, involving scurfing (or shot-blasting) to remove the entire gel coat, and then re-coating with a two-part polyurethane.

Boatswain   Please see bosun.

Boat your oars, to   May I ask the reader to look at To Ship. There is a fine opportunity for confusion in the use of these two words, so they had better be considered together.

Bobstay   The stay which braces a Bowsprit down to the Cutwater, or some point low on the stem. A bobstay may be made of solid rod, of chain or of wire-rope. With chain or rope a tackle is sometimes fitted so that the stay can be slackened off when at anchor so as to obviate the stress and the grating sounds as the cable bears on the bobstay. But a strong chain stay covered with plastic piping is a simpler solution. The stays which brace the bowsprit laterally are called Bowsprit

Shrouds. If the word shrouds alone is mentioned then it will refer to mast shrouds unless the context very obviously relates to a bowsprit.

Bollard An iron post, usually waisted below the head, upstanding from the quayside, to which boats make fast their mooring cables. Or a similar, but smaller device on the boat.

Bolt rope A rope sewn along the edge of a sail to take the principal stress when the sail is hauled tight. If along the Foot of the sail it may be called the Foot-rope, if along the Luff, the Luff-rope. In dinghies and some of the smaller cruising boats the luff-rope of the mainsail engages with a groove formed in the after face of the mast, and so holds the sail in place.

Bone in her teeth The bone is the curl of white water under the stem of a boat making a good pace through the water. The expression is used of sailing boats only, and implies that she is seen to be making a fair speed.

Bonnet An extra piece of cloth laced to the foot of a sail to increase its area. Mostly used by square-riggers hurrying to get their freight home; only a few perceptive owners bother with them nowadays. When things get really desperate, a drabbler can be laced to the foot of a bonnet. The Watersail is somewhat similar, and is usually laced beneath the mainboom when running.

Boom Principally a spar at the foot of a sail to give control. Almost all mainsails have a boom nowadays, and a few staysails have them too. On a staysail the advantage is that you can go from tack to tack without having to adjust the sheet. Some foresails have something akin to a short boom, called a Club.

Boomkin Please see Bumkin

Boot top The part of the hull along the waterline. Boot topping is the band of paint often applied along this line. Usually just a few inches deep, it separates the bottom paint from the Topsides.

Bosun Properly boatswain (swain meaning a servant or attendant) but pronounced bosun and now commonly so written. We don;t have bosuns, but we may have stowage space which we choose to call the Bosun's locker. In it will be stored rope, shackles, blocks and similar rigging components.

Bosun's chair A crude seat, fitted with slings so that it may be shackled to a halyard to take a man aloft.

Bottle screw Please see Rigging screw.

Bottom boards Boards fitted in the bottom of a dinghy with the dual aim of spreading the load fairly over the frames, and of keeping your shoes out of any accumulated bilge water. (See Grating.)

Boundary layer Please see Drag.

Bow (Rhymes with cow.) A boat has a bow on each side, and the whole forepart from the point where the sides begin to curve in towards the stem is nowadays known as the Bows. An object sighted 'On the bow' lies away from the ship and in the arc from dead ahead to forty-five degrees aft on either side (forty-five degrees is the same as four Points). All manner of combinations arise with Bow, such as Bow-rope, Bowsprit, and so forth which are self-explanatory. But the knot called a Bowline is not to be confused with a Bow-line, or a line leading from the bow. The knot is pronounced bo-lin, so there is no problem in speech, though there is often a problem about pronunciation of Bowsprit, for which the Oxford English Dictionary prefers 'bo'. Though I have not bothered with many etymological explanations in this book, its purpose being other, it is perhaps worth remarking that the OED gives the origin of the nautical word bow as deriving from words meaning shoulder. If the stem of the vessel is conceived as the head (and in the past, stems were embellished with heads and figureheads), then it is obvious that the shoulders are a little farther aft. And before we finally get shot of this matter, I myself find it interesting that the bough of a tree also derives from those ancient words meaning shoulder, a tree's shoulders being where its arms emerge. Three types of bow are illustrated overleaf.

Bower (anchor) The bower anchor is the boat's principal anchor, kept at and lowered from the bows. The secondary anchor is the Kedge, which is lighter, and may be stowed aft whence it can be taken off in the dinghy, dropped over the stern, or used as may be desirable. On larger vessels two bower anchors may be carried, in which case they may be known as the Best and the Small, though in a yacht it is more likely that they would both be of the same weight.

Bowline Pronounced bo-lin, it is the knot for making an eye or a loop in a rope's end. It is one of the very few knots which a boat-owner needs to know and is illustrated here. The merit of the bowline is that it is easy to make and easy to un-make; it does not jam. A Bowline on the bight is the same knot formed in a doubled end of the rope (bight), and thus forms two closed loops. A bowline reduces the strength of the rope by about forty per cent.

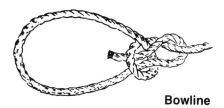

Bowline

31

Bows

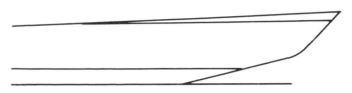

Spoon

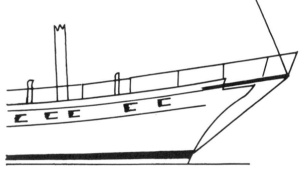

Clipper

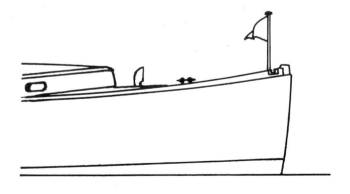

Straight stem

Bowse, to Often to bowse-down. To make the final tightening of a rope, such as a halyard. To gain and make fast the last fraction of an inch. (See Swig.)

Bowsprit A spar projecting forward over the stem of a boat with the purpose of lengthening the sail-setting base. A Reefing Bowsprit is one whose inner end may be unshipped so that the spar can be slid aft and inboard for convenience in harbour (and possible to save fees in a marina where the charge is by length). A Steeving Bowsprit is one that can be hinged up, sometimes even beyond the vertical. A Standing one does neither. Many stubby short-ended cruisers can gain in performance and interest from the addition of a bowsprit to carry a jib ahead of the staysail. A sail set on the end of a bowsprit is not easy of access, so it should stow by roller furling, or its tack may be fitted to a hoop or some other simple sliding device so that it can be drawn in to the stemhead when desired. (See Bumkin.)

Brace A rope used to control the yard of a squaresail. There is a brace for each end of the yard. The lower corners of the sail (the Clews) are trimmed by sheets.

Brails Lines leading from the leech of a mainsail to the mast and thence down to the deck. Each line is double, passing on both sides of the sail, so that when they are pulled the whole sail is gathered to the mast. Thames barges with their heavy, boomless, spritsails are the most noted users of brailing, but some owners have found the technique useful on smaller craft. If the sail has a boom, the clew must first be cast off, of course. To brail is the verb.

Brassy A brass eye, or eyelet, such as those in awnings or sails. Consists of a brass ring and a hollow brass rivet, whose flange is turned over the ring with the aid of a punch and die. Some sailmakers call them Turnovers.

Breaker A water-tub, or Barrico. Or in the ordinary sense of a breaking sea.

Break out (or break ground) Modern anchors, such as the CQR or Bruce, achieve a very high holding power in relation to their weight by burying themselves in the bottom. Subjected to a horizontal pull, such an anchor may burrow several feet below the ground, and it has ultimately to be pulled out. This is the process of breaking out, and it may take a good deal of time and effort. If there is any sea running, then the boat herself may be made to help. The idea is to shorten the chain when she drops into the hollow of a sea, and to make it fast quickly before she rises to the next. Alternatively the chain may be got as short as possible and the boat then driven ahead under the power of either sails or engine. A third method is to 'clap on a handy billy' as the saying goes, a handy billy being a block-and-tackle arrangement one end of which is hitched to the mast, for example, and the other to the anchor chain. The final method is to buy a windlass - best of all, an electric one if you can.

Breakwater   A small upstanding ledge or coaming across a deck or coachroof whose purpose is to deflect water coming from forward so as to keep it away from the cockpit.

Breast hook   A natural crook of timber, shaped like a broad V, which is fitted behind the stem of a wooden boat to link the two carlins, or a pair of Strakes or Stringers.

Breast rope   One of the six basic ropes used to moor any boat alongside a quay, a pontoon or another boat. They consist of three pairs, and the breast ropes are the two which run more or less at a right angle between the boat and the wall, one forward and the other aft. Breast ropes must be slack enough to allow for any rise or fall of tide. Even where there is no such movement (as when one boat is moored alongside another) the breast ropes should not be too tight. (See Warps and Springs.)

Breech   The opening in a block between Sheave and Shell which is not big enough to pass the rope. On the opposite diameter of the sheave is the Swallow, and that of course, is big enough to pass the rope.

Breeches buoy   A man-lifting harness consisting of a circular lifebuoy with canvas 'knickers' into which you put your legs. In bringing people ashore from a stranded boat, for example, the breeches buoy runs along a jackstay set taut from ship to shore.

Bridge-deck   A transverse structure at the forward end of the cockpit in many a small modern sailing cruiser. You step over it en route from cabin to cockpit., and it may house the engine or just be a stowage space. Big ships have a bridge where an officer may often be on duty when the ship is under way...

Brightwork   No, not brass, not stainless steel, nor chromium plate. This is the sailor's term for varnished timber parts above decks. Brightwork is kept bright by removing salt crystals with fresh water - in fact a seaman makes it a before-breakfast task, using the pure distilled water provided by the night's dew.

Bring up, to   To bring a vessel up is to anchor her. The term is also sometimes used of mooring to a quay or another boat. Not unlike 'pull up' in motoring.

Bristol fashion   In tip-top, shipshape condition. Dates from the days when the seamen and shipwrights of Bristol had a reputation for excellence.

Broach-to, to A vessel broaches-to when she slews broadside to wind and sea, taking a will of her own and overriding the helm. It is a phenomenon which occurs when a boat is running before the wind in heavy weather. For many years it has been held that the correct procedure was to slow the boat down in extreme conditions, by trailing large bights of heavy warp astern. But Adlard Coles in Heavy-Weather Sailing (Adlard Coles) put the view that modern yachts might do better to keep sailing as fast as possible in order to make the rudder effective. The emphasis is on 'modern', since boats of the past had straight stems and long keels and the forward underwater area naturally tended to dig in and slew the ship. Modern vessels tend to have their keel area well aft, with the forefoot cut away into a long gentle slope, and therefore to have more of an underwater weather-cocking character.

A broach-to

Broad reach   A point of sailing when the wind is abaft the beam, but less than dead astern. (See Reach and Large.)

Bronze   Copper-based alloys, among which Silicon-bronze and Aluminium-bronze are suitable for use in seacocks and other vital parts which must resist corrosion. Manganese bronze on the other hand is just a fancy name for brass which is good only for cabin fittings and the like.

Bruce anchor   Relatively new , this anchor has good holding power and stows neatly at the stem-head. It has three curving Flukes or palms, and acts by burrowing into the bottom. (It is also notably hard to draw !) Illustrated under Anchor.

Brummel hook   In the US of A this is the kind of inter-locking pair of C-shaped hooks which is known in Britain as an Inglefield Clip. In this book it is illustrated under that name...

Bulb bow   A Forefoot with underwater bullet nose, whose purpose is to reduce wave-making drag.

Bulb keel   A keel with an additional cylindrical or torpedo-shaped ballast weight along its bottom edge.

Bulkhead   A vertical partition running fore and aft or athwartships, but usually the latter in small boat parlance. The main bulkhead is the after end of the cabin, separating it from the cockpit.

Bulldog grip   A saddle-shaped steel clamp which, when assembled with a U-bolt and nuts, can hold two wires together. Every small craft with wire rigging should have a supply of Bulldog grips of the matching size on board. If an eye is to be made in the end of a wire, the end is brought round a thimble and clamped to the standing part with two grips. The saddle-piece must go against the standing part, since the U-bolt would tend to cripple it.

Bullseye   A wooden block or thimble, bored to take a rope and to act as a block (without sheave) or as a fairlead. Bullseye fairleads are nowadays more likely to be made of Tufnol or nylon, but the latter is quickly worn away by a rope, probably due to softening by heat of friction.

Bulwark *(or bulwarks)*   Raised woodwork running along the side of the deck to act as a wall so that gear or people are not washed overboard. They also keep the wind off for sunbathing.

Bumboat   A floating shop. Not often seen nowadays, but would be welcome around popular anchorages with newspapers, ice-cream, bootlaces and the like.

Bumkin   A short fixed spar extending aft over the stern of the boat to provide an attachment point for the backstay. On a short hull this allows the boom to be longer and the mainsail to be larger. The similar thing at the other end of the boat is a Bowsprit.

Bunk   A fixed, built-in sleeping berth, properly of partly boxed-in design. A settee-berth is not really a bunk, nor is a canvas fold-up pipe-cot. Still, they can't hang you for calling them bunks if you like - lots of people do.

Bunt   The middle part of a sail.

Bunting   A worsted material of rather open weave used for making flags. And the word is also used for flags collectively as in 'Let's string up the bunting, it's the Queen's birthday.'

Buoy   A floating mark, anchored to the bottom. Usually a hollow vessel of steel, glass-reinforced resin, or moulded plastics, it is likely to serve either as a marker for a laid mooring, or as a Navigational Mark. Navigation buoys may be lit or unlit, may carry a radar reflector or even a radar transmitter responding to the emissions of a ship's radar, and may come in a wide variety of shapes and markings. For details see almanacs or pilot books. (See also Bell Buoy.)

Buoy hopping   Pilotage by picking your way from buoy to buoy, reading the name of each and identifying it on the chart before setting off in search of the next. A rather amateurish (but reassuring) way to find one's way about, and usable only in well-buoyed areas.

Buoyancy   The power to float, inherent in a body whose density is less than that of water. The word is often used to define a buoyant material or construction, as in 'This dinghy is well equipped with buoyancy', meaning that she has a number of buoyant bags or tanks fitted. Speakers, and even writers, often show confusion about the action of such buoyant compartments in a dinghy. As long as a dinghy is floating by reason of her own displacement, such compartments simply add weight which, although very slight, tends if anything, to weigh her down. It is only when the dinghy is swamped that these sealed volumes show any benefit.

Buoyancy aid   Please turn to Lifejacket.

Burgee   A small triangular flag flown at the masthead usually to a design and colour peculiar to the owner's club. The burgee serves to indicate wind direction. A swallow-tailed burgee is flown by the Commodore of a club.

Burr   A saucer-shaped copper washer which is slipped over the top of a copper boat-nail before the end is riveted. In England the same thing is known as a Roove

Bustle   An underwater bulge in the after end of a (usually) sailing boat's hull. This swelling of the sections at the Run helps to diminish drag due to wave-making.

Butt strap   A Butt joint is a joint made by two planks (e.g.) joined end to end. The Strap is a third piece of wood bridging the joint (usually on the inside) and glued and screwed (or clenched) to the two principal pieces.

Buttocks   The underpart of the after end of the hull, where she turns up from keel towards the transom or counter.

Buttock lines   Fore and aft vertical sections of a hull on a drawing. The shapes which would be revealed if the hull were sliced parallel to the centreline on a bacon slicer. (See Lines, Waterline and Sections.)

By the head   A boat is said to be by the head when she trims bow down, in other words, with too much weight forward.

By the lee   The condition of a boat running, which has the wind off-centre and to the same side as that on which the mainsail is boomed out. A condition in which a gybe is therefore imminent.

By the stern   Trimmed too heavily aft. More common in small cruisers than 'by the head' since the weight of people and gear tends to collect aft, and because heavy outboards also thrust the stern down if not set at the correct angle.

C

C In the International Code of Signals the single letter C means Yes (or Affirmative). Charlie in the phonetic alphabet —•—• in Morse code.

CA Cruising Association.

Cabin cruiser Invariably a powered craft with sleeping accommodation. A sailing craft with similar accommodation may be implied if the word Cruiser is used alone, though the context is important, and usage varies geographically. On the Norfolk Broads for example, cruisers are powered craft, those with sails are called yachts.

Cable (1) May be of wire, rope or chain, but is the link between a boat and her anchor.

Cable (2) A measure of distance equal to one-tenth of a Nautical Mile. A nautical mile being 6,080 feet, a cable is just over 600 feet, and may be taken as 200 yards for most purposes.

Cable-laid Heavy ropes are often made of three laid up together in a left-handed twist. Each of the component ropes in cable-lay is Hawser-laid and consists of three strands (not ropes) laid up with a right-handed twist. Heavy hawsers are commonly cable-laid, whereas hawser-laid ropes are not often used as hawsers.

Camber (1) Almost always of decks, and means curved athwartships, as in a cambered road. Camber sheds water, augments strength because it forms an arch structure, and can permit greater headroom while avoiding unsightliness. Although a cambered deck is a nuisance when you want to sunbathe and your tea-mug may not stand level, it can be advantageous in a heeled sailing boat. In that case the weather side of the deck will be more nearly level than it would be if uncambered. But the lee deck will be correspondingly steeper.

Camber (2) The fore and aft curvature in a sail. Also known as Flow. Camber should be fuller for light winds, flatter for strong winds.

Camber (3) A small basin with its own entrance contained within a bigger harbour.

Canoe Although everybody knows of at least two types of canoe – the Indian birch-bark type and the smaller more compact Eskimo kayak, there are also sailing canoes of which the international ten-square-metre class is best known in Europe. The United States was the home of sailing canoes of many types, some of them very large. In ordinary sailing cruisers the term *Canoe body* applies to a hull of shallow form to which the keel is a separate appendage. *Canoe stern* (illustrated under Stern) is one which rises from the water like a counter, but has a rounded end.

Cap On a gaff-rigged boat the mast has a cap sprouting a ring through which the topmast can slide. The shrouds leading to the cap are called Cap shrouds, and people still use the term for the main shrouds of a Bermudan-rigged mast. (The capping piece on the top of a mast is the Truck.)

Capsize, to Any boat is capsized if she turns upside-down, but usage has it that a dinghy is capsized if her mast reaches the water, whereas a cabin boat at such an extreme angle (ninety degrees) would not be capsized but 'On her beam ends'. Capsize is also used of things turned upside down by sailors for their own good reasons: a coil of rope may be capsized, and so may a popsie.

Capstan A windlass with upright barrel, turned by bars radiating like spokes. Not to be found among today's pleasure craft, the nearest thing being the sheet Winch which is also normally mounted with barrel axis vertical.

Car Some sheets are led to a track, where they are attached to a sliding plate or a miniature flat-bed truck on rollers. This is a car, which may also be called a Traveller.

Carbine hook A hook with spring closure, basically similar to the hook on a dog-lead or a watch-chain, but made to a higher specification. Compare with Snap Shackle.

Cardinal buoyage system Is one in which a localised danger is marked by buoys situated to North, East, South and West of it. (Please see IALA buoyage system.)

Cardinal points   The four principal points of the compass, North, East, South and West. But the antique type of compass had thirty-two points in all, arrived by successive halving. Each Point was equivalent to 11¼ degrees of the modern compass.

Careen, to   To haul a boat down until her mast approaches the horizontal, and her hull is on its beam ends. May be done afloat or ashore. The purpose is to gain access to the hull bottom.

Carlins   Fore and aft timbers to which deck beams, cabin sides, etc., are attached.

Carry away, to   To break or collapse. An intransitive verb in this usage. If a shroud carries away, the mast may fall on your head. Subsequently they may come and carry you away, which is the transitive and non-nautical usage.

Carry helm, to   A boat 'carries weather helm' when the helmsman has to hold the helm to weather to keep her straight. Similarly she may 'carry lee helm'.

Carry her way, to   A boat carries her way when she continues moving by her own momentum after the propelling force has ceased to act.

Carvel   The form of wooden hull construction in which the planks are assembled with fine gaps between. These gaps are then caulked with cotton (or oakum) and Payed with stopping. The whole surface is then rubbed down smooth before painting.

Cast, to   The sounding lead is cast. To take a sounding somebody has to 'Make a cast of the lead'. When leaving an anchorage under sail, and supposing the boat to be lying head to wind at the time, there comes a moment when the helmsman must Cast the boat either to port or starboard in order to make a Board. While the boat is still lying to her anchor the rudder will be effective if there is any tidal stream running. In that case the vessel may be made to take a Sheer to one side or the other. But as soon as the anchor comes free you give her a Cast.

Cast off, to   To let go from a mooring. To undo a rope, free a dinghy.

Cat, to   To secure an anchor on board. Some boats have a Cat-head, which is in fact a small crane or spar to which the anchor is lifted and at which it may be stowed.

Catalyst An additive which initiates the curing of polyester resin. The resin is normally supplied (at least for amateur use) with an accelerator already mixed in. The catalyst's role is simple to trigger the cure and set it going. Only a minute amount of catalyst is needed, and the maker's instructions must be followed carefully. (Please see Polyester.)

Catamaran (1) In common parlance a Cat, but not a Cat-boat. To private owners the word means a twin-hulled boat, usually sail, but sometimes power. A sailing catamaran does not need ballast, but gains her stability by standing wide. Her long, lean hulls coupled with her light weight make her generally a faster boat than a single-hulled craft of the same cost.

Catamaran (2) Nothing at all like the high-speed craft above, but simply a collection of timber balks, railway sleepers or the like, held together with spikes or lashings so as to make a raft. Sometimes called a Flat or a float, these rafts are used as floating platforms by chaps painting topsides or doing other work on boats which are afloat.

Cat-boat The term cat has been applied to a variety of boats, but currently it will normally refer to an American type of sailing boat with shallow draft, very great beam, transom stern and centreboard. The boat is rigged with a single gaff sail on a mast stepped right in the bows, as in the illustration. The single-sail rig is also known as Cat rig or sometimes as Una rig after a famous cat-boat of the last century which was named *Una*.

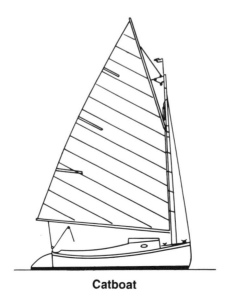

Catboat

Catch a turn, to To take a turn around a bollard, post, cleat or the like. Usually implies swiftness.

Cathedral hull A hull whose bottom is in the form of a triple V. When at rest or moving slowly, all three Vs are immersed, but at speed the hull rises and the outer Vs barely touch the water. Please see sketch.

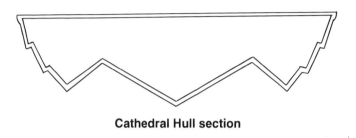

Cathedral Hull section

Cathodic protection Please see Galvanic corrosion.

Catspaw A gentle puff of wind.

Caulk, to Carvel hulls and Laid decks are formed of planks between which gaps are left, later to be filled by caulking. In a Carvel hull the gaps are V-shaped, with the wider part outward, and they are caulked first by ramming cotton or oakum into the bottom of the gap and then by filling with Marine glue, or by some modern compound. Although caulking is properly the first part of this process, and Paying the second part, most people nowadays tend to use 'caulk' alone, rather than troubling to speak of 'caulk and pay', which would be precise. *Caulking irons* are specially shaped tools with which the cotton or oakum is driven, with the aid of a *Caulking mallet*. A *Paying kettle* has a specially shaped spout to ease the pouring of the warmed marine glue between the deck planks. (Incidentally, marine glue is not an adhesive, but waterproof glue is.)

Cavetto This is the word that architects use for the hollow moulding that most boatbuilders call the Cove Line. Still, some boating people say 'cavetto', and some even say 'caveta', so I thought I would mention the fact.

Cavitation A phenomenon associated with a propeller which is being driven too fast, whose blade area is too small for the power it is expected to absorb, or which is working in badly disturbed water. Effectively the water parts from the blade surface, leaving a void filled with vapour or air; the void then collapses and the water falls back on to the blade with considerable force. This process is repeated with rapidity, eroding the blade and vitiating its propulsive efficiency. (A similar effect can erode the hull bottom of a very high speed craft.) In private craft, cavitation when running straight is a sign that the wrong propeller is fitted. When turning, even the right propeller may cavitate if the turn is very sharp: to avoid damage, throttle back or turn less sharply.

CB   Centre of buoyancy. Centreboard.

CCA   Cruising Club of America.

CD   Chart datum.

CE   Centre of effort.

Ceiling   Decorative linings to the cabin sides, but not normally overhead. In a boat the ceilings correspond to the walls of a room ashore, and the Deckhead corresponds to the domestic ceiling.

Celestial navigation   Finding one's position on the surface of the earth by using the stars and other heavenly bodies as reference points. The essential tools are a Sextant to measure angles between the horizon and a celestial body, a Chronometer to give Greenwich mean time (time is also monitored by radio signals) and a pre-calculated table of star positions which are known as the Ephemera and are found in various Almanacs.

Centre of buoyancy   The single point through which the buoyant force of the water pressure may be thought to act. If you are familiar with the idea of the Centre of gravity of a body as being the point about which it would balance, then centre of buoyancy is the same sort of thing the other way up. If you could push downward on a model boat with your finger precisely at her centre of buoyancy, she would go down without tilting. (But as she went down her centre of buoyancy would certainly shift, because of the changing shape of the immersed part of the hull. . .)

Centre of effort   And this will be a good place to consider the Centre of Lateral Resistance too, since the two are so commonly related in design work. The CE is the point at which the wind forces on a sail are assumed to be centred. It is akin to the concept of 'centre of gravity'. Conventionally the CE of a triangular sail is assumed to be at its centre of area (where lines from each apex to the mid-point of the opposite side cross each other), and the CE of the whole rig is found by proportioning between sails according to their areas. The CLR of the hull is likewise assumed to lie at the centre of all the underwater parts, but since it is usually only the fore-and-aft position which is thought to be significant, this is found by cutting out the shape of those parts in cardboard and balancing the pattern on a knife-edge. (The knife is set at a right angle to the waterline, of course.) Unfortunately neither of these simple methods for finding 'centres' has any relation to reality. The CE shown on the designer's sail-plan is well removed from the true centre of aerodynamic pressure on most points of sailing; and the CLR is no better. But convention has it that if the CE is some ten to fifteen percent of the waterline length ahead of the CLR the boat will balance quite well, with modest weather helm. In fact, the displacement of the aerodynamic thrust to leeward as the boat heels has far more luffing effect that the fore-and-aft relationship between the CE and CLR so neatly shown on the drawing of an upright boat with flat sails.

Centre of gravity   Please see Centre of buoyancy.

Centre of lateral resistance   Please see Centre of effort.

Centre of pressure   This is the same thing as Centre of effort, but is used of aerofoils in aeronautics... and sometimes in hydrodynamics.

Centreboard   *(and centre plate)* A centreboard is a retractable keel surface fitted on the centreline of the boat. (Compare with Leeboard.) It may or may not be ballasted, but its primary function is to provide underwater area to create lateral resistance and so to minimise sideways movement by a boat under sail. 'Board' is normally used of a wooden one, and 'plate' of metal, though one is not likely to be ostracised for talking about a 'steel centreboard'. Since the Board, as it is often called, works through a slot in the keel of the boat, it is necessary to keep water out. This is done by making a casing, called the Trunk, just big enough to accommodate the board, and rising above the level of the waterline. It makes a suitable plinth for the cabin table in small boats. In larger boats the top of the trunk may be below the waterline, and even beneath the cabin sole, in which case it must be fully sealed, though the lifting tackle may then run in a pipe whose upper end is sufficiently high. A centreboard boat which is allowed to take the ground regularly between tides may have so much mud forced into her trunk that the board will not drop, even though of great weight. Centreboards have been used for both racing and cruising craft, large and small, but especially for small sailing dinghies. Some have had pairs of boards, disposed fore and aft or laterally. The heavier ones are raised by winch or by block and tackle, but some make use of electric or hydraulic power.

Certificate of registry   Please see Registration.

Chafing gear   Just the opposite! It is anti-chafing gear. Anything rigged to prevent chafe of sails or ropes. (see Baggywrinkle.)

Chain plates   The metal fittings on each side of the hull to which the shrouds are attached. It is much more sensible to call them Shroud plates as is commonly done nowadays, though the old term still persists. (Old ships had chains below the Dead-eyes of their shrouds.)

Chains   Please see Channel (2).

Channel (1)   The deeper part of the water, often buoyed as the main route. The bit where you ought to have been when you go aground.

Channel (2)   A small balk of timber fitted to the side of the hull for the purpose of spreading the shrouds to a wider angle. Fitted in pairs, one each side of the boat, of course. Formerly such timbers were called chain-wales, a Wale being any raised strake, and they spread the chains below the dead-eyes. For that reason the part of the ship where the shrouds approach the hull is still sometimes called the Chains. 'Standing in the chains' still means standing on the edge of the deck by the shrouds – a good place for casting the lead, or for preparing to jump ashore.

Characteristic   The pattern, or signal or code of a flashing light or a sound signal by which it can be identified. Examples: Quick Flashing Light; Occulting light, and so forth.

Charlie Noble   The dome on top of a chimney. But don't ask me why, or who he was !

Chart   A map of the sea, showing shore lines, depths, useful marks and buoys. All British charts are based in the first instance on the work of the Hydrographer of the Navy, who prepares the Admiralty charts. These are used as references by some firms who specialise in charts for yachtsmen and private owners. Often these special charts give better value because they combine information from several Admiralty charts on to a single sheet, and also add harbour plans, pilotage information and so forth. Charts are listed in the Admiralty Catalogue of Charts, and they are obtained from chart agents, who are usually also chandler's shops. 'Class A' chart agents amend their charts and keep them up to date day-by-day. British agents are listed in the Admiralty catalogue, which can be obtained from HMSO (or from the agents themselves) for a very modest sum. In the USA charts are produced by the US Defense Mapping Agency in Washington, who collaborate with the US Coast Guard in publishing Notices to Mariners, containing details of changes and corrections.

Chart datum The sea level used as a reference point for the soundings given on Admiralty charts, and for the tidal heights in Tide tables. Likewise it is the reference level for the drying height of a sandbank. The current chart datum is the level of the Lowest Astronomical Tide, which is the lowest water level predictable. Lower levels are possible, for example by the combination of very strong wind with the LAT, but for practical purposes one assumes that the tide will not fall lower than chart datum. Thus if a sounding is shown as one metre, then there is a very high probability that there will never be less than one metre at that point, and there will usually be more. (See Tide and Height of tide.)

Charter, to To hire a vessel. The document recording the contract is the *Charter party*.

Check, to To check a rope is to ease it out slowly and under control. The nautical usage of check in relation to ropes is the opposite of the horseman's in relation to the reins. But when a seaman says of a boat 'Check her way' he means 'stop' or 'restrain' as a landsman would. (See to Start.)

Cheek Block of wood fixed against the side of something, such as a mast. A *Cheek block* is a hollowed-out cheek containing a sheave, such as is fitted to a mast for a Topping lift.

Cheese, to To coil a rope on the deck in a flat spiral, one layer thick, so that it looks somewhat like a tightly wound watch-spring. (See Fake and Flake.)

Chine The angle where the bottom of a hull meets the side. A round-bilge hull has no chines, but a boat built from flat sheets (plywood, say) has one or more chines each side, and is known as a hard-chine boat. (See also Bilge.)

Chinese gybe A situation, usually resulting from a gybe, where the upper part of the sail is to one side of the mast, and the lower to the other. It occurs because the boom is allowed to lift up too high. The term itself is an unwarranted occidental jibe, for Chinese boats with their fully battened lugsails are incapable of getting themselves into this specifically Bermudan predicament.

Chiplog A simple gadget for measuring speed. A flat, triangular-shaped board has a bridle consisting of a line from each corner, meeting at a single logline. The board is weighted at one edge so that it will float upright when dropped over the stern. In that attitude it remains stationary in the water and draws out the logline whose length is marked out with knots at regular intervals. The number of knots which run out in a given time provides a measure of the speed. For example, if you want to time over half a minute, which is 1/120 part of an hour, then make the distance between each knot equal to 1/120 part of a nautical mile. Then the number of knots that run out in the half minute will be the ship's speed in knots. 1/120 of a nautical mile is 50.6 ft. If that's too long, measure over 15 seconds and space the knots at 25.3 ft.

Chock A shaped metal fitting in Toe-rail or Bulwark which allows a mooring line to pass without chafe. In Britain it is called a Fairlead.

Chock-a-block When the two blocks of a tackle meet and no further movement is possible. The phrase has long since been adopted by, and adapted to, everyday life ashore. The situation also known as 'two blocks'.

Choke the luff, to To prevent a tackle running, by jamming a bight of the fall between a block and one of the rope parts.

Chop A sea which is short and small. Also a Lop. The adjective is Choppy, but nobody seems to say 'loppy'.

Chopped strand mat A non-woven form of glass cloth used for reinforcing polyester resin. The strands of glassfibre are two or three inches long and they lie in random directions, held into a sheet by a small amount of resin. There is just enough resin to retain them in this form for convenient handling, and when laid in place the mat is thoroughly permeated by a far greater amount of polyester resin. Most 'fibreglass' boats are built principally of CSM, though Woven rovings are also used.

Chronometer An accurate clock or watch of a standard that makes it suitable for navigation. By 'accuracy' I mean that it maintains a steady and known speed. It is not important that it gains or loses a little each day, so long as the gain or loss is constant and therefore predictable. This is known as the chronometer's 'Rate'.

Chute   Sometimes used as a slang term for a spinnaker, but more properly reserved for a full-bellied headsail which has some of the character of a genoa and some of the character of a Spinnaker. Like a genoa, a chute has its tack fast at the stemhead, which makes it much easier to control than a spinnaker which has its tack out at the end of its pole.

CLR   Centre of Lateral Resistance.

Class boat   A boat built to conform to limiting rules for handicap racing – or built to conform to a known Rating rule for racing.

Classification   A measure of the standard of a yacht's construction as certified by one of the 'classification societies' such as the American Bureau of Shipping, Lloyds Register, Bureau Veritas (France), or the like. In Britain, a boat built to Lloyds standards and under their supervision may, for example, be classed '100 A1', but she will lose that rating if she is not inspected by Lloyds at specified intervals. At such regular surveys Lloyds will specify what corrective work must be done to enable her to remain 'in class'.

Claw off, to   To beat away from a lee-shore. This is an expression used to emphasise moments of drama, and seems to be used mainly in bar-room arguments about the relative merits of various types of boat. It is the sort of phrase that mixes well with 'in my humble opinion. . .'

Cleat   A fitting for the quick attachment of a rope without the use of a knot or hitch. The cleat proper, ancient and respectable, is roughly like a short stemmed T, with two 'horns' which might also be described as arms. But there are various patent cleats of the jamming kind, including Clamcleat which has a V-shaped groove with ridges running down the inner faces to coax the rope into the nip of the V. Cleat can also be used as a verb.

Clench, to   A landsman would say 'to rivet'. To draw together two components, usually timber, with a copper Boat-nail. The nail is square in section and its end is spread over a cup-shaped washer called a rove. Clinker-built hulls are built by clenching all the planks together, which is why many people quite logically insist on calling them Clencher-built. Please yourself.

Clevis pin   The pin which closes the U-shaped fork on the end of a rigging-screw, for example, or which closes those small shackles made from bent strip. The clevis pin does not have a threaded end, but is usually drilled to take a split-pin or split-ring.

Clew   The lower after corner of a fore-and-aft sail, or the two lower corners of a squaresail if you are lucky enough to own one. The lower forward corner is the Tack, and the top corner is the Head.

Clinker construction   Also *Clencher*, according to taste. A form of hull construction in which the edges of the planks overlap, and are riveted together with copper boatnails. It makes a structure which is light for its strength, and which needs no caulking. The overlapping edges are called the Lands, and the lands nearly always face downward though there have been a few exceptions. The succession of small, downward-facing steps prevent water flowing up the side of the hull and make for a dry boat. On the other hand there can be a great deal of water noise with a clinker hull.

Clipper bow   The shape of bow in which the stem forms a hollow curve on its underside – often running into a bowsprit. The sections of such a bow are flared and hollow above the waterline. Illustrated under Bow.

Close, to   To approach, or come nearer, as in "we'll close the land in a little while and see if we can identify any features..."

Close-hauled   The point of sailing nearest to the wind – sometimes as close as thirty degrees off the wind, but more often on cruising boats in the region of forty-five degrees. (please see Reach.)

Close-winded   A loose term, used by salesmen or vain-glorious owners to imply that a boat sails closer to the wind than the listener might expect.

Clove hitch   The most common hitch for making fast to a samson post or a rail.

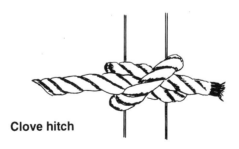

Clove hitch

Club   A short boom fitted to the foot of a staysail or jib. Rare in the UK but more familiar in the USA.

Clump The weight which holds a mooring chain on the bottom.

Coach roof The part of a cabin which stands up above deck level. (See House.)

Coaming A vertical ridge or barrier, of wood, steel, resinglass, etc., whose purpose is to keep water out. A cockpit usually has a coaming down each side, and perhaps all round. A deckhatch has one all round. Some hatches have a double coaming so that any water which gets past the outer one is channelled between the two and escapes through drains.

Coble A Yorkshire beach-boat of very distinctive shape. She has a snaking sheer, hollow shoulders and buttocks, but a full and firm mid-body. The rudder is of very high aspect-ratio, deep and knifelike. Some people think the world of these boats, which may be used under oars, motor or lugsail. Notice the deep rudder which is unshipped for beaching – it must be deep to balance the power of that deep forefoot.

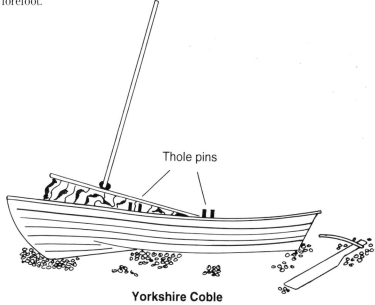

Thole pins

Yorkshire Coble

Cocked hat The triangular area contained within three position lines drawn on a chart. If there were such a thing as perfect precision all position lines would cross at a point. People generally assume that the ship's position at the time of taking the fixes was somewhere inside the triangle, and for want of anything better will put the plot in the middle. But avoid being deluded by the idea that the ship was really at that point. . .

Cockpit The 'dug-out' where chaps like me cower for shelter from the bombardment of sea, wind, snow and hail. If you have a reasonable area of deck around your cockpit it is a good piece of one-upmanship to call it the Well.

Codline Small three strand rope used for lashings. Like thick string. Hambro line is similar, but neither term is much used now that we are in the era of synthetic fibres.

Cod's head and mackerel tail The shape of a sailing-boat hull which was popular in times past, where the bow is very full and then fines away toward the stern. Current design of the sensible type has the maximum beam more or less amidships, with bow and stern waterlines well balanced, though some racing boats have the maximum beam well aft.

'Coffee grinder' A large and expensive winch drive system for sheeting the headsails of large and expensive boats. Commonly stands on a pedestal in the centre of the cockpit, serving port and starboard sheet in turn, and is actuated by crank-handles which drive internal gears.

Coir Coconut fibres used for making rope. At one time coir rope was used for heavy warps, but it is now rarely seen except as fendering of one kind or another.

Cold moulding A form of wooden-hull construction in which thin veneers are successively glued together over a male mould. Makes a very strong and watertight shell which is in fact tailored plywood. Wooden hulls may also be hot-moulded, but the oven large enough to take a hull is an expensive item of equipment, and glue which cures at ordinary temperatures makes the job easier. Hulls are also moulded in glass-reinforced resin, and planked timber hulls are built over Moulds.

Collision Regulations The odd name by which most people know the *International Regulations for Preventing Collisions at Sea*, a copy of which can be obtained from Her Majesty's Stationery Office for a few pence, and which should be read, re-read, studied and re-studied.

Colregs A compaction of *Collision Regulations*, as you doubtless guessed.

Combined lantern Please see Tricolour lamp.

Coming home If you pull on an anchor cable and the anchor comes towards the ship instead of the ship going towards the anchor, then you can tell the skipper 'The anchor's coming home'. In other words it's not holding.

Commodore   The president, or senior officer, of a yacht club.

Companion way   The entry into the cabin. In modern small boats just a doorway through the main bulkhead, because most small boats don't have a companion; or if they do, people call it a Dog-house wherever possible. And while we're on the subject, you may wonder, as I did for many years, what the devil this has to do with friendship. Not much, unless you go right back to Roman times since both words started life from the idea of 'with bread'. The human companion shared your bread, but 'companaticum' was what you had with your bread – cheese, butter, Gentleman's Relish and the like. Later the Italians liked to have a little storehouse on deck for cheese and suchlike stores which they called 'campagna'. The Dutch and English picked up the word, the Dutch using it to mean quarterdeck, and the English bending it into 'companion' and using it to describe any small deckhouse, and even a skylight. So there. . .

Compass   Well, you know, a little magnet, balanced on a pivot so that it is free to point always to the Magnetic North no matter which way the ship points. They come in all types and sizes, and you just can't do without one. Two are even better on any sea-going craft. (See Grid compass and Point.)

Con, to   Personally to steer your ship, as in 'I'll con the ship if you make the tea'. To control her. This word is of virtually no value to private boat-owners, unless uncommonly affected in their speech, but it is invaluable in the solving of crossword puzzles.

Consol   A radio navigation aid, working on 'long wave', which needed nothing more than the special Consol chart and a radio receiver. If the receiver had a beat frequency oscillator to make the Consol dots and dashes more distinct, so much the better, but it was essentially a simple system in which you had little more to do than to count the dots and dashes from two or more Consol transmitters. But when ships were able to use more sophisticated (and more accurate) aids, who wanted Consol? Only private owners in their little boats, so Consol was closed down.

Console   An upstanding plinth or box designed to support such things as a steering wheel, a set of instruments, the throttle levers and so forth.

Corrosion   Please see Galvanic corrosion.

Counter The overhanging part of the stern, especially when projecting markedly aft of the rudder. (There is an illustration under Stern.) A flat stern without overhang is called a Transom.

Course The direction in which the ship is pointing or heading. The compass course is the direction expressed in terms of compass degrees. When there is a cross-current, the vessel is not moving in the same direction as that in which she is heading, and it is customary to describe her direction over the sea-bed as the course made good. The distinction is important, and I prefer to use the word Track for the CMG, which is what you plot on your chart. But feel free to suit yourself.

Course-setting protractor A navigational protractor, normally scribed on a circle of transparent plastic, and having an arm or rule pivoted at its centre. The rule makes it very convenient to lay off courses, or bearings without recourse to the Parallel rules.

Courtesy flag When entering a foreign port, a boat should fly the flag of that country from her starboard Spreader, continuing to fly her own national ensign from its usual staff. Take care not to put two national flags on a common hoist or staff, for one will then inevitably be below the other, national dignity will be offended, and war will probably break out.

Coveline A moulding cut into a wooden boat's topsides a few centimetres below the sheer, and running from stem to stern (or almost). The section of this groove is the arc of a circle. Its function is to embellish, and for best effect it is gilded. A hull moulded in glass-reinforced resin normally has a painted cove line, or applied coloured adhesive tape.

Covering board A plank forming the edge of the deck surface, inside the gunwale. Whereas deck planks may be straight, covering boards are curved to the plan form of the hull at deck level.

CQR Please see Anchor illustration. For this very popular and very efficient type of 'plough' anchor.

Cradle A framework of wood or steel designed to support a hull ashore.

Crane   A short arm or bracket at the masthead, to which a forestay (or backstay) is made fast.

Crank   A vessel that is crank is one that is Tender – that's to say she heels too easily. If very crank she maybe dangerous. Tender is the usual word nowadays, but Crank gives you that certain air . . .

Cranse iron   A metal band with eyes which is fitted to the bowsprit-end to receive the bobstay, shrouds, etc.

Crevice corrosion   A form of Galvanic corrosion, notably suffered by stainless steels. When one end of a stainless-steel bolt, for example, is exposed to sea water and the other end is buried in timber so that is shielded, and two ends of the bolt act as if they were of two different materials. Wasting of the bolt follows.

Cringle   An eye in the edge of a sail, formed in the roping and usually fitted with a metal or plastic thimble against chafe. There is a cringle at each corner (Clew cringle etc.), and others for reefing. (It might be a good idea to see Earing and Grommet while we are on the subject. . .)

Crook   A piece of timber with a natural curve in it – used to make the curved part of the stem, etc.

Cross-bearings   Two or more bearings from which crossing position lines can be drawn on the chart to give a Fix.

Cross-tree   A strut fitted across the mast whose ends support the inward thrust of the shrouds. A cross-tree should be a single unit, whereas many modern yachts have a pair of separate struts, one on each side of the mast, and these are called Spreaders. The latter is a more satisfactory term for small boats.

Crown   The crown of an anchor is the farthest end from the chain – the point at which you would hitch a line in order to withdraw it from the mud.

Crown knot   The first step in making a Back splice. One of a few which it is essential to know. See sketch under Splice.

Cruise, to   To take a holiday on a boat, moving from place to place and spending nights away from base. The nights maybe passed under way, at anchor, or even in splendid hotels ashore, but the normal thing is to sleep aboard. One may cruise in an open boat, on the sea or on inland waters. The main thing, as Hilaire Belloc was at pains to emphasise, is that cruising is not racing. Another way of not racing is to go 'day-sailing', a term which implies that the boat returns to the same haven each night.

Cruise A cruise implies a voyage of at least several days , calling at various places *en route*. Each trip from one haven to the next is a Passage.

Cruiser The meaning of this word depends very much on circumstances and context. If there is no other clue, it probably means a motor cruiser – a motor boat with habitable accommodation. If the context is one of sailing craft then it means a boat whose design was not constrained by any arbitrary rating formulae devised for the amusement of racing yachtsmen. If compounded in the form Cruiser-racer it implies that the boat was designed to fit the rating formula but that the builder hopes he can sell her to cruising people in spite of that.

Crutch (1) A device to support the boom. Sometimes takes the form of a plank with a notch at the top like a Y, whence cometh the name which is the same as the crutch of a tree or the crotch of a person. Sometimes takes the form of a metal strut or crossed struts. But a goal-post type of support with two verticals and a cross-piece is known as a Gallows.

Crutch (2) A rowlock crutch is the purist's name for what I call a Rowlock. A metal object of familiar form (like a Y but with a top that's more of a U than a V) which supports an oar for rowing. It is called a crutch because it is like one of nature's crutches, and the hole it drops into is a Rowlock. 'strue. But I'll still call crutches rowlocks.

Cuddy A small space, too small to be a cabin and too big to be a locker. Usually right in the Forepeak of a half-decked boat.

Cunningham (hole) A tackle consisting of a line leading to an eyelet (the Cunningham hole) in the luff of the mainsail, a short way above the tack. By pulling on the line the Bunt of the sail can be flattened.

Current Please see Stream

Cut splice A form of splice used to make an eye in the middle of a rope rather than at an end. The rope is cut, and each fresh end is then spliced into the other rope sufficiently far along to make the eye. Alternatively, a separate short length of rope is spliced in. (Although the aetiology of the name is interesting, I would prefer not to delve into it in public. . .)

Cutless bearing A propeller-shaft bearing in the form of a rubber sleeve. It is used at the outboard end of the shaft and is lubricated by water which is appropriate for rubber. The metal housing of the bearing has small scoops to collect water as the boat moves forward and to direct it to the bearing, so care should be taken not to fill these scoops with paint.

Cutter Nowadays a cutter is a sailing vessel with one mainsail and two headsails – namely the Staysail and the Jib (see sketch under Rig). A vessel normally sailed with that rig remains a cutter even though one or more of the headsails is handed, and even if a Flying jib is occasionally added to make three headsails. This word is a good example of the way in which the language changes, for in the past it was either a ship-of-war's boat, used for fetching stores etc., or a fast sailing boat used by revenue men, which like as not carried a squaresail on her single mast. In those days the word Cutter could relate more to the boat that to the rig, whereas nowadays it refers only to the rig. (See Sloop.)

Cutwater The part of the Stem at the waterline.

Cyclone A revolving tropical storm in which the winds circulate around a low-pressure centre, the whole system moving linearly at the same time. This type of storm goes under different names in different parts of the world, 'typhoon' and 'hurricane' being the most familiar. A full-scale cyclone is rare in Northern European waters, but the type of weather system which centres around a low-pressure area is called Cyclonic, and that is extremely common in these areas. In the northern hemisphere cyclonic winds run anti-clockwise in a cyclonic system (generally bad weather) and clockwise for an anti-cyclone (good weather). In the southern hemisphere these directions of rotation are reversed.

D

D   The single-letter signal means, *'Keep clear of me; I am manoeuvring with difficulty'*. Few yachtsmen are likely to make it, if only because they would hardly find time to do it if they found themselves in such straits, but every private owner should know what it implies if made by a bigger craft. The Morse is —••. Phonetically it is Delta. In times of fog or bad visibility a long and two shorts on a ship's whistle means that she is not under command, or restricted in her ability to manoeuvre, or constrained by her draft, or under sail, or fishing, or towing or pushing another vessel. (Collision Regs, Rule 35c).

Dacron   Please see Polyester.

Dagger-board   A Centreboard usually in a dinghy, which retracts vertically. Some bigger sailing boats have dagger-boards, but their disadvantage is that they are not free to swing aft if they strike the bottom. (Although the vertically retracting board has a specific name, Dagger-board, the pivoted board lacks one. 'Centreboard' applies to both types.)

Dan-buoy   A small marker buoy (not usually for navigation) having a vertical stick or staff through its centre, with perhaps a flag or light on top. Dan-buoys are used to mark lobster pots, anchors and so forth, or as racing marks. They are also used in conjunction with horse-shoe rings as life-saving aids in man overboard situations.

Danforth   A patent anchor of the type illustrated under Anchor. The design originated in the USA, and the name has now become generic for a number of similar anchors, just as 'CQR' is often wrongly used for Plough anchors which are not of that specific design. A Danforth has excellent holding power, and so have some of its copies. An important point is that the shank should be strong enough and stiff enough to match the loads which its high holding power can impose. In other words, the poor imitations bend. . ..

Davits   The preferred pronunciation rhymes with 'have it', but the long 'a' is quite OK if you crave it. A davit is a mini-crane, usually a single steel tube formed into walking-stick shape. Davits may be of other shapes, and may be single to lift an anchor aboard, or in pairs to lift a dinghy or ship's boat.

Day-boat   Typically a small sailing boat, a few feet more or less than twenty, without a cabin, and used for pleasure sailing as opposed to racing. Like so many other sailing terms, this one is ill-defined (and not only by me). It is also used of small power craft, provided that they are not used for racing nor for overnight sleeping. But a fast runabout is not called a day-boat nor is a sea-angler's skiff. . .

Day-mark   An unlit beacon, normally rather large and erected on the land, to provide a reference point for pilotage by daylight. Daymarks often take the form of towers of brick, stone or steel, and may be several hundred feet high.

Dead-eye   A block without a sheave. Normally has three smoothed holes bored through the wood, with well-faired entry and exit, to take the lanyards used for bowsing down the shrouds of a sailing vessel. Alternatively, and more likely on a modern boat, the block has a single hole and is used, perhaps at the clew of a jib, to give a single whip purchase.

Deadlight   A solid cover which can be shipped over a Scuttle for protection. (Or you could say 'fitted over a porthole', but what's the good of having this excellent dictionary and not using the proper terms !)

Dead reckoning   Commonly abbreviated to DR. This is the type of navigational computation which deduces a position by plotting a heading and distance run (through the water) since leaving a former position. It makes no allowance for the effects of tidal stream, or current, or for leeway. When those influences are taken into account the result is an Estimated Position, or EP. (The 'dead' is supposed to derive from 'deduced', by the way.)

Deadrise   The rise of the bottom of a boat from the keel outward to the turn of the bilge. A flat-bottomed boat has no deadrise. The sharper the angle of the V in a V-bottomed boat the greater her deadrise. In planing boats a flat bottom gives best speed for a fixed power, but the ride is harsh. Increasing deadrise makes for a softer ride, but speed suffers slightly. The term deep-vee is applied to hulls with twenty-five degrees or more of deadrise.

Deadwood   A heavy timber fillet which fills the angle between the keel and sternpost (or transom) of a wooden boat. What you would call a big bracket if you were fixing a massive shelf in the kitchen. There may also be a deadwood between keel and stempost, but similar and smaller brackets in other parts of the ship are called Knees.

Deck   Need I ?

Decked   A boat may be fully decked, though the fact is not so likely to be mentioned as when she is 'half-decked', which implies decking over the bows (probably as far aft as the mast), a narrow strip of decking along each side, and a small after-deck.

Deckhead   The underside of the deck, as viewed from the cabin. Even if there is an inner lining or ceiling under the deck it will be called the deckhead. The word Ceiling has a special use which I could easily tell you now, but rather than be checked out of the lexicographer's union, I'll use that wicked *q.v.*

Deck light   A thick piece of glass let into the deck to allow light below. Sometimes of 'bullseye' or 'bottle-end' shape, and sometimes a prism.

Deck log   A rough note-book in which the crew in the cockpit can keep notes for neat compilation of the proper Log at some later time.

Deep-vee   Please see Deadrise.

Defaced   Of a flag, it means that some known pattern of flag is embellished with some other symbol. For example, the Cruising Association's ensign is the British blue ensign 'defaced by a white anchor on a red ball in the fly'. (See Fly.)

Departure   The known position from which a course is laid for Dead reckoning. For example the last reliable fix from shore bearings before the land disappears from view and you are obliged to rely on dead reckoning.

Depression   Meteorologically speaking an area of relatively low atmospheric pressure and harbinger of bad weather. Depression may result in the skipper who hears it is coming.

Depth   The vertical dimension of a hull between Sheer and Keel. Very often called the Moulded depth. (See Moulded.)

Depth finder   Same thing as an echo-sounder.

Depth gauge   A scale of feet or metres painted vertically on a harbour wall, or pile, or the like, which shows the actual depth of water at that place. Example, the present depth at the entrance to a lock. A Tide Gauge is similar in appearance, but conveys a different message.

Designed waterline   Please see Waterline

Deviation The compass error resulting form the influence of magnetic materials aboard the ship. In small craft deviation can often be avoided by siting the compass where it is several feet clear of the engine or other objects made of iron or steel. Otherwise one calls in a compass adjuster who will place little magnets in positions where they compensate for the effects of inbuilt metals. Or you can make a Deviation card which records the errors for various headings. (See Heeling error and Variation.)

DF Please see Radio direction-finding.

Diamond stays A pair of lateral mast stays, leading from the masthead, over Spreaders and back to the mast above deck level. (Thus outlining a diamond shape against the sky.)

Diaphone A foghorn operated by compressed air. Characteristically it emits a deep booming note which ends with a short grunt. (Compare with the Tyfon.)

Dinghy A small open boat, used under oars, sail, or outboard. A small sailing boat used for racing and having a centreboard and not a fixed keel. The term is automatically applied to almost any yacht's tender unless she is shaped like a launch and of fourteen feet or more in length. Thus it includes inflatables. But note that a small fast runabout driven by a powerful motor is not a dinghy.

Dip, to To lower, normally the ensign or national flag, as a sign of courtesy, and especially when passing one of the Queen's ships. The ensign is lowered about half down its staff as you draw level with the ship, which should dip in return. After she has dipped you return your ensign to its normal height. (Many small cruisers have such a short staff that the proper procedure cannot be followed: in such cases it is normal to remove the staff from its socket and tilt it down to a roughly horizontal position.)

Dipping Light A light seen at such a distance that it appears and disappears over the horizon as the ship lifts to the swell. The line of sight to the horizon is naturally below the horizontal (unless you are swimming) and this angle is the Dip. When using a sextant to measure the altitude of a heavenly body above the horizon, a correction must be made for dip.

Dipping lug A four-sided sail with a Yard at the head which sets on the leeward side of the mast, and has to be changed from side to side as the boat tacks. To get the yard and the sail round the mast they have to be dipped or dropped, partially or completely. See sketch under Lugsail.

Direction-finding Please see Radio direction-finding.

Dirty wind Off the lee quarter of a sailing boat the wind has been disturbed by vortices shed from her sails, and its direction is shifted somewhat to weather. Another boat will be hampered in this region of dirty wind, and may find it impossible to overtake through the lee quarter, even though she might be the faster if enjoying the same 'clean' wind.

Displacement (1) The weight of water which is displaced by a floating boat, and likewise the weight of the boat herself. A boat weighing, for example, one ton immerses until she makes a hole in the sea which formerly held a ton of water. The pressure to be exerted by the surrounding water is then the same as it was formerly. In design, and therefore in sales pamphlets, the displacement should be the weight of the complete boat in sea-going state, with fuel, stores and crew. (See Thames tonnage and Register tonnage.)

Displacement hull A hull which always floats in the water and never planes across it. Displacement craft are relatively slow but are sea kindly and economical of fuel. (See Drag.)

Displacement (2) In navigation, 'displacement' may refer to the distance by which a position is east or west of a Meridian of longitude.

Displacement/length ratio This is the standard formula used by naval architects (and percipient private owners) to assess whether a particular boat is light or heavy for her length. The underlying reason for the formula is that a boat which is twice as long as another, can be expected to weigh about eight times as much if she has the same displacement/length ratio. The two boats are then comparable in terms of 'heaviness' or 'lightness'. To find the D/L ratio you take her weight in tons and divide it by the cube of one-hundredth of her waterline length in feet. It looks like this

$$\frac{\text{TONS}}{0.01\text{ft}^3}$$

The tons which are used internationally by yacht designers for this formula are the old-fashioned British kind of 2,240 lb each, a fact which should be noted by North American readers. As a guide in case you are minded to work it out for your own boat, the sort of answer you can expect ranges from 400 Heavy, through 300 for Medium, and 200 for Light. (I allude, as always, to seaworthy cruising boats) The other widely used formula for comparing boats is the sail Area/Displacement ratio.

Distress signals   There are fourteen internationally agreed signals which may be made when a vessel or her crew are in danger and help is needed. A less urgent signal is to show the letter V by flag or Morse code, meaning that assistance is required, though there is no immediate danger.

Docking line   Just a rope which is used to make a boat fast to a harbour wall, a pile, or even another boat. Six docking lines are normally required to moor a boat alongside: two Breast Ropes; two Springs; and two Warps.

Dodger   A canvas screen erected to keep wind and spray at bay. More esteem will accrue to your image if you refer to it as a Weather cloth.

Dog-house   A raised shelter over the entrance to the cabin, so called because it has very roughly the dimensions of a dog-kennel. More properly called a Companion. (See Wheelhouse.)

Dog watches   In the Royal Navy the shifts of duty known as Watches are each of four hours, but the period from 1600 to 2000 is split into the first and second dog watches, each of two hours. This makes a total of seven watches in the twenty-four hours, instead of six, and this uneven number ensures that a fixed pattern of watches does not result in the same men doing the same watch day after day. There's little of value to you or me in this point, except that the phrase is very common, and equally commonly misunderstood.

Dolphin   A fixed pile of timber, concrete or metal which is used for mooring a ship, and especially for warping in or out of a dock. Also used of a navigational beacon if standing in water and rather massively built.

Dory   A flat-bottomed double-ended pulling boat whose sections show straight flared sides. The thwarts are removable so that the boats stack one inside the other on a ship's deck, so to be carried to the fishing grounds where they are launched for (e.g. long-line) fishing. A mast may be stepped and rigged with a small lugsail. The name dory has also been applied commercially to a triple-vee or Cathedral-hulled boat which bears no relation at all to a dory – other than the fact that both are boats.

Double the angle on the bow, to   A navigational technique for finding one's distance off a mark, such as a headland. Laying a course to pass off the headland, a bearing is taken of the mark – let us suppose that it lies fifteen degrees off the bow. Maintaining the same course the distance by log is measured until the mark shows double the angle on the bow (thirty degrees off). The direct distance between ship and mark is now equal to the distance she covered between taking the two readings. To get the best accuracy it is necessary to take into account the effect of any tidal stream, since it is the true distance the ship has moved over the bottom that is required. (See Four-point bearing.)

Douglas protractor   A navigational protractor made on a square sheet of transparent plastic instead of the conventional circular form. The square edges make it easy to align the protractor with a meridian, or with Magnetic North. (See also Course-setting protractor.)

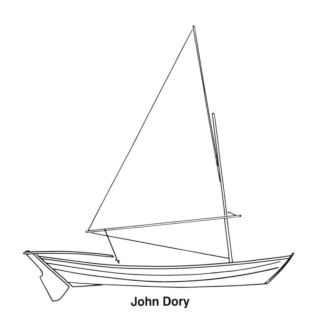

John Dory

Downhaul You guessed it – a rope rigged for the purpose of hauling something down, commonly a sail or the tack of a sail. (See Inhaul.)

Down helm Please see Up, and Bear away.

Dowse, to To capture a sail and hold it quiet, by lashing, tricing, bagging, or just sitting on it. Also, as ashore, to extinguish a lamp.

DR Please see Dead reckoning.

Drabbler Please see Bonnet

Drag, to An anchor drags when it slides across the bottom and will not stay put. Try more Scope.

Drag (1) The downward slope of the bottom of a keel which is deeper aft than forward.

Drag (2) The old word used to be 'resistance', but drag has been dragged into naval architecture from aerodynamics. The water drag of a hull can be considered as composed of four different types of drag. First is *Form drag* which in essence is due to the difference in pressure on the back and front faces of a moving object (your hand when swimming, for example). Second is *Skin drag*, which is akin to friction but results from the clinging of a thin layer of water (the Boundary layer) to the surface of the hull. This layer moves with the boat, and there is thus a shearing force between it and the stationary fluid farther away from the skin. Third is the *Induced drag*, which results from the difference of pressure (lift) on the weather and lee sides of the keel. Fourth, and of great significance in surface craft, is the Wave-making drag. *Wave-drag* effectively limits the speed of any displacement craft, and for the following reason. When moving through the water, a hull creates bow and stern waves, with a hollow between. Any wave in water has a natural speed, proportionate to the square root of the length between wave crests, and when the wave is hull-generated the length between crests is directly related to the length of hull. Hence a boat's speed is related to the square root of her hull length. It works out that a practical speed in knots is found by taking the square root of the waterline length in feet and multiplying by a factor between 1.2 and 1.4. Thus a twenty-five foot waterline boat can be expected to move at between six and seven knots. The corollary is that the factor can be found if you divide the speed in knots by the square root of the waterline length $(V/\sqrt{L})$, or in words 'V over root L'.

Draught The depth of water a vessel draws, in other words the depth of water she needs to float.

Draw, to A boat draws three feet when the lowest part of her hull, keel, rudder, etc., is three feet below the water surface. A sail draws when it is filled with wind and it pulls on the sheet.

Dress, to A mast is dressed by attaching the standing and running rigging. Rigging is dressed by coating it with linseed oil, lanolin or the like. A ship is dressed (overall) by rigging all her signal flags (bunting) in a line from stem to masthead and down to the stern. Sails used to be dressed with catechu or cutch, red ochre, linseed oil, potassium bichromate, and beeswax in various magic proportions to preserve the cotton against mildew and rot . . . but those days are past.

Drift (1) The Nautical Institute of London confines this term to 'the distance covered in a given time by the movement of a current (USA) or tidal stream (UK)'. The same Institute uses the word "set" for the direction of that movement. Most of us who navigate our own boats use drift to represent the combination of both those meanings – that's to say the change of position due to stream or current. (Please also see Dead Reckoning.)

Drift (2) A noun, meaning the distance between two blocks in a tackle or the amount of take-up available in a rope. As the blocks of a tackle approach drift gradually lessens and it is zero when they are Chock-a-block.

Drift (3) *(of stays)* The linear displacement of the lower end of a stay, which sets it at an angle. For example, a lower shroud might have a drift of two feet, relative to the Cap shroud.

Drifter An especially lightweight headsail for winds of up to about Force one. Would be in cloth of 2 oz. (See Ghoster.)

Drogue Any device designed to drag astern so as to create a slowing or rearward pull. Used occasionally by motor vessels in heavy seas, and more often to cross a harbour bar. The rearward drag prevents the stern from being slewed round by a following sea. A more prosaic use of a drogue is to keep a dinghy from bumping the backside of her parent boat in the night. For this job the drogue usually takes the form of a bucket, which is more effective when streamed from the stem of the dinghy than from her stern.

Drying mooring A mooring where a boat is sometimes afloat and sometimes aground. When the tide leaves her, and she grounds, the boat is said to be 'dried out'. Used in that sense the words simply mean that the water has left her. The same words may be used in their ordinary sense of the planks of a boat which has been ashore and under cover for a long time, so that the wood is thoroughly dry.

Duck up A real old seaman's term this. Most of us would think of ducking down, but when an old salt lifts the corner of a sail, or raises a boom to clear his head, he 'ducks it up'.

Duplex working   Please see Radio telephone.

Dutchman's log A small chip of wood (or other buoyant material) which is cast over a bow, and whose passage down the hull is timed. If the length of the hull is known it is then possible to calculate the vessel's speed.

DWL   Designed Water Line.

DZ   Danger Zone. For example, a practice firing range.

E

E   In the International Code of Signals the single letter E means, '*I am altering my course to starboard*'. Echo in the phonetic alphabet, and just a single dot in the Morse code.

Earings   Not rings, but ropes. May be any rope used to lash the corner of a sail to a spar or a halyard, but shackles are normally used for that job nowadays, except for the clew earing which is used to haul the foot of the sail towards the end of the boom. When reefing, the earings draw the Cringles (which are rings) down to the boom at clew and tack.

Ease, to   To slacken a rope slightly. A sheet is eased when it is let out, Hardened when it is pulled in.

Ebb, to   Both verb and noun. When the tide falls it ebbs. The event is the Ebb. One may leave harbour 'on the ebb', or one may 'take the ebb to the West', etc. The contrary term is Flood, both verb and noun again.

Echo-sounder   A depth-measuring instrument which transmits a pulse of sound from a transducer in the ship's bottom, receives the reflected pulse (echo) and deduces the distance to the bottom by the time taken for the return trip. Offers wonderful value to the single-hander who would find it hard to take continuous casts of the lead at those times when sounding are most needed.

Electrolytic corrosion   Corrosion caused by current leaking from the boat's own electrical system. Its results are similar to those of Galvanic corrosion.

End-for-end   A rope such as a halyard is turned end-for-end by the thrifty owner to prolong its life by avoiding concentration of wear at one portion. The same is done with anchor chains. Used sometimes as a verb, as, 'We'll end-for-end the jib halyard next season'.

Ensign   The flag of nationality worn by a vessel. Most countries use their national flag for their ships but British ships have a special ensign with the Union flag in the upper corner of the Hoist. Merchant ships and most private craft fly the Red ensign, but members of some clubs are privileged to fly the Blue ensign if granted a warrant to do so on application to the Admiralty. The Royal Navy flies the White ensign, and so does the Royal Yacht Squadron, a yacht club which enjoys royal patronage. The ensign is hoisted at 0800 in summer and 0900 in winter, and is lowered at sunset or 2100, whichever is earlier. The ensign is used for saluting a senior vessel.(Please see *Dip, to.*)

EP Estimated position. Please see Dead Reckoning.

EPIRB Emergency Position Indicating Radio Beacon. Sends out its signal on frequencies monitored by aircraft, or satellites, or both.

Epoxy resin A resin which is stronger than the cheaper polyester. It makes an excellent glue, and is the basis of very good 'putty' for filling screw-holes, cracks in resinglass hulls, and so forth.

Equinox The times of year when the length of day and night are equal, about 20 March and 22 September. The weeks either side of these dates are loosely embraced by the same term, and it is around that time that some people expect to suffer 'equinoctial gales', though I don't think that these expectations are supported by the statistical records. But tides are certainly higher (and lower) than average at the equinoxes.

Establishment An old-fashioned term of little practical value to the modern boat-owner, who will simply use his tide tables. The establishment of a given place is the time difference between the transit of either the full or the new moon and of High Water on the following day. Also known as High Water Full and Change.

Estimated position This is the position of the ship as deduced from Dead reckoning. It has a much higher probability of inaccuracy than a Fix from cross-bearings or the like.

Euphroe The Dead-eye through which run the multi-part sheets of a fully-battened Chinese 'junk' sail.

Expanded polystyrene A lightweight plastic material ('man-made-cork') which is used in blocks to provide buoyancy. Small dinghies and fun-boats are made entirely of EPS, but it lacks sufficient strength for bigger craft.

Eye-band A metal band with eyes for attachment of shrouds or stays to a mast, boom or bowsprit. (See also Cranse iron and Spider band.)

Eyebrow A lip or ledge formed above a Scuttle or window to divert water that might otherwise drip in. (See Rigol.)

Eyes The eyes of a vessel are the extreme forward parts of the bows, immediately abaft the Stem.

Eye-splice An eye formed in a rope's end by turning it back and splicing. Eye is used afloat in the same manner as ashore, for eye-bolts, eye-plates, and so forth.

F

F In the International Code of Signals the single letter F means, *'I am disabled; communicate with me'*, In the phonetic alphabet it is Foxtrot. In Morse code ••—•.

F Fixed. (On charts, though for the most part I am omitting chart abbreviations.)

Fairlead A device made to lead a rope smoothly or fairly. May be made of plastic or wood or metal, and in a variety of forms. Some fairleads are open, for example those mounted on side-decks to prevent chafe of mooring lines, and others are closed as is the case with the Bullseye sheet lead. A fairlead is fixed to the boat, whereas a Dead-eye is usually free to move: for example a dead-eye may be attached to a sail.

Fairway The main navigable channel in an estuary or harbour. The fairway should be kept clear of anchored craft, fleets of racing dinghies and the like, in the same way that racing and parking are discouraged on a main road.

Fair wind A wind that allows a boat to fetch between two points without the need to tack. A boat maybe close-hauled with a fair wind, but she is less than close-hauled when the wind is Free. (Please see Slant.)

Fake A single coil of rope, or loop of chain, as it might lie on the deck. The difficulty here is that in the past the verb *To Fake* was used for the arranging of a a sail or rope in folds, whereas the modern word is Flake.

Fall The hauling part of a halyard or other tackle. (See Halyard.)

Fall off, or fall away, to To sail not quite so close to the wind as hitherto.

Fashion pieces Shaped parts of timber used to thicken the inside face of a Transom around the edges so as to provide extra bearing surface for the plank ends.

Fast Perversely, a boat is fast when she is held stationary, either by mooring lines or because she is stuck on the mud. Items of gear are fast when they are fixed – that's to say 'made fast'.

Fastenings Nails, screws, rivets, bolts (and even Trunnels).

70

Fathom   A unit of length equal to six feet, and used mainly where depth is involved, as in soundings or lengths of anchor cable. The unit is expected to die out slowly now that Admiralty charts and pilot books have gone metric (But having see French carpenters working in inches after about 150 years of the Metric System, I emphasise the 'slowly'.)

Fathom lines   Contour lines drawn on charts to show the shape of the sea-bed. (On metric charts they ought to be 'metre lines', but I have not yet seen the term used.)

Fay, to   To shape and fit two surfaces accurately together.

Feather, to   To turn the blade of an oar so that it is parallel with the surface of the water and presents less windage on the return stroke. (See Propeller.)

Fend off, to   To hold a boat off an object she is about to strike.

Fender   A cushion, shaped like a ball, a pear or a sausage, and with an eye for attachment of a lanyard, which is properly used to protect and pad the ship's side when she is alongside a wall or another vessel. But some people flaunt them like a tart's trinkets on all occasions, even when under way, to the disgust of all seamen. . .

Ferrocement   A structural material for boat hulls and decks which has been used by a few boat builders in the last few decades, though it has been known for about a hundred years. Essentially, a basket or armature of iron rods is made in the shape of the hull. The rods are then overlaid with a mesh of thinner welded rods, or even a heavy chicken wire. The whole is then plastered with cement, which is allowed to cure at a slow and carefully-controlled rate. Care is needed at every stage, and skill is needed especially for the plastering process, but if both are present the hull will be durable, pleasing to the eye, and not expensive.

Fetch (1)   The distance a sea wave has travelled before it reaches you, or the uninterrupted extent of sea to windward. The point is that the longer the fetch the greater the chance for the seas to build up.

Fetch (2)   A course that can be sailed to windward without tacking. A Close-fetch is the same, but close-hauled and meaning that you can just fetch the desired mark or position. As you see, the word is also a verb, and to 'fetch a buoy' means to be able to sail to it on the one Board.

Fibreglass   The technique of drawing molten glass into fine threads has been known for more than three thousand years, and in the last few decades the high tensile strength of these filaments has been put to use in the reinforcement of resins. A fibreglass hull is only partly glass, the rest is polyester resin, so it is better to call this composite material Resinglass. The glass content of a moulded hull may lie between thirty and seventy per cent, from which it follows that the same may be said of the polyester content. The most common form in which glass is laminated or 'laid up' is the Chopped Strand Mat (CSM). This is a mat of randomly-laid strands tacked temporarily together by an adhesive which is soluble in the moulding resin. Individual fibres are about one-hundredth of a millimetre in diameter (ten times as thin as a human hair, say). They are made up into strands which in turn can be woven into cloth. A coarse form of cloth, loosely woven from bundles of strands is known as 'woven Rovings', which is used by some builders in hull moulding. If all woven rovings were used, the glass would account for some seventy percent of hull weight: if all CSM it would account for thirty per cent. Some moulders use a mixture of the two forms of glass.

Fid   A fat, tapered bodkin used for opening the lay of a rope when making a splice. May be of wood or metal. (Another type of fid, rarely seen now, was the square-section metal pin used to retain a topmast or a bowsprit.)

Fiddle   An upstanding ledge around a table or stove-top, or along the front of a shelf, to prevent items from sliding off.

Fiddle block   A block with two sheaves of different sizes, and fitted one above the other in the same plane, thus presenting a shape not unlike the body of a fiddle or the middle part of Miss Mae West, the renowned actress.

Fiddle head   The decorative scrolled carving at the stemhead of a clipper bow, similar in appearance to the scroll of a violin.

Fife-rail   A bar or rail, of wood or metal, in which several Belaying pins are set in a row so that halyards can be made fast to them. Commonly situated at the foot of the mast, athwartships if a single, or fore and aft on either side if there be a pair. (See Pin-rail.)

Figure-eight knot   A Stopper knot, made in the end of a rope to prevent it slipping through a fairlead, or to make a handhold. Its merit is that it does not jam. It is also the packer's knot, which has nothing to do with boating, but is an essential part of life's equipment – unless your servants make up all your parcels for you.

Figure of Eight

Fillers (1) Pasty compounds of various consistencies used to smooth out the porous grain of wood and to fill minor cracks and blemishes. Stoppers or Stopping are stiffer and heavier, for filling deeper cavities.

Fillers (2) Fillers in the form of fine powders may be used to improve the properties of reinforced plastics materials such as the resinglass composite used for moulding boat hulls. On occasion, and mainly in the 'bad old days', fillers were used to save money by bulking out the resin. For that reason they got a bad name, but when used for the proper reasons they are welcome.

Fisherman staysail Like other nautical words, the meaning differs from one region to another. On gaff cutters when I was a lad (long, long ago) the fisherman staysail was a long-footed staysail – so long in the foot that it was almost an equilateral triangle. But on a schooner, the fisherman is a four-side sail set between the two mastheads.

Fisherman's anchor The traditional type of anchor. The kind that looks like an anchor – please see the entry under Anchor and its accompanying sketch.

Fisherman's bend Useful for hitching a warp to an anchor, or for any purpose where the hitch may be heavily loaded. As the sketch shows, it is akin to the Round turn and two half hitches, but is less likely to jam.

Seize or tuck the end

Fisherman's bend

Fit out, to *(and fitting out)* Either the preparation of a new ship with all she needs to perform her duties at sea, or the subsequent and similar preparation after Laying up. For the average yacht owner, fitting out is a yearly task, following the winter lay up.

Fix A fix is an estimate of position inferred from observations of fixed objects. The observations may be compass Bearings of shore marks, radio bearings on beacons, a Sounding, a Transit, or some specialised technique such as Decca. Crossed bearings are a common example of a fix which you 'get' or 'take'.

Fixed light A light which is permanently on (when it is on at all). Compare Flashing and Occulting. And see 'Fixed and Flashing', though you could hardly avoid it, for here it is:

Fixed and Flashing A light that is permanently on, but with flashes of increased brilliance. The Mariner's handbook also defines a Fixed and group flashing light whose flashes of brilliance are in coded groups – but I have never seen one, alas.

Fl. Flashing. (On charts, and another exception to my intention to omit the many, many chart abbreviations.)

Flake, to To fold, or lay in folds. The mainsail, is flaked down over the boom when it is laid in folds left and right to make a neat package. An anchor chain is flaked down on deck when it is Ranged in long loops ready to run. A rope is flaked when looped on deck in figure-eights, likewise ready to run. There is possibility of confusion with Fake which was used by some people in the past as a verb with the meaning of 'to fold'.

Flam A hull section which is a convex curve all the way, growing wider from keel to sheer, has flam. Compare with Flare, immediately following. . .

Flare (1) A hull section which starts from the keel as a convex curve, but changes to concave near the sheer. This results in outward-curving 'lip', like the inverted section of a bell. See also Tumblehome.

Flare (2) A firework intended to create a bright light, red in colour as a sign of distress, or white to indicate 'I am here- please don't run me down'. White flares as used in small boats are always hand-held; red flares may be, but they may also be projected skyward by rocket, and may descend by parachute. Star shells, and hand-held fireworks which look like red Roman Candles also come under the general term of 'flares', though they may have more proper and precise names of their own.

Flare-up light   An obsolescent term for a white flare such as may be used to draw attention to your presence if you are afraid of being run down. Rule 36 of the Collision Regulations says that a vessel may attract attention by light or sound signals, provided that they cannot be mistaken for any other type of signal. In practice this is likely to mean shouting, or showing a white flare.

Flashing light   An intermittent light showing a single flash at regular intervals. The period of light is less than the intervening periods of darkness. Abbreviated Fl. on the chart. A *Group flashing* light shows two or more flashes at regular intervals and is abbreviated Fl.(3) with the number of flashes in the group shown in the brackets.

Flat   A barge, sometimes a sailing barge, but more often a towed barge on inland waters. Sometimes a raft-like contraption used for work alongside ship in harbour. (Please see Catamaran (2).)

Flattie   A dinghy with a flat bottom, hard chines, and flat sides, In fact 'flat' is not strictly correct for, in common with other 'flat-bottomed' boats a flattie may have Rocker to her bottom and fore and aft curvature in her sides. They are flat only in the sense that they could be made by bending flat sheets in one plane only. (See Scow and Punt.)

Fleet, to   To shift something horizontally, whereas to Sway is to move vertically. You could sway the dinghy aboard, then fleet her aft, though I must confess that I don't hear anybody using these words nowadays – more's the pity.

Float   The floating walkway of a marina in the USA – or what would be called a pontoon in Britain. See also Catamaran (2)

Flog, to   A sail flogs when it flaps widely from side to side. Flogging is like fluttering on a grand scale.

Flood   Both verb and noun. When the tide rises it floods, and the event is the Flood. One may plan to enter harbour or explore a creek 'on the flood', or to 'take the flood' up Channel. The contrary term is Ebb. (See Main flood.)

Floor   A structural member in a boat. It lies athwart the keel and links the keel itself to the frames on either side. There are many floors in a steel or wooden boat, of course. (Please note that the flat surface that forms the cabin 'floor' is called the Sole, and that it is a social solecism to call it anything else, even though it may be composed of pieces of wood which you can call 'floor-boards' with perfect propriety. The cockpit also has a sole.) A dinghy has Bottom boards.

Flotsam Floating wreckage, goods or equipment accidentally lost overboard. Material deliberately thrown into the sea (sometimes to lighten ship) is Jetsam.

Fluke The flattened and broadened area of an anchor which digs in the bottom. Also known as the Palm.

Fly (1) The horizontal dimension of a flag. The vertical dimension is the Hoist. The fly is also the lower corner of a flag, farthest from the hoist, and it is in this corner that it may bear a special emblem. The flag is then said to be defaced.

Fly (2) A small wind indicator, usually at the masthead, in the form of a pennant or wind-sock.

Flying Of a sail. A sail which is attached only at head and tack, and is not hanked to a forestay. Jibs are often set flying, spinnakers invariably.

Flying bridge A lightweight raised deck structure, higher than the principal structure, and provided to give a good view all round.

Fog signals Commonly so called, but to be made when visibility is restricted by 'fog, mist, falling snow, heavy rain, sandstorms or any other causes whether by day or night...' Under way, signals are made by Whistle or horn; at anchor by bell. See the Collision Regulations, Reed's Almanac or the like for extensive details.

Following wind The opposite of headwind – that's to say a wind up your tail. But some people call it a leading wind, because it leads on ahead to your destination, I suppose. That following and leading can mean the same thing may be a bit confusing until you get used to it.

Foot The lower edge of a sail. (The forward edge is the Luff, and the after edge the Leech.) Also the lower few feet of the mast.

Fore Mostly used as an adjective, when it has the opposite sense to After: fore cabin and after cabin, fore deck and after deck. But can be a noun, well to the fore, or an adverb, fore-and-aft, though that last is a peculiarity and the usual adverb is Forward. Its most common and important adverbial role is in Fore-reach, an expression used mainly to describe the slow forward movement of a sailing vessel which is Hove-to.

Fore-and-aft rig The almost universal rig of sailing boats nowadays, with all sails fixed at the forward edges and sheeted from the after edges. Contrast with the Squaresails of yore.

Forecastle   Used to be a built-up fighting platform over the bows of the vessel, but is nowadays generally used of the space under the fore deck where your fights are with your sleeping bag. Pronounced focsle, as in 'folks'll never believe you can sleep in that tiny space. . .' It would be less pretentious to talk about your fore cabin and more descriptive to call it the forepeak – unless you have a large boat.

Forefoot   The lower part of the stem, where it joins the keel below the waterline, or the foremost part of the keel where it joins the underwater part of the stem – take your choice. . . (And see Tuck.)

Foremast   The meaning is so obvious that, like Foredeck, it barely seems worth troubling over. Yet in a ketch or a yawl, where the after of the two masts is the smaller, the forward mast is the mainmast. In a schooner where the aftermast is the greater, the forward one is indeed the foremast. In boats with three or more sticks the foremost is always the foremast.

Forepeak   The peaks are the narrow volumes under the deck in the bows of every boat and in the stern of those which have pointed after ends. Every boat has a forepeak, but only some have an afterpeak. (See Sternsheets.)

Fore-reach   Please see Fore

Foresail   This is one of two quite different sails, according to the type of rig. In a Schooner it is a sail set abaft the foremast, usually with a boom at its foot just like an ordinary mainsail. But it may also be a Headsail, and usually the one set to the stemhead of the boat – in another word the forestaysail which is commonly shortened to Staysail. The chaps who sailed (and some still sail) Thames barges tend to call their staysails foresails – see illustration under Sprit – as did (and do) some fishing and workboat skippers. Where a boat has a single headsail it is commonly called the Jib, but where she has two headsails the jib is the foremost one.

Foreshore   That part of the shore which lies between high and low water at Mean Spring Tides.

Forestay *(or headstay)*   The stay running from the masthead to the stem of the boat. The corresponding one aft is the Backstay.

Fork end   Rigging screws are made with fork ends or eye ends. A fork end is closed with a clevis-pin, an eye accepts the pin of a shackle.

Forward   Adjective and adverb. The winch is mounted forward on deck, forward of the foremast, and you go forward to get to it. But the boat herself does not go forward, she goes Ahead. The word is often pronounced forrard, but is not so spelled (except just this once.)

Foul Ropes and cables are fouled when tangled, especially around your own propeller or your own anchor. In such cases the anchor or propeller is foul or fouled, too. A boat with a *Foul bottom* has weed and barnacle growing there, but a foul bottom may be the same as Foul ground, an area of the sea-bed where it would be unwise to drop your anchor because rocks, wrecks or cables might foul it. A *Foul berth* has nothing to do with hygiene or comfort – it results when a vessel anchors so near another moored vessel that there is risk of collision between the two. It is up to the later arrival to avoid giving a foul berth to any boat already at anchor, and to shift if necessary.

Found Used only in the phrase 'well found', of a ship which is well fitted, provisioned and maintained. The converse, 'ill found' is rarely used, but enlivens conversation or writing the more so for that reason.

Founder, to Not just another word for 'to sink', it has implications of sinking in a goodly depth, for it comes form the Latin, fundus, bottom, from which we also have 'profundity'.

Four-point bearing A special case of Doubling the Angle on the Bow. The log is read when an object bears forty-five degrees off the bow (i.e. four points) and again when it bears ninety degrees. The distance off is then equal to the distance run between these two observations.

Frame A rib of the hull, either of steel or of sawn timber. If grown naturally to the shape, or steam-bent, such a rib will be called a Timber. Whether using timbers or frames, a hull is said to be 'in frame' when building has progressed as far as the skeleton.

Frap, to To bind something tightly by wrapping a rope or cord around it. Those damnable halyards that clink and clank against metal masts should be frapped – so should owners who neglect this simple social decency.When a spinnaker becomes frapped it is a nightmare.

Free The wind is free when it comes from abaft the beam, whereupon the boat is sailing 'free'. Furthermore the wind 'frees', or even 'frees the boat' when it shifts more aft so that the boat is sailing 'free-er'.

Freeboard The height of the boat's side above the water. Best measured to the lowest point at which water could get on the deck or into the cockpit.

Freeing port   An opening in the bulwarks, sometimes with a hinged flap, through which water can escape from the deck seaward.

Freshen the nip, to   To move or adjust a rope so that the wear does not continue to come at the same point.

Front   A meteorological term. The line where a cold air mass meets a warmer one. If the colder air is advancing it is a *Cold Front*, and if the warmer air is advancing, well, give you three guesses.

Full and by   A nice point about a point of sailing. The 'by' implies that the boat is being sailed 'by the wind' and not by compass course. In fact she is sailing close to the wind, but the sails are kept comfortably full so that she makes a good speed. In sailing 'full and by' the aim is to make the best possible progress to windward – what our modern instrumentised skippers would call best Vmg – the best balance between high pointing and fast footing.

Full and change   The times of the full and new moon,. Significant dates in tidal predictions, relating to Spring and Neap tides respectively.

Furl, to   To gather up a sail into a near package along its length. A mainsail is furled along its boom – a headsail is often furled by rolling it up around its own luff. But furling implies merely a tidy stow. A partly furled sail cannot be set to the wind as a reefed sail can.

Futtocks   Where a curved frame or rib is made of more than one piece, each component piece is a futtock. Possibly it was originally a 'fat-hook', in the form of one curved piece turning the bilge between a vertical rib and a Floor. The word is not likely to be important to the modern yachtsman, but a shout of 'and futtocks to you!' has great force with perfect propriety.

G

G   In the International Code of Signals the single letter G means, *'I require a pilot'*, and may be made by flag or any other method of signalling. It is Golf in the phonetic alphabet. In Morse code it is − − •. (Note that a fishing vessel when on her fishing grounds may make G to mean *'I am hauling my nets'*.)

Gaff   The spar at the head of a four-sided fore-and-aft sail. May be short or long. (A Gunter mainsail is strictly speaking four-sided, though two of the sides almost form a straight line. The spar at the upper end of a gunter luff is called the Yard.) (Please see illustration under Sail.)

Gale   Not a very precise term, and used by some to describe any fresh breeze they happen to have been out in. But the Met. men use it for winds of Beaufort force 8 and 9, embracing wind speeds in the range 34-47 miles an hour.

Galley (1)   The tea-tray sized area in one corner of the cabin where you fry bacon and heat beans. For what is often little more than a cupboard the word might seem pretentious, but the usage is quite normal, and it embraces cooker, sink, and pan stowage as well as working top.

Galley (2)   Rare, but could be used more. A clinker boat of some thirty feet, propelled by oars or sail and part-decked. On the flicks you would have seen Admiral Hornblower being pulled ashore in a galley on important occasions. (When he was a captain he would have had a Gig, similar, but smaller.)

Gallows   A support for the lowered main boom, consisting of two uprights and a cross-bar. Unlike a crutch it is normally a fixture.

Galvanic corrosion   Corrosion which results when an electric current flows between two metals. For example, if dissimilar metals such as brass and aluminium are immersed in salt water but connected above water level by a conductor such as a metal bolt, an electric current will flow between them. In the process the less 'noble' metal will corrode away. The least noble metal in fact has the lower electrical potential and forms the anode, while the more noble metal forms the cathode. To protect against this phenomenon it is wise to avoid the use of dissimilar metals under water on the same boat. Furthermore, by fitting a sacrificial Anode of very low-potential metal, such as zinc or magnesium, all the adverse effects can be confined to the sacrifice. Although the anode is sacrificed, this technique is known as Cathodic protection.

Galvanise, to As far as we are concerned it is to plate iron or steel with a layer of zinc, as protection against rust. Properly it would apply to any type of electro-plating, but usage now has Galvanise for non-electric processes, such as 'hot-dip' galvanising' or even 'cold galvanising' in which a zinc-rich paint is brushed on. Now that stainless steel has taken over most of the duties of galvanised mild steel, the most common galvanised item to be seen on boats is the anchor chain, and probably the anchor too. Be that as it may, zinc-plating is still a powerful defence against rust.

Gammon iron A metal ring or band which holds the bowsprit to the stemhead. A word not much used in recent decades, but as the benefits of bowsprits are re-discovered, it may come back too. (And see Cranse iron.)

Garboard In wooden boats, the plank or strake nearest the keel. One each side, of course.

Gaskets Short lengths of rope or tape used as sail-stops or ties.

Gate start A method of starting a race when a large number of boats is involved. The starting line is not static, but lies between a moving boat and a free-floating buoy. (See also Line start.)

Gel coat The g is soft, but the coat should not be. It is the glossy outer skin of a resinglass moulded hull which not only gives desired beauty but also protects the underlying laminate against ingress of water. It is between half and a quarter of a millimetre in thickness (up to a fiftieth of an inch, say) and should be treated with care. Scratches and cracks should be filled before water gets a chance to penetrate, for a subsequent frost would burst further areas of gel coat away from the laminate. Most of the troubles with resinglass hulls are related to the gel coat.

Genoa A large triangular headsail, extending abaft the mast and often coming right down to the deck. A very efficient sail, because it gets a clean wind free from interference by any other sail, the 'genny' can be awkward to handle and, if low-cut, can block the helmsman's view ahead. It was first recognised as a sail in its own right at the 1927 International Regatta in Genoa, though in fact it is simply a development of the Dutchman's *fok*, the reaching staysail and the fisherman jib.

Ghoster, and to ghost An especially lightweight headsail for winds of up to about Force 2 (or between 1 and 2). Would be in cloth of 2 to 3 ozs. To Ghost is to sail very slowly in the lightest of airs. (And see Drifter.)

Gig   A clinker-built open boat of four or six oars. Long and lean, she is easy to pull. She may also be rigged with sail. Naval officers go ashore in them and practical civilians sometimes get a chance to buy one that the Navy no longer needs. (Both gs are hard.)

Gimbals   Concentric, pivoted metal rings which allow a compass, lamp, or the like to swing freely and so to remain upright no matter how the ship pitches or rolls. The g is soft and the plural form is used of the device alone, but the singular is used in combination as Gimbal-ring. Used as a verb (or participle for purists) in 'a gimballed stove'.

Gingerbread   Gilded floral or curlicue carvings at a boat's bow or quarters, or across her stern.

Gipsy   A wheel on a windlass with notched and grooved rim to receive and hold the links of a chain cable.

Girt, to   To constrain or distort a sail by a rope or other hard edge running across it. The hull may be girt by a mooring line or anchor cable.

Glue   'Marine glue' is not glue at all. It is a special compound used for Paying or caulking the seams between deck planks. Having got that off our chests we are left with a wide range of waterproof adhesives which can be used for boat-building and on which you can get information from a hardware or tool shop – or even by writing to some magazine editor who has nothing much else to occupy his time...

Go about   Also 'put about'. To turn the ship's head through the wind, to tack. Turning the other way, tail to wind, is to Gybe or Wear.

Goodrich bearing   Please see Cutless bearing.

Goose neck   The double-hinged fitting which attaches the boom to the mast.

Goose-winged   Running before the wind with mainsail out to one side and staysail to the other. Also Wing and Wing.

GPS   Global Positioning System. A highly accurate navigational aid which makes use of automatic measurements from a multiplicity of artificial satellites.

Gradient wind   A wind resulting from a difference in barometric pressure across the face of the earth. The more marked the change of pressure in a given distance, or the closer the isobars on the synoptic chart, the steeper the gradient and the higher the resulting wind speed.

Granny knot   A granny knot afloat is the same as ashore, and the same that you learned about in infancy – I hope. It is not a knot at all – just a useless mistake.

Grapnel   A multiple hook, with two, three or four prongs, designed to catch in a bush ashore, or to snare a lost cable on the bottom. If you are thinking of taking up piracy to augment your retirement pension, lay in a good stock for grappling before boarding.

Grating   A collection of square holes held together by wood – preferably teak. Ideal for the floor of a shower-room, but shows to its best in the cockpit of a really smart yacht, or in the bottom of her tender. In a perfect world every boat would have gratings.

Grave, to   To inlay a piece of wood so as to make good a damaged part. The inlay is known as a Graving-piece and if fitted by a craftsman you won't know that it is there.

Great circle   Please see Rhumb line.

Green stage   The chemical process of curing a resinglass hull can take days or weeks. Although the resin may appear to have set quite firmly in less than an hour, the assembly may be susceptible to permanent distortion for a period of weeks. If left unsupported during that time it may take on a permanent change of shape. This is part of the green stage, though the greenest part is in the first hour. Moral: if you buy a freshly moulded hull, set it up true, support it well, and build in stiffening bulkheads and the like before supports are moved.

Gribble   A small marine creature, similar in appearance to a woodlouse, which eats underwater timber. Unlike the Teredo, it does not burrow into the wood but bores in to about an inch, then emerges and starts again. It thus reveals its presence. Like teredo it dies when the timber is removed from salt water.

Grid compass   A compass which has a movable frame of reference or cursor which can be rotated to any desired setting. Thereafter it is necessary only to maintain a course such that the compass 'needle' (or a boldly marked card) remains coincident with the grid marking above. If the grid is correctly set in the first place this arrangement makes it much easier to hold the right course, and errors due to mis-reading are eliminated.

Gripe, to A sailing boat gripes when she shows a strong tendency to turn up into the wind and requires great tiller force to restrain her. The noun Gripe from which it derives means the forefoot or the forward extremity of the keel, but it is now obsolescent.

Grommet (1) An eyelet in the edge of a sail, usually a small one such as is used +to attach a luff-slide. Modern sails have grommets at head, tack and clew, but habit has endowed those larger grommets with the name of Cringle. In the past that word was reserved for a ring attached outside the bolt rope, whereas a grommet was an eye within the rope, in the margin of the cloth itself. The brass eyelets you can fit yourself with a punch and die are grommets aboard ship.

Grommet (2) A rope ring. Handy for deck quoits.

Ground swell Technically, this is a swell which, on reaching a depth of less than half its wave-length, starts to become shorter and steeper, preparatory to breaking in even shallower water. In that sense it is a wave-train which is influenced by the nearness of the ground. But to most yacht skippers, a ground swell is just a swell which arrives from far off when there is no local wind to set up seas of the same height.

Ground tackle Your anchoring equipment, principally your anchors and cables.

Group flashing *(and occulting)* Please see Flashing light and Occulting light.

Grow, to An anchor cable is said to grow in the direction in which it lies from the ship. 'Which way does the cable grow?' a good wife should ask her straining husband. If she can understand his reply she should motor the boat slowly in that direction to relieve the load.

GRP Glass-Reinforced Plastic (or perhaps Polyester).

Guard rail The 'fence' around the deck which should save you from falling overboard. It should be at least two feet high, and good and strong.

Gudgeon Every book must have its sex interest nowadays, and here it is. The gudgeon is the female part of a pair of rudder hangings, into which the male Pintle fits. You need a pair of these pairs to hang a rudder, and sometimes more may be used.

Gunter lug A type of sail , the upper half of whose luff is fixed to a yard which rises bodily up to the mast and extends more or less vertically above it. The resulting short mast is welcome on dinghies which are left on open moorings, or are trailed on the road, or which are used on waters spanned by low bridges. A jolly good rig for boats up to twenty feet or so, but rare in anything larger. Note that the yard stands almost vertically, in contrast with the acute angle of a Gaff. (See Lugsail.)

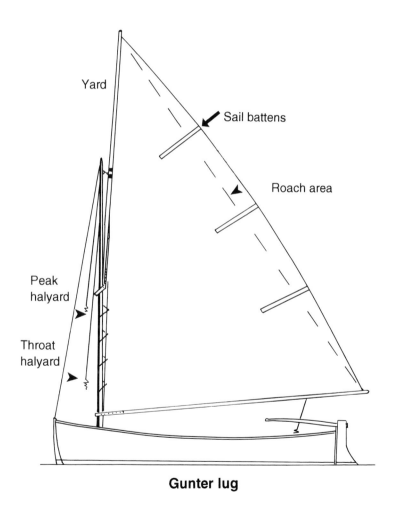

Gunter lug

Gunwale A wale is a strake standing proud of the planking, and the gunwale should be the uppermost member along each side of a hull, linking all the ribs and the topmost plank. But the usage now has it simply as the upper edge of the ships side, even in resinglass boats where no such structural wale exists. It is pronounced gunnel, as you are perfectly well aware. (Please see Sheer strake, too.)

Guy A rope used to restrain a boom. It may lead forward from the boom as a precaution against an unexpected gybe, or else aft from a Spinnaker boom.

Gybe, to (or jibe in American) To turn a boat so that the wind changes from one quarter to the other across her stern, so swinging the mainsail over abruptly. This manoeuvre is called a gybe. A Gybing course is one where the boat is running before the wind with a chance that the wind will get behind the mainsail and swing it across. In a cabin boat a deliberate gybe is made by hauling in the main sheet until the sail is almost fore and aft so that it cannot gain much momentum in its short swing across. Once the wind is on the new side of the sail the sheet can be eased. Light dinghies, by contrast, often Gybe all standing, allowing boom and sail to sweep right across from square out on the one side to square out on the other. The greater mass and inertia of gear aboard a cruising boat makes the gybe all standing a risky business. (See Wear, to.)

Gybe-o! Helmsman's warning call to crew members who have just had their hats knocked off by his unpremeditated gybe.

H In the International Code H means, *'I have a pilot on board'*. It is a commonly-made single-letter signal since a ship normally flies the H flag whenever she does have a pilot. In Morse code H is four dots. In bad visibility a pilot vessel may identify herself by sounding H on her whistle. Otherwise, this signal may not be made by sound. In the phonetic alphabet H is Hotel, pronounced the English way rather than the French.

Half-breadth plan A drawing showing horizontal sections of a boat's hull, or what are known as Waterlines, though only one section is really the waterline. Only half the boat is shown, thus allowing the designer more time to watch television. (Please see Lines for illustration.)

Half-decker An open boat with a certain amount of decking – commonly over the forepeak, over the stern sheets, and along each side of the well. About half the total area is decked, and the decking is around all the outer margin.

Half-hitch Half of a very useful hitch known as 'two half hitches'. One half-hitch by itself has little other than very transient value, but make a second one and you have enduring security. Please see Round turn and two half-hitches.

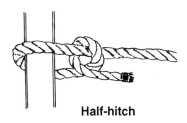

Half-hitch

Half-tide A half-tide mooring is one where your boat floats for (roughly) half the day and is aground for the other half. A half-tide rock is sometimes immersed and sometimes not. Pretty obvious, really.

Halyards Originally 'haul-yards', now any rope for raising a yard, a sail, an ensign or a burgee up a mast or staff. A rope which adjusts the height of something or simply holds it up, rather than moving it from bottom to top is a Lift, as in Topping lift. But the rope that lifts a cargo aboard, or raises a dinghy in davits is a Fall.

Hambro line   Small hemp rope or cord, in the region of four to five millimetres in diameter, used for lashings and so forth. I wish I knew why it is called Hambro line, though. Codline is technically not the same, but yachtsmen treat it as if it were, and either can be used for odd jobs. If not sure what to call cord when aboard, the term 'small stuff' will mark you down as a mariner of unrivalled experience, and saves you the trouble of searching for the precise term.

Hand, to   To lower and furl a sail. The knowing chap doesn't 'get the mainsail down', he 'hands' it.

Hand compass   More commonly called a Hand bearing-compass, and nearly always with the stress on the word 'hand' as if it grew hands like a fruit-bearing tree. It is a bearing-compass, that's to say one with some form of sight for taking bearings of other vessels or objects ashore, and one which is small enough to be held in the hand.

Handsomely   A very pleasing adverb which deserves to be used more often. It means to take the job at a steady, controlled pace. Not leisurely, but just so fast as is prudent and proper. If only people would sail handsomely, come into a berth handsomely, haul up sails and anchors handsomely, step ashore handsomely, and generally adopt handsomely as the family motto, there would be fewer broken boats and broken bones.

Handy billy   A small tackle which many owners like to have aboard just in case. Normally consists of a single and a double block, each of which has a rope tail (or perhaps one has a hook). Such a tackle can be used wherever an extra purchase may be required – or perhaps for breaking out an anchor or to set up a jury stay for the mast.

Hank   A clip of metal or plastic which attaches the luff of a sail to a stay. Most staysails (vulgarly called 'jibs') are hanked to their forestays with piston hanks, taking the form of P-shaped hooks closed with a spring-loaded plunger. But there are moulded nylon hanks and hanks made of tape which are held by press-studs. The latter are surprisingly rare, considering how neat and light they are.

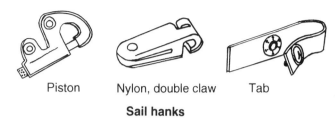

Piston   Nylon, double claw   Tab

Sail hanks

Harbourmaster   The chap in charge of a harbour. I say in charge deliberately because under an Act of Parliament now some 130 years old he has real authority. You must berth where he tells you, and move if he tells you. If you don't move your boat he can move her – and charge you with the cost. By the same Act, a skipper who brings his boat into a port where harbour dues are payable must report his arrival to the harbourmaster within 24 hours. In short, a harbourmaster is master within his own harbour.

Hard (1)   A stretch of shore which is firm enough for landing or launching boats.

Hard (2)   As an adjective corresponds to 'right' as in 'put the helm hard over', or 'hard to port', or 'hard down'. It means all the way.

Hard alee   A warning cry by the helmsman that he is putting the helm over in order to go about. Best preceded by Ready About. (See Lee-Oh).

Hard-chine   Hulls are either Round-bilge or Hard-chine, the latter form resulting where the hull is built from flat sheets so that the sides meet the bottom at a distinct angle. The line along which the side and bottom meet is in fact the chine, and if there is an angle it is 'hard'. Obviously there is no common term 'soft chine', though it would be useful where the angle of a hard-chine form is a little rounded, perhaps by using a substantial chine stringer with a rounded bevel. Some people tend to suppose that a hard-chine hull is inherently inferior to a round-bilge form, but in fact a hard-chine hull can be very satisfactory.

Harden in, to   To haul a sheet in, so as to flatten the sail.

Harmonic rolling   Please see Rhythmic rolling.

Harness   Or **Safety harness**, is a harness of webbing worn around the chest and shoulders, with a lifeline whose end is attached to a suitable strongpoint on the boat. Ideally the lifeline should be so short that, from its point of attachment, there is insufficient length to allow the wearer to go over the side. But that is not always possible, and then the only consolation is that you will still be attached to the boat, even if somewhat wet.

Hatch   An opening in a deck, through which people or goods can pass. Note that the hatch is the opening. The cover is properly the Hatch-cover, though many people mis-use the word Hatch to mean that.

Haul   This verb is used afloat in the same way that it is used ashore, but it has a special application to the behaviour of the wind. If the wind *Hauls ahead* it shifts to come from a point farther ahead. Likewise it may 'haul aft'. But a boat which *Hauls her wind* changes course to bring it more on the nose. In other words, usage has it that the wind may haul itself either way, but a vessel hauls her wind only one way.

Hawse-hole   A hole through the bulwarks, or even through the bows of the hull itself, where the anchor chain enters. The chain then disappears down through the deck and into the chain locker via the Navel pipe.

Hawser-laid   The rope we commonly use is of a construction known as hawser-laid. If you hold the rope in front of you, the strands run upward to the right, and are said to be 'laid right-handed'. Each strand is made of a number of yarns which are laid left-handed. Each yarn is made of fibres, laid right-handed. Just to complete the story, heavy warps are made for ships by laying up three or four hawser-laid ropes left-handed. The result is then known as Cable-laid.

Head (1)   The stem or forward end of a boat. (please see Bow where this concept is covered more fully.) Also the upper end of a spar, as in Masthead. (Though see Truck, which may be useful to you.) The Head of a sail is the top corner of a triangular one, or the whole top edge of a four-sided one. (And see Tack and Clew.) The upper extremity of the Rudder stock is the head.

Head (2)   Of a pier or jetty, the seaward end. The other end is the Root.

Heading   A vessel's heading is simply the direction in which she is heading, in short it is usually her compass course.

Heads A Royal Navy term for lavatory, deriving from the days (which the R.N. finds hard to forget) when the projecting timbers at the bows of sailing vessels, known as knight-heads, served as perches for the performance of natural functions. Regardless of that, 'heads' really have no place on a yacht – unless you want to assert your past naval service, as may indeed be your right.

Headsail A sail that is set at or near the head of the vessel, that's to say before the mast or before the foremast. Most modern yachts are sloops with a single headsail which is hanked on the forestay and logically called a forestaysail or Staysail. A Cutter has two headsails, a staysail and a Jib ahead of that, often set from the bowsprit end. Nowadays, when most boats enjoy only a single headsail, it is common to call that sail a jib, and especially so in sailing dinghies, so in practice the word jib has two meanings. The word foresail is not a generic term for all forward sails as headsail is, but has two specific meanings. In some fishing and working boats the headsail set from stemhead to masthead (not the topmast head, for these would be boats with a mast and separate topmast) was called the foresail. The staysail would then be set outside on the long stay from stemhead to topmast. The jib would always be the sail set from the bowsprit end. The other kind of foresail is set abaft the foremast of a Schooner, and usually has a boom at its foot, so that it is a miniature sister of the mainsail which sets on the after mast (mainmast) of a schooner. (Please see sketch under Sail.)

Headstay The stay from the masthead (or from some point not far below it) to the stemhead. Nowadays commonly called the Forestay.

Heave Apart from its ordinary use (verb), the noun describes the vertical motion of a vessel in the water as the seas lift her. Her other motions are Pitch, Roll, Yaw and Scend.

Heave-to To bring the boat as nearly to a stop as possible, by use of sails or engine. In a sailing boat the headsail(s) is Backed by hauling it over to the windward side of the boat by the sheet. Then by adjustment of mainsail and helm the vessel is held quiet and steady with very little forward movement. A very useful manoeuvre which seems to be used less often than it might be. Please also see Fore-reach (under Fore).

Heaving-line A light line, with a weighted end, which can be heaved to a helper on a dockside and subsequently used by him to haul a mooring line over. The weight is often made of the line itself, by forming it into a decorative knot called a Monkey's fist.

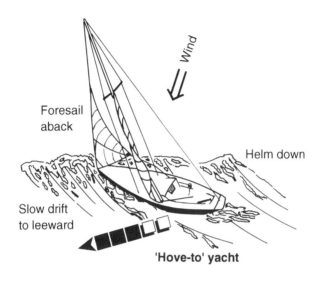

Foresail
aback

Wind

Helm down

Slow drift
to leeward

'Hove-to' yacht

Heel The lower end of a mast, embracing the end-face and the couple of inches next to it. The lower few feet, where halyards are belayed and winches may be mounted, is the Foot of the mast. The lower extremity of a rudder-blade is the heel.

Heel, to The sideways tilt of a sailing boat (and sometimes of a motor boat too) under the influence of the wind. Most people find a heel angle of fifteen degrees to be enough for sustained and pleasurable sailing. Note that if a boat lies over to one side because she is heavy on that side, she Lists. If she heels regularly and alternately first to one side and then to the other, she Rolls.

Heeling error A form of compass Deviation. When a boat heels, both the compass and any magnetic material on board may move sideways in relation to each other. (Picture a compass mounted on deck and an engine below.) Thus deviation is not the same when heeled as when upright. In practice most owners ignore heeling error, largely because of the difficulty of making out deviation cards to correspond to different angles of heel.

Height of tide *(also Rise and Range)* The Height of the tide is the difference of the water level at that moment above Chart datum, which is effectively the lowest level the sea reaches. A term not much used nowadays is the Rise which is properly the Height at High Water specifically; the figure shown under Height in many tide tables should properly be Rise, because it relates to High Water, but the word Height seems more common nowadays. The Range of the tide is the difference between successive Low and High Waters. This figure is the same as Height only at Lowest Astronomical Spring tides, because at other times the Low-Water tide level is not so low as Chart datum. It is important to remember this, because it is a common error to use the height shown in a tide table as if it were the amount by which the level will rise and fall on that day – in other words to confuse it with Range. If you really need to know the range it can be deduced from the height of Mean level: subtract the Height of Mean Level from the Height of HW on that day, and double the result. (Because the tide rises as far above the Mean Level as it falls below, you see.) Now all you need is the Mean Level, which is rarely shown on the tide tables I filch from chandlers' counters. But it can be found by looking for the maximum Springs height and halving it. What you are looking for is the Highest Astronomical Tide which is the opposite of Chart datum, so to speak. Half-way between those high and low points is the Mean level. (Please see Tides, where Neaps and Springs are discussed as well for convenience.)

Helm A word with several shades of meaning. It may be just the tiller, the tiller and the rudder, the whole steering gear including wheel and cable controls, or even the abstract idea of directional control, as in 'she needs more helm'. Nonetheless, it is primarily the Tiller when its meaning is concrete. In any wider sense, as 'she needs a lot of weather helm' one does not say 'weather tiller' even though it is the tiller that must be held to weather. Likewise 'more helm' or 'less helm', or 'she's very light on the helm'. The tiller is just that single and particular component – a handle to turn the rudder. Likewise, 'helmsman' and not 'tiller man' is the modern term for the rather attractive and now obsolescent 'steersman'.

Helm's alee Variation of Hard Alee.

Hemp Hemp, especially Italian hemp, was the best of the natural fibre ropes, though cotton was favoured for the mainsheet because it is soft and that sheet is the one most likely to be handled by the owner. Artificial fibres are stronger, more durable and more reliable, so the only reason for anyone to have a bit of hemp aboard nowadays is for the simple pleasure of handling it.

Hertz Pronounced hairtz, it is a unit of one cycle a second, so frequency of one kilohertz is one thousand cycles a second. Named, like Watt, Ampere, Henry and other scientific units, after a pioneer researcher, the unit is spelled with a small h, unless abbreviated whereupon it takes a capital thus, Hz. (H, in case you are interested, is the abbreviation for henry, a unit of inductance which has no direct interest for yachtsmen.)

High To sail high, or higher, is to sail close to the wind, or closer.

Highfield lever A device for tensioning stays, most commonly runner backstays. The lever swings fore and aft, and throws over top dead centre to lie on the deck when in either the forward (slack) or aft (taut) positions.

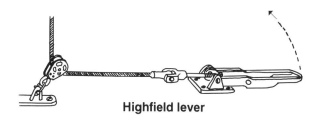

Highfield lever

High Water High tide. Likewise Low Water.

High Water, Full and Change The 'full' refers to the time of the full moon and the 'change' to the time of new or 'changing' moon. The time of High Water bears a constant relationship to the full and new moons at any particular place, and if you know the time of high tide after full moon you will know it for every subsequent full moon through the year. Still, you don't really care, do you, because you get a free tide table from your chandler, or your club, or perhaps even from your bank.

Hike, to or to Hike-out. To sit on the gunwale of (usually) a sailing dinghy with weight as far out to windward as appropriate. Toes may be hitched beneath webbing bands fitted along the bottom of the boat – i.e. hiking straps.

Hitch A sort of knot. And a knot is a sort of hitch. You can argue as long as you like (and some people do, believe me) but I don't believe there is any way of deciding for certain which knots are hitches and which hitches are knots. In any case they are all bends. Nevertheless, when used as a verb, to Hitch means to make fast a rope to a ring or a spar, whereas you Bend one rope to another. You can use a reef knot to bend to ropes together, a topsail sheet bend to hitch a rope firmly to the eye in the clew of a sail, or a rolling hitch to bend one rope to another rope or to a spar. (Now you're as confused as I am)

Hobby-horse, to   A yacht hobby-horses when she pitches up and down with an unpleasantly sharp and rapid motion, making little forward progress the while. It tends to happen when the frequency of short steep seas comes into coincidence with the natural pitching frequency of the hull. One tries to avoid hobby-horsing.

Hobgob   A confused choppy sea, such as will be found at the confluence of tidal streams, or where reflected waves running back from a harbour wall cross at an angle the waves which are running towards it.

Hog   A fore-and-aft timber running above the keel in a wooden boat.

Hogged   Arch-backed, like a hog. A vessel may be hogged accidentally through grounding with her ends unsupported, or she may be designed with a hogged Sheer in the first place. She Sags if she bends the other way. (See Wring.)

Hoist   As a verb has its ordinary sense, but as a noun it is also the vertical dimension of a sail or flag, and the term for a group of signal flags. (See Fly.)

Holding (or holding ground)   Mud, clay and sand provide an anchor with good holding. An area of shingle, on the other hand, is poor holding ground.

Holiday   To owners, a period of rain and gales, but in a boatyard an area of skimped work, especially a patch where paint or glue are deficient.

Hollow run   An area of the hull which is concave gives a hollow run to the water flowing aft, and is itself called a hollow run.

Hood ends   The ends of the planks where they fit into the stem or stern-post rabbets.

Hoops   *(or mast-hoops)* Hoops of ash, Canadian rock elm, or oak, steam-bent into a circle and riveted with copper nails. On gaff-rigged boats they encircle the mast, and the luff of the mainsail is seized to them at regular intervals. When the sail is hoisted they make useful climbing steps.

Horn, horn timber   A traditional cleat has two horns, though not so curvaceous as a cow's. The jaws of a gaff end in two horns. A horn timber is similar to a transom Knee, but the latter implies a more or less vertical transom, whereas a horn timber has a more oblique angle and is appropriate to the shallower-sloping archboard of a counter stern.

Horse (1)   A thwartships metal bar or tube on which a sheet end slides. Most commonly used for the mainsheet, but is also used with a boomed staysail or club-footed jib.

Horse (2)   A bank of sand or mud in what otherwise would be the fairway. Usually one that is exposed at Low Water.

Hounds   Wooden chocks on the mast to engage eyes formed in the lower shrouds, which are slipped over the mast of a gaff-rigged boat. A modern Bermudan-rigged boat cannot have wire eyes passing right round as they would obstruct the track for the sail-slides. Nevertheless, the locality where the lower shrouds and spreaders meet the mast is still called the hounds.

House   A cabin or similar structure built on the deck, or standing substantially above it. Broadly speaking if you stand in a cabin and the deck is at chest level or higher, the superstructure is a Coach-roof. But if the deck comes at hip level or below you would be better advised to call it a House. If it's in between, please yourself.

House, to   To set anything in its proper place, as you might house an anchor in its deck chocks before lashing it down, or house the lower end of a stanchion in its socket.

House-flag   The private flag of a shipping line or of a private owner. A very pretty thing to have, if you are good at sewing. Choose your own designs, taking care only to avoid one that has already been adopted by somebody else.

Hove-to   In English 'hove' is the past tense and past participle of the verb 'to heave'. It retains those functions when in the compound verb to Heave-to. Thus: 'Please heave-to'. 'I have hove-to'. 'That boat over there is hove-to as well'. 'We were both hove-to yesterday afternoon', It ought to be clear enough, but not to some people it ain't: hence my lengthy examples. Personally I rather fancy 'I have hoven-to' for the past tense. Either is permissible, but the older 'hoven' pleases me. At all events, please refer to Heave-to.

Hovercraft   A trade name for what some people call an 'air-cushion vehicle'. Properly it is only one brand, deriving from Sir Christopher Cockrell's original invention. But, like Hoover, it has entered our language, which is what happens when it is nobody's responsibility to invent words for newly-invented things.

Hull The body of a boat, excluding her decks and superstructure, her internal fitments and bulkheads, and her bolt-on ballast keel. If you order a hull all you can expect is an open-topped, rather floppy shell. The nomenclature of the hull is shown in the sketches.

Hull-down A boat is Hull-down when she is so far away from you that her hull is below the horizon and only her mast and sails are visible.

Hurricane A tropical revolving storm with wind of Force 12 or more. Such storms are called cyclones, typhoons and other names in various parts of the world.

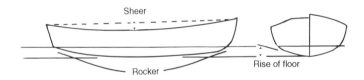

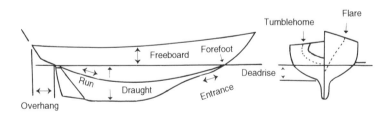

Hull descriptions

HW   High Water.

HW, F & C   High Water, Full and Change.

HWN   High Water, Neaps.

HWS   High Water, Springs.

Hydraulic drive   A form of coupling between engine and propeller in which the engine drives an oil pump and the oil passes to a hydraulic motor mounted close to the propeller. With this arrangement the engine can be mounted wherever it maybe convenient, and may even lie with its crankshaft athwartships, since it is merely a matter of running the oil pipes to the hydraulic motor in the stern of the boat. But hydraulic drives are not cheap.

Hydraulic gearbox   A mechanical forward-neutral-astern gearbox in which the shifts are made by a hydraulic link from the hand lever. A small boat may have a direct-acting lever like a motor car, but a hydraulic link allows the control lever to be fitted at some more remote point in a larger boat. Engine lubricating oil, supplied by the engine pump, is often used as the hydraulic fluid.

Hydrofoil   A wing designed to work in water and to provide lift when moving forward. The term is also commonly applied to a boat fitted with hydrofoils. Such a boat floats in the ordinary way when at rest or moving slowly, but as she accelerates the underwater wings provide enough lift to raise the whole hull from the water. Drag is then much reduced, and high speed can be maintained with economy of power.

Hydrographer   One who practises hydrography, which is the mapping of the seas and the preparation of charts and other information necessary for safe navigation.

I

I   As a single-letter signal in the International Code it means, *'I am altering my course to port'*, and as such is more often given by sound than by any other means. It is two dots in the Morse code, and India in the phonetic alphabet.

IALA buoyage system   The initials stand for International Association of Lighthouse Authorities, and 'the' buoyage system is one result of this group's efforts to reduce the thirty or so buoyage systems of the world to one uniform pattern. Fully titled IALA Maritime Buoyage System 'A', being one of several considered over a period of years, this system is an amalgam of the Lateral and Cardinal systems which were in use by various European countries. *System A* follows the 'red to port'. *System B* has red to starboard, as in (e.g.) US waters. This dictionary is not the right place to give a complete description of the systems – Almanacs and most books on navigation contain full information.

Imminent   In weather forecasts this means that the expected conditions will arrive in the specified area within six hours. Soon means within twelve hours, and Later means beyond twelve hours.

IMCO   Inter-Governmental Maritime Consultative Organisation.

Inboard   As a comparative of position it indicates that a thing is nearer the centre of the ship than another. As an absolute term it means anything within the shell of the ship, as Inboard motor, whereas a bathing ladder would be Shipped outboard.

Inboard-outboard   Another name for Stern drive.

Index error   Of a sextant, is simply a misalignment of the index or pointer – that's to say, when the mirrors are parallel, the index shows an angle whereas it should show zero.

Indraft   A current setting into a bay or a sound.

Inflatable   The commonly-used abbreviation for inflatable boat. (Though since it is a boat only when inflated, I sometimes wonder if the word should not be 'deflatable'.) Inflatables are light, stable and popular as yachts' tenders. But they are no cheaper than rigid dinghies of the same carrying capacity, and they wear out in ten years or less whereas a rigid boat should last you a lifetime.

Inglefield clips Interlocking C-shaped metal clips used for attaching signal flags to a halyard or to each other.

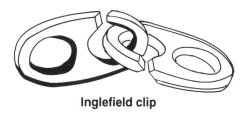

Inglefield clip

Inhaul A rope used to haul the jib in from the bowsprit end, or any rope doing a similar job. Downhaul is equally obvious.

In irons A sailing boat is in irons when she comes head to wind and fails to Pay off on either tack. The answer is to make a Stern board, to let the wind push her backwards and then to use the rudder to throw her stern off to one side or the other.

Initial stability Like a flat-bottomed vase, some hull forms are stable to a certain angle of heel, and will return to the level if released. But, like the vase, if pushed too far they go right over. They have only initial stability. The round-bottomed toy clown who comes up from any angle has more than initial stability – his is ultimate. Beamy flat-bottomed boats have high initial stability, and so do catamarans, but neither type has the ultimate stability of the boat with a deep ballasted keel which will pick herself up even if knocked flat. (The beamy barge-type boat should not be knocked flat, of course, nor should a catamaran. That would be carelessness and poor seamanship.)

Inshore As a comparative, towards the shore, or nearer the shore than the observer. As an absolute, that region of sea which is, broadly speaking, where the land is in sight from a small boat. The region where many of us do most of our sailing. (Please see Offshore.)

In stays A sailing boat is in stays when she is going from one tack to the other, and in the arc when her sails are not drawing. She must always be in stays before she can get In Irons, though the one condition does not necessarily follow the other – indeed, it should be a rarity.

Internal halyards Halyards which run down the inside of a hollow mast (usually aluminium alloy) to emerge near deck level. They reduce windage and save you the trouble of Frapping them to avoid the abominable and slovenly clatter which characterises so many moorings and marinas nowadays.

International Code of Signals A system of standard signals using mainly two letters (three for medical messages) in place of certain phrases and sentences. I have given the single-letter signals – if you want the full list you must buy a copy of the code book from Her Majesty's Stationery Office or a chandler.

Interrupted quick flashing light A light which flashes at a rate of more than 60 times a minute, but with periods of darkness at regular intervals.

Intumescent paint A paint which protects glass-reinforced resin ('fibreglass') against fire. The polyester resin of which most modern boats are built will burn merrily, so it is wise to protect the galley and engine areas with intumescent paint. When heated, this paint swells up into a crust, not unlike meringue, cutting off the oxygen supply to the resin, and to some extent insulating it from heat.

Inwale The upper edge of a wooden hull may have a strake inside the top ends of the frames. This is the inwale. The strake outside is commonly called the Gunwale. (Neither has anything to do with whales. Please see Wale.)

IOD International One Design.

IOR International Offshore Rule.

Irish pennants Tatty ends of frayed rope flying in the breeze.

Ironbound An ironbound coast is a rocky one without anchorage or haven.

Iron topsail In the past, when the wind fell light a gaff-rigged boat would set her topsail. Nowadays someone just presses the starter button of the diesel, otherwise know as the iron topsail.

Isobar A line drawn on a weather map linking points of equal atmospheric pressure.

Isobath   A line drawn on a chart to link places of equal depth.

Isogon   A line drawn on a chart to link places of the same magnetic Variation.

Isophase light   A flashing light with equal durations of light and darkness.

IYRU   International Yacht Racing Union.

J

J As a single-letter signal it means, 'I am on fire and have dangerous cargo on board; keep well clear of me'. In the Morse code it is •——— and in the phonetic alphabet it is Juliet.

Jack The Union Flag or Union Jack is the national flag of the United Kingdom, but it is worn at sea only by ships of the Royal Navy, or ships with royalty aboard. (Please see Ensign.)

Jack-in-the-basket A pole with a cylindrical cage on top, forming a beacon. There never seems to be anyone, or any thing, in the basket. Odd . . .

Jackstaff The staff right forward on a warship where the Union Jack is flown. Pleasure craft fly an Ensign, and thus may have an ensign staff, and it will be shipped right aft.

Jackstay A tightly stretched wire to hold the edge of an awning or a sail, or along which something may slide. If the Coastguard ever rescue you by breeches buoy they will haul you along a taut jackstay. But the most immediate use of a jackstay for the average boat-owner is when stretched along the deck as a lifeline for his personal harness.

Jackyard A short yard which is bent to the foot of a topsail to carry it aft of the gaff.

Jaws (1) The fork of a gaff which seats around the mast. Shown are the solid traditional style and a modern lightweight (dinghy) version.

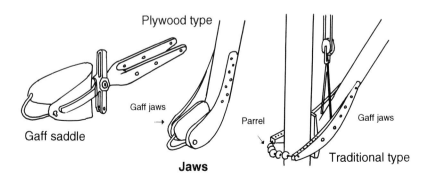

Jaws

Jaws (2) Of a block, the slot in which the Sheave is fitted. (The phrase 'Long in the jaw ' refers to rope and will be found on another page.)

Jetsam Goods thrown overboard, originally to lighten a vessel, but also applicable to wantonly abandoned rubbish – which is illegal. (And see Flotsam.)

Jib Properly the foremost sail, and the one set to the bowsprit end. Aft of the jib there would have been a forestaysail (Staysail for short) hanked on to the forestay. Some people still call any such sail a staysail, and all credit to them, but since on many modern boats the staysail is the only Headsail, it is commonly called the 'jib' by the great army of people who find it hard to cope with words of more than one syllable.

Jibe Just the simplified, American spelling of Gybe.

Jib-boom A bowsprit upon a bowsprit, so to speak. A spar which can be extended forward of the bowsprit to carry an outer jib in light weather.

Jib-headed In the days when gaff rig was common any sail without a spar at the top – like a jib, with three sides instead of four – was called 'jib-headed'. The term is rare now, but those who read the older books will come across it. Also see Marconi.

Jib-stick A light spar which is used to hold a jib or staysail outboard when running with the wind free.

Jib topsail A small jib set flying above the ordinary jib.

Jiffy reef A popular and efficient type of Slab reef. The reefing-line is fixed to the main boom at a predetermined point (either tied around the boom through a slot in the foot of the mainsail, or to a sliding eye in a track under the boom, both near the clew) and thence up through the reefing eye on the leech,then back down and through a turning block on the boom and forward to the mast. It can then be secured either by a lever cleat within the boom or to a cleat on the mast, or via turning blocks back to a cleat on the coachroof. The last method gives total control from the cockpit. The slack sailcloth can be reefed conventionally or if racing, and on a short windward leg, tidied only at the mast end so as not to create excessive drag.This is the most efficient system of mainsail reefing in that it flattens the sail for stronger winds.

Jigger The small mast (and also the sail) which is carried right aft in American yawls. On both sides of the Atlantic, Mizzen is the more modern term of both mast and sail, and especially the sail. Where differentiation is needed, one says Mizzenmast, but never 'mizzen sail'.

Jockey pole Please see Reaching Strut

JOG Junior Offshore Group.

Jumbo A large staysail, usually associated with a cutter. Long in the foot, it is set to the hounds, and is thus lower than the typical Genoa of conventional Bermudan-rigged yachts.

Jumper stay A stay on the fore-side of a mast, to prevent it from bowing forward. It is taken over a *Jumper strut*, the strut providing the rearward push at the desired point, commonly where a forestay meets the mast about three-quarters of the way up.

Junk and junk rig Junks are the native craft of China and they take many forms, with up to as many as five masts with a variety of features which could fill a book in themselves. It is the rig which has attracted many Europeans for its effectiveness, cheapness and ease of handling and reefing. In brief the junk rig sets a Lugsail on an unstayed mast, as shown in the sketch. The sail is made up of many panels, with full-chord bamboo battens between. Each batten acts effectively as a boom, and each has its own sheet, with all the sheets leading to a single control.

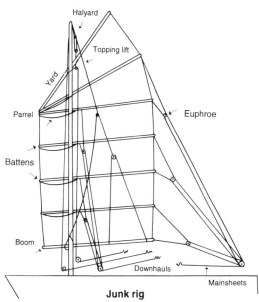

Junk rig

Jury An adjective describing any temporary or makeshift device, such as a rudder made from a table, a mast from an oar, or an anchor from an outboard motor.

105

K

K   As a flag, or flashed in Morse code, —•—, it means, *'I wish to communicate with you'*. In the phonetic alphabet it is Kilo, pronounced 'key-low'.

Kedge   A relatively light and secondary anchor used for a variety of purposes, such as backing up the main or Bower anchor, or for a temporary stop when great security is not required. To anchor in that way is 'to kedge'. To Kedge off is to haul the boat off the mud, or into another position, by laying the kedge anchor out from the dinghy. To make such work easier and lighter, the kedge is normally used with a rope cable rather than chain.

Keel   A word with several associated meanings. In the first place it is the principal fore-and-aft timber member of a boat's backbone. To the keel proper may be bolted a Ballast keel of iron or lead. The first kind of keel is a structural component, the second a dynamic component with the functions of holding the boat upright and reducing her leeway. In the second category are Bilge keels, or Twin keels. These may be fitted to a hull which has a structural keel, or to a moulded resinglass hull which has no such member. But even if the boat has a real keel, her bilge keels would in that case not be attached to it: they would be carried by bilge-stringers or bilge-plates, one to each side of the hull. A False keel is added externally, beneath the keel proper, to increase the draft – for example to give a rowing boat additional area to resist lateral drift.

Keelson   A fore-and-aft timber fitted above the keel, and above the transverse Floors which link the frames. The complete backbone structure may consist of the keel timber, the Hog, which is wider and shallower to provide a landing for the Garboards, and above that, sandwiching the floors, the keelson.

Ketch   A two-masted sailing boat, with the after or mizzen mast forward of the rudder. Well, that's one definition, and its corollary says that a Yawl has the mizzen aft of the rudder. But it is not always as simple as that, and when deciding whether to call a boat ketch or yawl one must pay attention to the proportions of her main and mizzen sails. A yawl will have a mizzen amounting to only a quarter, or at most a third the area of the main, whereas a ketch's mizzen will be from fifty per cent upwards. In boats of less than about forty feet, the drawback with either two-masted rig is that the mizzen and its rig takes up useful space in the region of the cockpit and after deck – and costs more.

Kevel   A large upstanding timber, usually the head of a frame prolonged above deck level, whose purpose is to belay warps. Not to be found in yachts and small pleasure craft, but would be found on a larger and older boat, often in the form of two uprights with a cross-bar.

Kicking strap A tensioned strop to prevent the boom from lifting. Usually running from the foot of the mast to meet the boom at about forty-five degrees, but in a more sophisticated arrangement its lower end runs in a curved track or Horse on deck, thus giving a vertical pull.

Kingplank In a wooden boat, a strong central timber in the deck. More than just a deck plank, it will often be several inches thick, especially in the region just abaft the Stem where it may make a base for Bitts or anchor Windlass.

Kingspoke A distinctive spoke on a steering wheel to show when the wheel is centred.

Kitchen rudder A steering device in the form of a pair of metal clamshells enclosing the propeller. When the shells are open the water flows directly aft. By closing them aft of the rudder they form a rounded 'bucket' which turns the water flow forward and thrusts the boat astern. With the shells open they may be turned in unison, to port or starboard to steer the boat. (Spelled with a capital K after the name of the inventor.)

Kite A light-weight, light-weather sail, flown high up. Slang for spinnaker if you hadn't guessed !

Knees Approximately L-shaped pieces of timber, or metal, used to support Thwarts or deck beams, or indeed to strengthen the joint between any two components meeting at something near a right angle. Hanging knees are fitted vertically, Lodging knees horizontally. A wooden knee may be cut from a piece of timber with suitable grain, or it may be laminated by bending and gluing thin strips.

Knot (1) Generally used as a term for a speed of one Nautical Mile an hour. Some people get very cross if you talk about 'knots an hour', while others delight in producing seemingly sound arguments in support of that usage. In fact, and in real life, when people talk about knots they mean speed, not distance.

Knot (2) Knots, like Bends and Hitches, are ways of joining rope to something else. But don't ask me which is which, I've said my little piece under Hitch.

Knuckle A relatively sharp curve in a frame or in the contour of a hull (illustrated in Hull sketch). This is one of those terms which are freely used by boatbuilders and designers but which are hard to get hold of until you actually know. If you think of a traditional timber boat and liken her frames to fingers you get the point. The numerous breed of Laurent Giles-designed Westerly Boats (Pageant, Centaur, Renown, etc.) all show knuckle in their Bows.

L

L If someone flashes this at you in Morse code, •—•• it means, *'You should stop your vessel immediately'*. For radio-telephone work it is Lima, with the Li pronounced Lee.

Lacing eye (and hook) A lacing eye is a small bridge-shaped metal fitting with a hole at each end to attach it to coaming, deck or whatever. A lacing hook is half a bridge, or finger, with two screw holes to hold the foot.

Laid deck A deck made of narrow planks of teak, each about two inches wide, and caulked between with black Marine Glue. Lovely to behold, kind to bare feet, and rather tedious to maintain. (Anyway, I can't afford it.)

Laminate, to To make a wooden component, usually curved, by gluing together relatively thin strips or sheets of wood. Or to build up a composite structure of glass-reinforced resin by putting down successive layers of glass material and impregnating them with the resin. A 'laminator' in modern parlance is one who earns his living (and earns is right) by doing this messy work with resin and glass.

Laminate As a noun, a sheet of material, usually resinglass, made by laminating.

Lanby Made from the initial letters of Large Automatic Navigational Buoy, this word defines a type of buoy which is steadily replacing light-vessels. Big enough to provide refuge for seamen in distress, such a buoy houses a diesel generator and a variety of sophisticated equipment, much of it controlled by radio from the shore.

Land The overlapping part (or 'lap') of two planks in a Clinker-built boat. (Alternatively, the place which lovers of the sea so frequently yearn for.)

Land breeze Please look up Sea breeze.

Landfall The land which is first seen or met at the end of a sea passage. A Landfall buoy is one with a tall superstructure sited a mile or so to seaward of a harbour or channel to help mariners locate it.

Lanolin A grease extracted from sheep's wool which protects human skin, wire shrouds, ironwork and other metal components. Very thick and heavy in its natural state, it is easily applied if first dissolved in warmed white spirit. But take care to buy only anhydrous lanolin, which is free from water. (Cosmetic lanolin 'creams', by contrast, have been deliberately emulsified with water, and apart from being poor value, are useless as a protective for metals.)

Lanyard A short length of cord or rope, used as a safety line to prevent loss of an object overboard, as a line to raise a bucket of water from the sea, to secure a whistle or knife, and especially to set shrouds taut with Dead-eyes. Before the introduction of Rigging screws, lanyards and dead-eyes were always used for that purpose, and some owners still prefer them for their lightness and low cost.

Lapstrake A form of hull planking where each Strake (plank) overlaps the next plank below. In England this construction is now more commonly know as Clinker, though lapstrake is still normal term in some parts, as it is in the USA.

Large A useful word that seems to have been forgotten. 'Sailing large' is to have the wind somewhere between the beam and dead astern. The nearest common term is Broad reach.

LAT Lowest Astronomical Tide. (Please see Height of Tide.)

Lateen A triangular sail with the foot more or less horizontal, and the leech more or less vertical. The luff is laced to a long spar which extends forward of the mast and slants upward toward its after end. Seen on the Nile boats and Red Sea dhows, and on some European dinghies, though its former popularity in the West has waned.

Later In weather forecasts it means 'arriving after a lapse of twelve hours at least.' Please see Imminent.

Lateral buoyage A fairway or 'street' system of buoyage, with flat-topped red buoys to port, and conical green buoys to starboard, when you are moving in the same direction as the Flood tide. (Please see IALA buoyage system.)

Lateral plane The projected underwater area of hull, keel and rudder as it would be seen on a flat drawing of the side elevation. It is the total area available to resist Leeway.

Lateral resistance The ability of a hull to resist Leeway, or sideways movement through the water. It is especially desirable in sailing craft because of the lateral force of the sails.

Latitude The position of a place on the earth's surface, measured as an angle from the equator. (See Longitude.)

Launch A small open boat driven by mechanical power at displacement speed. A launch is invariably of traditional character, and usually of some elegance.

Lay Of a rope or cable, is the spiral twist of the strands which compose it. In making a splice the strands tucked in may spiral in the opposite direction, 'against the lay', or in the same direction, 'with the lay'.

Lay, to When one draws a course on a chart, following the appropriate calculations, one is said to 'lay it off on the chart'. If the boat subsequently sails to that course she will be said to be 'laying her course'. (Compare with Fetch.) If the wind is in the wrong direction you may find that 'she can't quite lay the course'. As a result of that, she won't 'fetch her mark' either. But when she finally reaches harbour, her skipper will use the verb in quite another way, and will say, 'I'll lay her alongside the quay'. By that he means that he will bring her to rest at the quay, and nothing more. The next step will be to moor her, the laying alongside having ended when she comes to a stop. Nevertheless, she may thereafter lie at (or to) the quay for the next two or three weeks. (and see Lie.)

Lay out, to To take an anchor out from your boat, in a dinghy or across the beach on foot, as distinct from dropping it underfoot, from the boat herself.

Lay up, to (1) To take a boat out of service. She may be laid up either ashore or afloat, and with or without her mast stepped and fuel in her tanks. But she will not be in her normal state of readiness for sea-going. An insurance company charges less to cover a laid-up boat, but the company will not consider her laid up if you are cooking and sleeping aboard.

Lay up, to (2) To make a laminate of glass fibres and resin. The ordinary process of making a fibreglass shell or component.

Lay-up A laminate of glass and resin. 'The lay-up is uniform and free from bubbles, but it looks a bit thin to me. . . .'

Lazy block A block fitted to a deck-plate so that it is upright when loaded, but will lie down when not actually working (the type of block commonly used for genoa sheets). If possible a lazy block should be held upright by a length of shock-cord leading to the guard rail or other convenient point. Alternatively the eye may be bound with rubbery tape. At all events it is very irritating to those below if it is free to keep thumping the deck.

Lazy jacks A pair of ropes passing from the mast down each side of the mainsail to a point somewhere inboard of the end of the boom. Their purpose is to gather the sail as it is dropped. Several lazy jacks may be used together, spaced along the boom as in the junk rig. Lazy jacks are much appreciated on gunter-rigged boats where the yard might otherwise clout somebody on the head if lowered without great care. The same term is used of the set of lines which may be looped between mast and forestay so as to prevent a spinnaker from wrapping itself around a stay. (see also Anti-fouling net.)

Lazy lead A free swivelling block for wire rope, used in steering gears and held up by the tension in the cable. Like a lazy block, it will fall down if not kept at work.

LBP Length Between Perpendiculars is a term rarely used in full, indeed rarely used at all nowadays, though one may come across it in reading. It is the length between a perpendicular dropped from the stemhead of a hull and another dropped from the after face of the stern post. You will see that we are talking of timber construction, and you have to remember that many a boat had a counter extending aft of the stern post and rudder. The counter was a sort of elegant addendum to the basic fishing-boat type of hull, and, when added, it made the distinction between Length Over all (LOA) and LBP. The significance of LBP is that it was the figure used for the calculation of Thames Tonnage.

Lead The lead is a lump of lead, attached to a light line and used for taking Soundings. Naval practice specifies the precise weight of the lead, and the manner in which the line is to be marked, but that has little value for small craft. It is better to make up your own mind, in accordance with your own needs. Even though you have an Echo sounder, it is prudent to carry a lead-line aboard. Even if the echo sounder does not go wrong, its transducer is located at a single point. With the lead-line you can sound all round the boat and so know whether the bottom is level or if you are about to ground on a bank that slopes at forty-five degrees.

Lead Pronounced 'leed', refers to the direction in which a rope runs, a matter of some importance on boats where ropes are so much used. To get a fair lead, with minimum chafe and friction is the objective, and fittings called Fairleads are made for that very purpose.

Leading marks *(or lights)* Clearly seen objects, natural or artificial, which lead a vessel on a safe course when kept in alignment, or in Transit.

Leading wind The same thing as a Following Wind. Sounds silly, perhaps, but please see Following Wind.

Lee   Both noun and adjective. A lee is shelter from the wind, so you may anchor close under a wooded shore to get a lee. Qualifying something else it means on the side, or in the direction, towards which the wind is blowing. Driftwood blows up on to a lee shore: a lee-going tide is a tidal Stream running in roughly the same direction as the wind. But usage is not simple; a lee shore is to Leeward of the viewer; it therefore has he full force of the wind blowing on to it. (Leeward is pronounced 'loo-erd', by the way.) Please also see Weather.

Leeboard   Normally in pairs, port and starboard, though a small boat may have a single one that is shifted to the leeward side as required. Most commonly seen on Thames barges, and the wide variety of flat-bottomed Dutch boats, the leeboard is pivoted on the side of a shallow hull so that it can be lowered into a more or less vertical position where it acts as a hydrofoil to resist Leeway. It has the same function as the Centreboard in a sailing dinghy, but avoids the problem of building a centreboard trunk and leaves more space free for fish or cargo. The plan form of leeboards varies from broad to narrow, but long before aerodynamicists had studied wing sections, simple boatbuilders were making their leeboards with cambered aerofoil sections to generate lift to weather. The pressure so generated holds the leeward leeboard firmly against a heavy Wale on the hull side. There is much more that could be said about the design and use of leeboards, but its practical value would be limited to the one boat owner in ten thousand whose boat may be so equipped.

Lee-bowing   Sailing on a tack such that the tidal stream is carrying the boat towards the wind. This makes possible a track closer to windward and also increases the relative wind speed of the boat. There is a corresponding term 'weather-bowing' for the other tack where the stream takes you downwind.

Leech   Probably originally 'lee edge', this is the extreme after edge of a sail – what aircraft people would call the 'trailing edge. (See Luff and Foot.)

Leech-line   A light line passed through the hollow hem of a sail's leech for the adjustment of its tension and curvature.

Lee helm   A sailing boat which has 'lee helm' must have the helm held down to Leeward to maintain a straight course when on the wind. Lee helm is necessary because she is trying to Pay off, or Bear away; the rudder must hold her head up to the wind. Designers avoid lee helm because any increase in wind speed tends to turn the boat more across the wind, increasing the heeling force. This may be dangerous, whereas Weather helm works in the opposite sense and is a safety feature. Some boats show a modest amount of lee helm when the wind is very light, but change to weather helm as soon as the wind is fresh enough to cause a few degrees of heel. That is quite acceptable, of course.

Lee-oh   Before tacking, the helmsman gives the warning call 'Ready about', followed after a sufficient interval by 'Lee-oh' as he puts the helm down to leeward.

Leeward   Downwind. In the direction toward which the wind is blowing. The opposite from Windward. Strangely, it is pronounced as if spelled loo-ard. But the lee side of the boat is not called the loo-side. . .

Lee rail under   The sort of chap who likes to be awash with beer likes to tell you how 'We had her lee rail under, old boy', because he thinks it sounds a bit dashing. The Rail from which the term originates was the capping timber along the bulwark, but is now more likely to be the narrow outboard plank forming the deck-edge, or the Toe-rail. Few boats sail well with this part under water.

Lee-shore   A shore towards which the wind is blowing. A natural place of danger, since a vessel tends to be blown on to it.

Leeway   The sideways movement of a sailing boat when sailing on the wind. When close-hauled in a calm sea it may be slight, so that the difference between her Heading and her Track may be less than five degrees. But this Leeway angle becomes greater as the sea becomes rougher. Much also depends on the form of hull and its Lateral plane. It is no simple matter for the navigator to estimate leeway, even though he may know his boat well, for the helmsman will often tend to steer slightly Higher when going to windward. Attention to the compass will show whether variations of heading tend more to the weather or to the lee side – or they may reveal that you have (or are) a perfect helmsman, maintaining a correct average heading.

Left bank   Of a river, is on the left when facing downstream, but the 'port hand' would normally mean to port when facing upstream – i.e. the right bank.

Left-handed   Of a propeller, turning anti-clockwise when viewed from the rear – i.e. the upper blade moving towards the left. Of a rope, with the strands slanting upward and to the left when you hold the rope vertically before your eyes.

Leg   (1)   A tack to windward, as 'we made a long leg on port, followed by a short one to starboard'. One side of a racing course.

Leg (2) A strut of timber or metal which can be shipped on the side of a boat to hold her upright when she dries out. Usually in pairs, held to the hull by bolts passing into plates in the hull-sides, and braced fore and aft by rope guys.

Length The length of a boat is her length. Obvious enough, but boating jargon is not so rational as that. With that strange human desire to use three words where one would do, we tend to say 'length over all' to mean the length from stem to stern, when you might reasonably think that it would mean the length over all – including bowsprit, bumkin and any other extras. But it does not. This silly term is abbreviated as LOA and is nearly always found in the company of LWL, which is length of the hull at the waterline when the boat is loaded to her average working weight.

Let draw, to When going about, there comes a point when the headsail sheet must be let fly so that the sail can pass to the other tack. When that is to be done the order is, 'Let draw', whereupon the old sheet is let fly and the new one is trimmed as quickly as possible. Probably very few pleasure sailors bother with orders of this kind, since they can rely on each other to do the right thing. But there are times, especially when leaving an anchorage or manoeuvring in close quarters, when the headsail must be held aback for a period in order to force the boat's head round smartly. 'Let draw' then find its use.

Lie, lie-to, to A boat which is stationary lies. In the open sea in heavy weather she 'lies-to' under bare poles. In harbour she lies alongside a wall or another vessel. In winter she lies in a mud berth, and if you are buying and want to view a boat, the broker will tell you she is 'lying Exmouth' in the jargon of his trade.

Lie a hull, to To lie in a heavy sea with all sail lowered and stowed.

Lie alongside, to A boat lies alongside another in a harbour berth, but husband and wife rarely get a chance to lie alongside in a berth below decks, a deprivation for which yacht designers must take the blame.

Lifebelt and lifebuoy These terms tend to become confused, but since the ring-type has largely given way to the horseshoe type, perhaps buoy is the better. If you do get a ring type, take care to get a man-sized one of 30 inches (760 mm) diameter. The object of the exercise is life-saving, not neat appearance or easy stowage.

Lifeboat Ships carry lifeboats (also called ship's boats), and lifeboats of quite different type are owned and manned by the Coast Guard in the USA, the Royal National Lifeboat Institution in Britain, and equivalent bodies in other countries. Private pleasure craft are not big enough to have dinghies which can serve as lifeboats, though the better-quality inflatable dinghies are a good compromise. The true ship's lifeboat for a yacht is the inflatable Liferaft.

Lifejacket A vest or jacket worn like a garment and giving some 35lb of buoyancy. To earn its name it must be designed in such a way that the wearer naturally floats on his back, with mouth and nose held up clear of the water. A distinction is made between a lifejacket proper, and various kinds of buoyant waistcoats and vests giving lesser degrees of buoyancy (but greater freedom of movement). It all depends on the type of boating you do. In the USA the generic term is PFD (Personal Flotation Device). Several grades of PFD are approved by the US Coast Guard, for differing circumstances.

Lifeline Sometimes the Guard rail around the deck, sometimes the short line linking your personal harness to the boat, and sometimes the Jackstay along the deck to which you can attach your lifeline. Usage is inconsistent – as usual.

Liferaft The modern liferaft is an Inflatable, experience in the Second World War having indicated that the inflatable raft, with protective canopy, is a better life-saver than the rigid lifeboat. Private boat-owners find an inflatable liferaft expensive to buy and to maintain, for it must be professionally serviced every year without fail. A large inflatable dinghy is a good compromise, especially if you can arrange some weather protection.

Lift A line of wire or rope giving support to a part of the rig. The Topping lift supports the boom, and can usually lift it. But a lift may be static – for example a short wire stay above a spreader to ensure that it cannot drop down to the wrong angle.

Light-vessel *(or lightship)* A moored, and usually engineless vessel fitted with a lamp powered by generators and manned by a crew, marking a hazard. Light-vessels are now being replaced by Lanbys.

Lignum vitae A hard wood, used for Parrel balls, for Blocks and for Fairleads. Rather rare nowadays, in the face of Tufnol, which does the job better, and nylon, which is often a waste of money as it can wear away so rapidly.

Limber hole One of a series of holes made in the frames (or floors) where they meet keel, hog, or perhaps keelson so that water can drain aft to the bilge-pump suction. They must not be allowed to remain blocked, and some owners thread a light brass chain through all the limber holes form one end of the boat to the other so that fluff, matchsticks and toffee papers can be cleared by jiggling to and fro.

Line Generally the smaller sizes of rope carried aboard. The actual size depends on the size of the vessel, but for private boats, 'line' is roughly equivalent to the garden clothes line, or smaller.

Line start In racing, a start across a line lying between two fixed points. (See also Gate start.)

Lines A boat's lines are simply the lines drawn on paper to show her hull shape in plan, end elevation and side elevation. The drawing shows which lines are which.

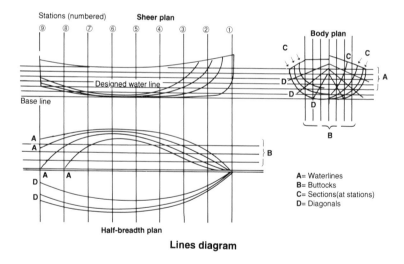

Lines diagram

Link shackle   A shackle in the form of a C, whose opening is closed by a screw-nut.

List, to   Please see Heel, to.

Lizard   The term is not so much used as it might be, but the thing itself is useful to have about. It is just a short length of rope with a hard eye spliced into one end. The other end can be hitched to another rope or chain, say, and by passing a further rope through the eye you can get the purchase of a single whip for a good heave. It may also prove useful as a temporary Fairlead.

Lloyd's Register of Yachts   Was a useful Who's Who of private pleasure craft, their builders and their owners which was published annually in Britain until 1980, but had absolutely nothing to do with any government registration of vessels. 'Registered at Lloyd's is a meaningless phrase. On the other hand 'classified' by Lloyd's is very significant for it means that the boat has been built under the supervision of a Lloyd's surveyor and that she has been kept up to standard by periodic surveys and appropriate remedial work. This is not the place to go fully into the intricacies of Lloyd's procedures, but it is worth remarking that there are various grades of classification, as well as sub grades indicating that a boat has been well build insofar as her hull is concerned, though she may not have been well maintained. Please see Classification, which is a word to know.

LOA   Length Over All. (Please see Length.)

LOP   Line of position, which is the same thing as a Position Line.

Locker   Any sort of cupboard, closet, wardrobe, cuddy,, pantry, nice nook or glory-hole which you may use as stowage. It needs no lock and may not even have a door.

Lock-off   A device which holds a rope by bearing down on it with a cam-and-lever, or something of that sort. In England it is called a Stopper.

Loft (and to loft)   Noun and verb, closely related. The large flat floor of a loft was a good place to draw the outline of a sail or the frames of a hull in chalk. The process of laying out and drawing at full scale thus became lofting, no matter whether done in the basement or on sheets of hardboard in the back garden.

Log (1)   Short for log-book, in which all necessary navigational information and ship's progress is recorded. Was originally a 'log-board', taking the form of two black-painted boards hinged together to open like a book, on which the readings of the Log (2) could be written in chalk.

Log (2) Short for log-chip (or log-ship), a fan-shaped wedge of wood, weighted to float upright, which was streamed astern on a line of known length so that the ship's speed could be determined from the time taken for the line to run out. About a hundred years ago the Patent log began to come into use, streaming a spinner at the end of a plaited line which rotates the mechanism in the recorder onboard, showing distance run which is far more valuable than speed. This type of log is still used by many private owners, though there are several more sophisticated types now available using modern electronic techniques.

Long in the jaw A rope which is old and well stretched becomes long in the jaw, the 'jaw' being the length occupied by a strand in making one full turn.

Longitude The position of any point on the earth's surface measured as an angle east or west of the Greenwich meridian, which is also known as the 'prime meridian' and is zero longitude. (see also Latitude.)

Longitudinal Any fore-and-aft structural member of a boat's hull.

Long splice Please see Splice for both the Long and Short kinds, as well as the others.

Loom (1) The reflection on the clouds of a light which is too distant to be seen directly because it is below the horizon. Occasionally the loom of a distant light is clear enough to reveal its characteristic, and so offers a useful navigational aid. Also the hazy appearance of land through mist, just as in ordinary land-bound English.

Loom (2) That part of an oar's shaft which the oarsman grips – the opposite end to the Blade.

Loose-footed A mainsail is loose-footed when its Clew is extended by a boom, but its Foot is not attached along the length of the boom. There are also boomless mainsails, and these are better so termed to distinguish them from those which have a boom with foot unattached.

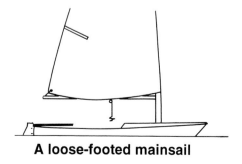

A loose-footed mainsail

118

Lop   A short choppy sea with no weight in it. A term appropriate to sheltered water, whereas a Chop would be found in more exposed water.

Loran   A long-range navigational aid making use of pulsed radio transmissions from linked stations.

Low Water, Low Tide   Please see Height of Tide.

Lubber's line Or **Lubber line.**   A reference line against which the compass scale is read.

Luff   The forward edge of a fore-and-aft sail. What an aviator would call the 'leading edge'. (See Leech and Foot.)

Luff, to   To bring the boat head to wind, or more near to the wind. The expression is often 'luff up', as in,'Luff up a little, old chap, and let's see if she'll point a bit higher'.

Luff rope   Please see Bolt rope.

Luff spar   A slender spar, usually of metal or wood, to which the Luff of a Headsail is attached. Its purpose is either to give a clean aerodynamic edge, or to permit reefing by rolling the cloth around the spare.

Luff tackle   Uses one single and one double block to obtain an advantage of three-to-one.

Lugsail   A four-sided fore-and-aft sail whose upper edge is attached to a Yard which extends ahead of the mast. The Dipping lug has no boom, and the yard has to be 'dipped' and passed round the mast when the boat tacks. The *Standing lug* has a boom whose forward end pivots at the mast. The *Balance lug* has a boom which projects forward of the mast but is not attached to it: the boom is Bowsed down with a lanyard. The *Chinese lug* has a boom and a number of battens extending from luff to leech, all of which, like the boom, extended forward of the mast. These boomed lugsails are not dipped. You didn't ask, but I may as well tell you that the lug is my choice for a sailing dinghy: the balance lug for boats up to ten or eleven feet, the standing lug for anything bigger. It is the ideal sail for pleasure boating as opposed to formula racing. (See Gunter lug, and the sketch of the Balance lug, which names the parts of the sail.)

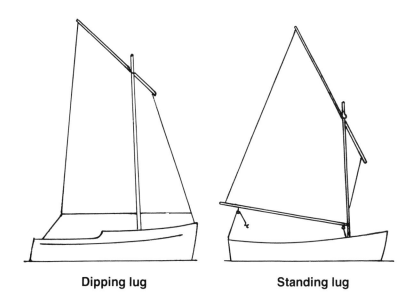

Dipping lug **Standing lug**

Lutchet Neither the word not the device is much used these days. It is similar to a tabernacle, but extends below deck level and has one side open to clear the foot of the mast when it is lowered. A lutchet makes it possible to fit a counter-balance weight to the foot of a mast below deck level.

LWL Length, Waterline. The same abbreviation is sometimes used for Load Water Line, meaning the waterline of the boat at her average working weight with stores and crew aboard, and water and fuel tanks half filled. When seen alongside LOA (as it usually is), LWL refers to length, but in books or articles on design the context should reveal whether the author has chosen to use the abbreviation in another sense.

M

M Two dashes in Morse code, and means, *'My vessel is stopped and making no way through the water'* in the International Code. Mike in phonetic.

M Magnetic

Magnetic Of bearings, courses and the like, means that the direction is measured as an angle related to Magnetic North rather than True North. (Please see North.)

Main Of two masts the taller is the Mainmast. If it is the after of two then the forward one is the Foremast, but if the main is to the fore then the lower after mast is the Mizzen. The Mainsail is carried on and abaft the mainmast. All pretty obvious.

Main flood The direction of the tidal stream is often used as a reference in pilotage notes and so forth. An object left on your port hand when you are moving in the direction of the flooding tide would obviously be left to starboard if you were moving in the opposite direction, and the distinction is crucial. But there are eddies and reverse currents in nature, so the pilot books refer to the Main flood – that's to say, the general direction of the flood tide as·a whole.

Make, to Of tides. After Neaps, the daily Range becomes greater, and tides are said to be making. In this sense we have plural tides. The term may be used of any one tide on any one day, as when you have been aground for the best part of the day and a cheerful crew member at last tells you, 'Tide's making, skip'. He means to tell you that it is visibly rising even though in the broader sense tides in general may be Taking off, or moving away from Springs towards Neaps.

Make the land, to To pick up the land after a passage away from it.

Make sail, to To set sails. And to make more sail is to add a sail here and there as to set a Topsail or a Watersail.

Make water, to To leak.

Man overboard! It is wise to teach all your family to use this alarm call, rather than to mutter 'Oo, look at Willie' or other natural phrases. A cry of 'Man overboard!' is the most important and serious order you can ever hear, and it is an order which means instant action by everyone no matter who gives it. Think on't, and try to devise a plan which will suit your boat and your crew.

Manila A natural rope fibre much used in the past for warps and general purposes, but now displaced by the synthetics.

Manrope A thoughtful skipper will always provide a manrope alongside a boarding ladder so that ladies will have something to cling to.

Marconi rig Though not much used now the word refers to tall-masted Bermudan rig, which in contrast to the old gaff mast needed sophisticated wire bracing akin to that of a wireless-mast ashore. (Marconi – get it?)

Marina An artificial yacht harbour, sometimes totally concealed from view by bingo halls, boozing dens, and boatels, but revealing itself to the ear by the unceasing jangling of halyards on the masts of boats whose owners have long since forgotten their existence.

Marine glue Not glue. A caulking material for the seams of Laid decks, which, I believe, used to consist of rubber, pitch, naphtha and shellac. But modern chemistry offers us caulkings superior to the old marine glue.

Mark buoy or **marker buoy.** Usually a racing mark rather than a navigational buoy. The latter tend to be called buoys – others have the prefix, mooring, marker, wreck, telephone, DZ or the like.

Marline Small line not unlike landsman's twine, properly made of two tarred strands laid up loosely. Can be used for Whipping or Serving.

Marline spike A fat bodkin with an ogival taper to its point, used for opening the strands of wire or rope cable when splicing. Some people use the pointed end to turn shackle pins, but the curved taper is not appropriate to that application and the spike is likely to slip out of the pin and into your flesh. A shackle-key is better, and some good hands prefer a pair of pliers. (See also Fid.)

Marling hitch See sketch.

Marling hitch

122

Mast A mast is a mast, and it may be long or short. A motor cruiser may have a mast that is no longer than a sailing cruiser's ensign staff, but it is still called a mast. A mast has a Head at the top and a Foot at the bottom. The head of a wooden mast is usually capped with a disc called the Truck which covers the exposed end-grain of the mast itself against water. A mast is supported by Shrouds and Stays, and it may have Spreaders to spread the shrouds and widen their angle of pull. Lower shrouds meet the mast at the roots of the spreaders, and this region is called the Hounds. The foot of the mast may step on deck in a large socket structure called a Tabernacle, or it may pass right through the deck and be stepped on the keel itself. Note that a mast steps on things with its foot, and that the after part of the underside of the foot is even called its Heel.

Mast coat A sleeve of canvas, often painted, or of some more modern material such as neoprene sheet or Terylene, which encompasses a keel-stepped mast at deck level. Its purpose is to prevent water from passing down below decks, and both the lower and upper edges of the coat must be well sealed, the upper to the mast and the lower to the deck.

Master Dad, usually. The chief officer of the vessel. The chap who does the worrying.

Masthead float Catamarans and trimarans, being normally unballasted, float with great stability either way up. A float at the masthead should prevent the immersion of the mast, and thus ensure that the craft never gets into the stable, inverted attitude. Some such floats are made of lightweight foamed plastic, or are air-filled hollow chambers. Others are bladder-like, to be inflated automatically from a carbon dioxide cylinder if the boat goes beyond a certain angle of heel.

Masthead light Please see Steaming light

Mat Please see Chopped strand mat.

Matthew Walker A knot used to form a knob or clump at the end of a rope. One of many such. I make no attempt to describe all possible knots, but if you are interested in such things get hold of a copy of *The Ashley Book of Knots*.

Mayday The international spoken word of distress, corresponding to SOS. It derives from the French *m'aidez*, help me. Should you need to make this call (usually by radio telephone), the drill is to repeat the word 'Mayday' three times in succession and without haste, then give the name of your boat, her position, the nature of the trouble, and what action you are taking. In short, tell them what they are to look for, and where they are to look.

123

Mean level, of tide   Please see Height of tide.

Measured distance   An accurately measured distance marked by two pairs of beacons ashore. Sometimes it is exactly a sea mile, but the actual distance will be shown on your chart. The chart will also show the correct course to sail when checking speed – you must sail parallel to the measured line, of course.

Mercator's projection   Named after the chap who invented this method of showing the spherical world on flat paper, it shows parallels of latitude parallel, as they are in fact. It also shows meridians a longitude as parallel, which they are not, because in practice they meet at the north and south poles. Still, it is Mercator's method that we all normally use, Heaven rest him.

Meridian   One of the imaginary lines which run due north and south between the poles of the earth, denoting longitude. The meridian which passes through Greenwich (England) is zero longitude and all others are measured as so many degrees east or west of that. (You might care to take a look at Parallel, too.)

Metacentre   In naval architecture the metacentre shows the relationship between the Centre of gravity of a vessel and her Centre of buoyancy when heeled. By relating those two centres it provides an index of her righting or restoring tendency. By plotting the positions of the heeled metacentres for sections along the length of the hull, the designer traces a curve called the *Metacentric shelf*. This curve is considered to give a good guide to the fore-and-aft Balance of a boat under sail.

MHWN   Mean High Water, Neaps.

MHWS   Mean High Water, Springs.

Microspheres   Sometimes called 'microballoons', these are tiny bubbles of air, encased in shells of glass or resin. So small that the resultant material looks and feels like powder, they are mixed with resin to make a relatively low-density filler for cavities in moulded or foam sandwich hulls. Not used for highly stressed components, of course.

Middle ground   A shallow bank which divides a channel or fairway into two parts. It is marked with Middle-ground buoys which usually indicate the deeper of the two channels so formed.

Midsection   Please see Sections.

Mile, Nautical   Please see Nautical Mile.

Millibar A unit of pressure which is itself one thousandth of a bar. (And one bar is a pressure of one million dynes per square centimetre, as you probably know.) The actual value does not concern a yachtsman, who soon learns to recognise the weatherman's lows and highs in terms of millibars. His own on-board barometer will be graduated in millibars, perhaps with inches (of mercury) as well.

Miss stays, to To fail to Go about. A sailing boat misses stays when she Luffs up into the wind and then falls off on the same tack instead of on the intended new tack.

Mitre A seam in a sail where the cloths meet at an angle, usually approaching a right angle.

Mizzen (and one z is OK if you prefer) The fore-and-aft sail set on the after mast of a Ketch or Yawl. The mast is called the mizzenmast, and associated rigging and fittings take the same prefix when necessary, as in 'mizzen boom, mizzen halyard' and so forth. (Jigger might be worth a look, too.)

Mole A stone pier or breakwater protecting a harbour from seaward, and normally one against which vessels may lie. Would not be used of a breakwater of roughly-heaped boulders, for example.

Monkey's fist An easily-made knot which has many turns so as to build up into a ball of rope. Used to weight the end of a heaving-line, sometimes with a piece of lead or a stone buried within the 'fist'.

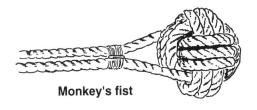

Monkey's fist

Moor, to To make a vessel fast to a laid Mooring, alongside a quay, or to the bottom by means of two of her own anchors. The first two uses of the word require no further explanation, but the third always denotes a clear distinction between 'anchoring' with only one anchor, and 'mooring' with two. If a boat lies to a single anchor there is a likelihood that the pull on the anchor will be reversed from time to time by changes in wind and tide. An anchor is designed to support a directional pull, and those changes mean that it may have to re-bed itself several times a day. Thus if a boat is to be left unattended for longish periods, it is prudent to moor her with two anchors, placed in up- and down-stream positions. There are several ways of doing the job, of which this is but one: drop the main or the normal length of cable, then take out the Kedge in the opposite direction in the dinghy and drop it at the extremity of its cable. Now make fast the kedge cable to the bower cable (normally with a Rolling hitch) and veer a couple more fathoms of the bower cable so that the hitch is well below the boat's keel and rudder. If you have plenty of bower cable you can manage the job without a dinghy, by first veering at least double the normal amount of cable, then dropping the kedge Underfoot and hauling in half the main cable again before making the rolling hitch.

Mooring An arrangement of anchors, Clumps and chains which are left permanently in position so that a boat may lie to them. There is commonly a ground chain running along the bottom between anchors, clumps or the like, and a riser chain leading up from a Swivel on the ground chain to a mooring buoy. In some cases the boat makes fast to the buoy, in others the buoy is brought aboard so that the riser may be made fast to the Bitts or Samson post.

Morse code light A beacon light which flashes a letter of the Morse code. Rather rare.

Motor-sail, to To sail, usually to windward, with the motor providing some additional push. A very sensible say of making progress, quicker and easier than sailing, quicker and more comfortable than just motoring.

Motor-sailer An odd term, this, meaning different things to different people. Most modern sailing cruisers have at least as much mechanical power as the motor-sailers of the past, and many have more. They also have more sail area. Perhaps the main distinguishing characteristic of most motor-sailers is that they retain the sort of shelter and comfort that motor cruiser owners are sensible enough to demand but which sailing people seem to think degenerate.

Mould or **mold** Here is a word which, with its derivatives, has to work very hard. The spelling is different in England from that in the USA, of course, but no matter. To a real boatbuilder a mould is a pattern or template of an internal hull section. Moulds are set up along a centreline in the builder's shed, and braced to the roof. The hull is then built around them and they are eventually removed. On the other hand, a mould to a modern slush-bucket boatbuilder is hollow, like a jellymould, inside which laminates of glass and polyester resin can be laid up. That kind of mould has the dimensions of the exterior of the boat, and is itself made by 'moulding' over a solid wooden Plug which has to be made as accurately as is humanly possible. A hull laid up of resin and glass inside a mould is said to be 'moulded'. But so is one made from strips of wood veneers glued in layers over a male plug. A wooden boat may be Cold moulded, as is usual, which means that the glue sets at ambient temperatures without heating. More rarely it may be Hot moulded, which involves baking the glue at quite a high temperature. Anything made in or over a mould is called a Moulding, whether it be as large as a hull or as small as a ventilator. By contrast there is the more ancient moulding, the half-round or quarter-round timber strip used by a traditional boatbuilder to fit into such corners as that between a hatch coaming and a deck.

Moulded and sided   Notwithstanding all that has been said immediately above about hulls that have been 'moulded', the same word has a different and very special usage among boatbuilders, when it means the dimension of a timber between its curved faces. Thus a frame or rib might be described as 'four inches moulded, and three inches sided', meaning that it is four inches between the curved faces and three inches between the straight faces. In a deckbeam 'moulded' is the thickness top to bottom, and 'sided' is the fore-and-aft dimension. In a keel 'moulded' is the vertical dimension, 'sided' is the lateral or side-to-side, if that is any help.

Moulded depth   This term is one whose meaning has changed slowly over the years. Except in strictly technical parlance, it would nowadays be taken to mean the body depth of a hull. That is to say the depth between deck and keel. The term is used of any type of boat, whether of moulded construction or not.

Mouse, to   To close the open mouth of a hook by taking several turns of a lashing across it. Double, or sister hooks are moused with a lashing of marline to keep them closed.

MRINA   Member of the Royal Institute of Naval Architects.

Mud-berth   A hollow in the shore near High-water mark where a boat may lie when laid up. When the mud is soft she may create her own berth by the combined action of her weight and of the water flow around her bottom.

Mushroom anchor   An anchor used in soft mud, sometimes as part of a laid mooring. It is shaped like a mushroom with a very hollow crown.

Muzzle, to   To restrain and hold down a sail or other piece of flapping canvas. (See Dowse.)

Muzzler   A headwind. A wind on the nose. A wind on your muzzle – if you happen to be a sea-dog, I suppose. (You might take a look at Eye Of The Wind).

Mylar   Polyester film used for sails. Has high strength for its weight. Mylar is in fact a trade name of its American maker. The same stuff made in Britain goes under the name Melinex. Polyester fibre when woven into cloth for sails has the trade name Dacron in the USA, Terylene in the UK.

N

N   Means 'no' or negative when made as a single-letter signal. Dash dot in Morse code, and November in phonetic.

Nacelle   A word deriving from the Latin navicella, a little boat, it is used for a small subsidiary hull, such as might be found in a trimaran, or for the pod which bulges beneath the bridge-deck in some catamarans to accommodate feet.

Nail sick   A boat has this sickness when her fastenings become loose. If you can identify those that leak, cut them out and replace by one size larger. Or you may clench up any that may be only slightly slack and insert new ones between every pair of old ones in suspect areas.

Narrows   A narrow part of any channel, fairway or river.

Nautical almanac *(or nautical calendar)*   A comprehensive book of tides, celestial phenomena and a thousand and one useful items of information for the navigator. No boat should go to sea without one.

Nautical mile   The international nautical miles is 1852 metres. For practical purposes it can be called 6080 feet, or just over 2000 yards. A mile is divided into ten 'cables', each of which is therefore approximately 200 yards.

Navel pipe   A metal deck fitting through which the anchor cable passes down to its locker.

Navigation   Is the art of finding a ship's position in the open sea, and of finding her way across the sea. Pilotage is the same thing in inshore waters where buoys and landmarks may be observed. But the two tend to overlap

Navtex   A radio-printer service which enables a yacht to have an on-board print out of weather and navigational information, plus any other useful operational messages such as distress and rescue traffic.

Neap tides   Or just 'neaps'. These tides occur approximately every two weeks and have a smaller Range than Springs. It's all summed up under Tide.

Neaped or **beneaped.**   Left high and dry, especially if the boat has gone aground on High tide at a time when the tidal range is decreasing, so that tomorrow's High water will not be as high as today's. In other words the tides are moving towards Neaps (or 'Taking off') and the boat will not float until neaps are over and Springs are approaching again.

Ness   A cape, promontory or low headland.

Nip   A sharp bend in a rope, as when formed into an eye or when running round a sheave. (See Freshen.)

North   Except when talking in general terms about 'northerly winds' or 'I'll bet you a beer that Halifax is farther north than Seattle', one has to distinguish between True north and Magnetic north. As the magnetic north pole is not at the same spot as the earth's axial pole, and as charts are drawn with reference to True, while the likes of us have to navigate with Magnetic compasses, a simple correction must be made. The correction differs as you move across the earth's surface, and it is even very slightly different from one year to the next. Fortunately the correction is easy to make, using the information that is printed on your chart.

North cone   A black cone, hoisted point up by Coastguards or other shoreside officials to indicate that a gale is expected from the North. By night three (red) lamps are hoisted in the form of a triangle, also point up. Note that the only choice is between 'north' and 'south'. The South cone points downwards.

Not under command   A vessel is in this condition when she cannot be controlled, perhaps by failure of her steering gear, even though her master is aboard and in charge. By night she carries two all-round red lights, one vertically above the other, instead of her forward and after white Steaming lights, but with her red and green Running lights and her Sternlight if she is making way. By day she carries two Black balls or shapes, one vertically above the other. But as these need to be no greater than two feet in diameter, you will be lucky to notice them above the massive bulk of a tanker, say.

Nun buoy   A buoy which is diamond-shaped when viewed from any side. It has a pointed top and a pointed bottom, and does not remind me of any nun I have ever seen.

O

O As a single-letter signal, means '*Man overboard*'. It is three dashes in the Morse code, and Oscar in phonetic.

Oakum Teased-out fibres of old hemp rope which are used for caulking seams before Paying.

Oar The difference between an oar and a paddle is that the former is generally longer and that it is used in conjunction with a fulcrum such as a thole pin or a rowlock. The paddle is supported solely by the arms of the paddler. An oar has a Shaft, with a Blade at one end and a Loom at the other for the hands to grip.

Observed position A more elegant term for a Fix, that's to say a position determined in relation to observable fixed objects or radio beacons, rather than the calculated position of dead reckoning.

Occulting light A steady light with periods of darkness at regular intervals, but the general effect being more light that dark. A steady light with dark flashes, you might say. A Group Occulting light has two or more of these dark flashes at intervals, and is the dark complement to a Group Flashing light.

Off the wind Sailing with the wind anything freer than a Reach.

Offing That part of Inshore waters which is well clear of shoals and shore dangers, but still visible from the land.

Offshore Farther to seaward than Inshore. Not precisely defined, but the change from inshore to offshore would be understood to begin somewhere more than ten miles out, and roughly where the land disappears from sight. 'Offshore' is also sometimes used as an adjective, for example to describe a wind blowing seaward from the shore.

Oil bag A porous bag containing oil which is trailed astern so that the oil will gradually seep out and calm the sea. Detergent would probably do the job better, and would counter-balance the growing amount of unwanted oil that is polluting (but not calming) our seas...

Oilies Short for oilskins, which are nowadays made of PVC or polyurethane on a basis of nylon, Terylene or Dacron or some such. But we still call them oilies, and I hope that fact gives you some slight satisfaction, as it does me.

On the beam Nothing to do with aviation. It simply places an observed object to one side or the other – in a word, Abeam.

On the bow Said of something observed anywhere from dead ahead to forty-five degrees to port or starboard. More helpful if 'port' or 'starboard' is specified.

On the wind Sailing Close-hauled or on a Fetch -i.e. with the wind coming from forward of Abeam.

One two three rule Please see Rule of Twelfths.

Onshore In a direction towards the shore from seaward. Compare Offshore and Inshore.

OOD Officer of the Day or Offshore One Design.

Osmosis Please see Boatpox.

Outboard Anything mounted or fitted beyond the normal area of the deck, or rail or bulwarks. A Bowsprit is 'outboard'. So is an outboard motor, known for short as an 'outboard' of course.

Out-drive Please see Stern drive.

Outfall buoy A buoy marking the seaward end of a sewer pipe. Take your bathing party elsewhere.Much loved by fishermen.

Outhaul A rope used to pull something in an outward direction in relation to the centre of the boat. An outhaul pulls the tack of the jib to the bowsprit-end.

Outrigger One of a variety of objects rigged outboard of the hull. In some rowing boats it is a bracket which carries the rowlock crutch outboard of the hull itself. In some sailing boats it is a subsidiary balancing hull set outboard of the principal hull by means of beams.

Overfalls A turbulent area of the sea, with over-curling waves, usually caused by the Tidal stream running over a submarine ridge. The same thing is seen in shallow and fast-running rivers. The chart may indicate 'overfalls on the ebb', say, or 'overfalls with strong easterly winds'. Take note and keep clear – unless you actually prefer rough water.

Overhangs Inexpensive boats have stems and sterns which rise fairly abruptly from the waterline. Expensive boats have overhanging ends, the after one being known as a Counter.

Overhaul, to (1) Although you may 'overhaul' the engine of a boat just as you would an automobile, the word has a special use in connection with running rigging or block and tackle. It means to extend a tackle or sheet rather than to haul it in. Sometimes in light airs the main boom will not swing out because of the friction in the blocks of the mainsheet. In that case you 'overhaul' the sheet to ease it out.

Overhaul, to (2) To overtake another boat, usually to windward.

Overtaking light The same as the Stern light. Any vessel approaching in the arc through which this white light shines (67½ degrees to port and starboard of dead astern) is an overtaking vessel in the meaning of the International Regulations, and must keep clear. The same arc holds force in daylight, of course.

Overtaking vessel Please see the entry above where it was more convenient to cover this point.

P

P Flag P, the Blue Peter, is one of the best-known flags ashore and afloat. Used as a title for a variety of commercial products, for at least one magazine and a television show, its principal meaning when flown by a ship is, *'about to proceed to sea'*. When you see it you know that the moment has come to join, or jump, ship. If you are a chandler ashore this is your last chance to get your bills paid. But the same flag, flown in the open sea by a fishing vessel means *'My nets have come fast on an obstruction'*, to use the polite and restrained words of the International Code of Signals. P is Papa in the phonetic and •— —•in the Morse code.

Pad-eye Similar to a lacing-eye, but larger and stronger so that a sheet block may, for example, be shackled to it. It consists of a base-plate on which stands a roughly semi-circular bridge to form the eye.

Painter Everybody knows that this is the rope spliced into the eye at the head of a launch, dinghy or other small craft, by which she is either towed astern or made fast. But one wonders what it could possible have to do with paint. My *Oxford English Dictionary* says that the origin of the word is obscure, but directs attention to two facts: first that in antique times it was spelled penter; second that in Old French a penteur was a rope on which to hang something, and that the nautical use of penteur relates to a lifting rope rove at the masthead. I draw my own conclusions from those facts, and leave you to draw your own – if this sort of mystery intrigues you.

Palm A leather pad made to be worn on the hand and to protect the palm when sewing sailcloth. The palm of an anchor is the flattened area of the Fluke, by analogy with anatomy.

Parallel One of a number of geographer's lines drawn around the world parallel to the equator. Each line is defined by its angular displacement from the equator, measured at the earth's centre. You might also care to take a look at Meridian.

Parallel rules A pair of rules linked by pivoted arms so that each rule always stays parallel to the other. By 'walking' the instrument across the chart a bearing or course can be transferred from one part to another. A more convenient instrument for small boats is the rolling rule – a single rule with inset rollers which allow it to be moved bodily across the chart without changing its attitude.

Parbuckle A useful word for a useful technique, even though neither of them is much used nowadays ! If one end of a rope is made fast and the other is passed around a log, say, then as you pull the free end the log rolls towards you. In effect the log plays the part of a sheave in a block, and you get the two-to-one purchase of a single whip. If we still had to get barrels aboard boats that would be the way to do it – indeed you may still see the occasional drayman lowering a barrel into a cellar by parbuckling. A possible use for the yachtsman is to get an inert body from the water to deck level, perhaps using a sail in place of the rope.

Parcel, to To cover a rope with canvas, plastic pipe, or smaller rope so as to protect it from chafe.

Parrel A rope strop holding a spar, usually a Gaff as far as you and I are concerned, to a mast. Also a similar strop holding the luff of a gaff mainsail to the mast. Wooden balls or beads are commonly threaded on such strops to save chafe and allow easy movement – they are then called *Parrel trucks or beads or balls*, or sometimes just 'parrels'. See sketch under Jaws. And see Junk.

Part, to When a rope breaks, a sailor says it 'parts'. (But it doesn't make any difference. . .)

Partners Paired timbers as may be put either side of a mast at the deck for reinforcement, or either side of Bitts or a Samson-post.

Passage A trip in a boat from one place to another is usually called a passage. The round trip there and back is a 'voyage', though it would be fanciful to use that word for a Saturday afternoon trip across the bay and back.

Patent log A name reserved for that type of distance-measuring device which trails a Rotator (spinner) at the end of a line. The rotator turns the plaited line and the line turns the mechanism in the recorder. There are many other ingenious logs, mechanical, electrical, electronic and acoustic on the market nowadays, and some of them embody patented ideas. But the patent log's name derives from a less sophisticated era.

Pay, to To fill a seam (the gap between two planks) with Caulking compound, such as Marine glue, pitch, or some modern polymer-based compound.

Pay off, to The head of a vessel pays off when it swings away from the wind. With a cross-wind you may leave the jib slack and allow the head to pay off, and then sheet in and Let draw.

Pay out, to To ease or slacken a rope.

P-bracket Please see A-bracket.

Peak (1) The forward or after extremities of the interior of a hull. Normally the fore and after peaks are used for stowage, there being little space for anything else.

Peak (2) The after upper corner of a Gaff sail and the upper end of the gaff itself.

Pelican hook A metal hook with a cam-action tongue which can be opened, as shown. Used for joining guard rails among other things.

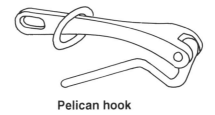

Pelican hook

Pelorus A large circular protractor fitted with sights so that you can take bearings of objects ashore in relation to your boat's centreline. It is used when Swinging the compass.

Pen A marina berth formed by the space enclosed between two fingers or pontoons.

Pendant *(or pennant)* A short line, hanging from a reef point or the tack of a sail, and used for shortening down. Ashore, as afloat, a pennant (but not a pendant) is also a triangular flag. (See Burgee.)

Perch Also a withy, is a pole or sapling standing in the mud to mark the edge of a channel.

PFD Personal Flotation Device. That's to say a Buoyancy Aid or Lifejacket.

Pick Jocular for Anchor.

Pillar buoy   A buoy bearing a tall and relatively slender structure to make it visible from a greater distance, and often placed at the seaward end of a series of channel buoys to act as a Landfall buoy.

Pilot (1)   A person with high qualifications, much experience, and detailed knowledge of local waters, who helps the master of a ship negotiate those waters. Pilotage is compulsory for big ships in some harbours and their approaches but private pleasure craft take a pilot only when they choose to. Fly flag G if you need a pilot – and can afford him.

Pilot (2)   A book of pilotage instructions or sailing directions for particular waters. Such a pilot is one of the things without which no prudent mariner will put to sea. Pilots are either government publications, prepared for shipping by bodies such as the United States Defense Mapping Agency (or the US Army Corps of Engineers for the Great Lakes), and by the Hydrographer of the Navy in Britain, or by commercial ventures specially suited to yachtsmen.

Pilot Chart   A planning aid for ocean passages. Shows expected directions and strengths of winds and currents, and likelihood of storms during each season of the year.

Pilotage   The art of finding one's way around in waters where the coast, rocks, buoys and the like, provide visual references.

Pinch, to (1)   To pinch a boat is to sail her so close to the wind that the sails lose their drive, even though they are still drawing. One may say 'You're pinching her', or simply, 'You're pinching'. (See Starve.)

Pinch, to (2)   A hull which has been slightly crushed or squeezed is said to have been pinched. When buying a second-hand boat, one must look out for distortion resulting from pinching – which is not so unlikely as it may sound, since a small boat may easily find herself berthed between two bigger ones. (It might be as well to see Hogged while we are in the midst of these tribulations.)

Pinch,to (3)   Unless you are a yacht designer you cannot do this one. A yacht with pinched ends is usually one that was designed to the IOR handicapping rule as it stood in the '70s. A pinched stern may have given a racing yacht of that vintage a good rating – but they 'rolled in wet grass' down-wind. Basically a wide beam and narrow at the ends.

Pinholes   Tiny holes in the gel coat of a resinglass moulding, usually caused by trapped air bubbles. If not corrected they will allow water to penetrate to the laminate and deterioration will follow. If your eye was sharp enough to spot pinholes your brain will be sharp enough to set you looking for another boat to buy. . . (please see Boatpox.)

Pin-rail Also known as a Fife-rail, a bar of timber with holes bored through it to take a number of belaying pins to which halyards maybe made fast.

Pintle Since pintles and gudgeons go together like bacon and eggs, please see Gudgeon.

Pipe cot A sleeping berth made of canvas stretched within a marginal frame of galvanised pipe. It is usually tapered to one end, and the pipe at the shipside edge is attached by hinged brackets so that the whole cot can fold up against the side of the hull. The most comfortable form of sleeping accommodation when a boat is going to windward and therefore heeled, especially if a tackle is fitted to the inboard side. This allows vertical adjustment so that the sleeper can adjust his cot to the horizontal. Strangely seldom seen on cruising yachts. (Compare with the Root berth whose canvas rolls up towards the shipside.)

Piston hank The metal clip with sliding plunger that is often used in some number to attach the Luff of a headsail to the forestay. (There is a sketch at Hank.)

Pitch (1) The rocking-horse motion of a vessel in the sea. (please see Roll, Yaw, Heave, and Scend.)

Pitch (2) Of a propeller, the distance that a blade would move forward in one revolution if it were cutting through a solid. In practice there is a certain amount of 'slip'. In choosing a propeller it is important to get correct pitch and diameter. These dimensions are related to the power of the engine, the rate (RPM) at which the propeller turns, and the speed of the boat. The short answer is to get technical advice, usually from the propeller manufacturer.

Pitch-pole, to A sea pitch-poles a boat when it turns her end-over-end, stern over stem. It happens so rarely that it would hardly be worth mentioning were it not for the extraordinary experience of the Smeetons who had it happen twice, as recounted in their widely-read book *Once is Enough*. When it does happen, the boat pitch-poles too, so the verb is both transitive and intransitive.

Plane, to Light boats with plenty of propulsive power can ride and skim on the surface of the water, supported by dynamic pressure. The slower-moving or stationary boat is supported by the static pressure of the water, summed up in the one word 'buoyancy'. When a boat planes, the dynamic water pressure is higher than the static, with the result that her weight is supported by a smaller area in contact with the water. Friction and Drag are thus reduced and speed increases. Sailing dinghies, which have suitably shaped hulls and sail areas which are large

137

for their weight, can 'get on the plane' in a fresh wind, though they do not quite reach the condition of a planing power boat. (see also Displacement hull.)

Plank   Much the same meaning as when used ashore. A wooden hull is skinned with fore-and-aft planks, and is said to be 'planked' in teak, or larch or whatever. In passing, it's worth mentioning that boatbuilders tend to refer to planks as Strakes. (See for example Lapstrake.) But all the strakes together make up the planking.

Plank on edge   The very narrow, minimal beam hulls which were at one time favoured because it was thought they would be fast, were known as 'plank on edge' because of their proportions. Thank heavens we don't see them nowadays.

Plim, to   To swell, or swell up. Likewise to plim up. Used of plums and suchlike by fruit growers, and of the planking of wooden boats by yachtsmen. A boat which has been long ashore may take water when first put afloat, but, just 'give her time to plim up' and she'll get tight.

Plot, to   To record position, course, bearings and such like observations and calculations on your chart. The result is 'the plot'.

Plough, plow, anchor   One with a single blade, shaped like a ploughshare. For example the CQR. (Please see sketch at Anchor.)

Plug   Obviously enough, something that fits into a hole to bung it up, as the drain hole in the bottom of a dinghy. More important and more widely used, it is the full-scale model, or male mould from which a hollow female mould is taken for the building of resinglass hulls. To make a plug is a costly business; it must be very fair and accurate, with a fine surface finish, for the mould will faithfully reproduce any imperfections, and they in turn will be transmitted to all the hulls which are laid up inside it.

Pod   Please see Nacelle.

Point (1)   A point of the compass is one of the 32 divisions which derived from taking a half-way position between North and East, say, then halving that, and then halving again. A tedious process, whose main result was to provide fun for petty-minded navigation instructors. Fortunately we all use the 360 degree circle now, I hope, and there's no need to bother with points. Incidentally, simple arithmetic will show you that if there are 32 points for a 360 degree circle, each point amounts to 11¼ degree s.

138

Point (2) The crews of racing yachts refer to 'the point' as the bow end of the fore deck. The crew 'doing point' is the man with his backside wedged into the pulpit at the start, shouting or indicating to the helmsman to go high (luff) or down (bear away). He will be the poor soul responsible for the sail handling in the wettest part of the boat.

Point, to A sailing boat 'points to windward' when she sails to windward. Colloquially the question, 'How does she point' means to ask whether she is close-winded. Likewise, 'Point up a little more' tells the helmsman to bring her a little closer on the wind, and, 'She's pointing well' reveals the satisfaction of a proud owner.

Points Please see *Reef, to.*

Points of sailing One may sail directly before the wind (run), or one may sail across it: each is a point of sailing. Running dead before the wind, for example, is generally said to be 'a difficult point of sailing'. Probably the term derives from the way the boat points in relation to the wind, for each point of sailing is in fact a geometrical relationship between the boat and the wind. Truly there are three main points of sailing. The first is *Running*, when the wind is dead astern or up to about forty-five degrees either side of astern. The second is Reaching, when the wind is on the beam, or a little abaft or ahead of it. The third is *Beating*, when the wind is coming over either bow, say within an angle of 40-55 degrees to port or starboard. Needless to say, there is no precise angular definition of these expressions, and they are usually qualified by such phrases as, 'We were running with the wind over the port quarter'; or 'We should be able to reach to the buoy with the wind just before the beam'.

Pole mast Times were when gaff-rigged boats had short masts, upon which Topmasts could be set. In heavy weather the Topsail was not wanted and the topmast was 'Sent down' to the deck, making a tiring and irksome job for one of the hands. But there came a time when some bright chap decided to have a single mast as long as main and topmast together, though with the gaff going no higher than before. That was the pole mast, and when no topsail was set and the bare upper end of the mast was left naked, the boat would be described as 'bald-headed'.

Polyester resin The man-made plastic (or polymer) of which Terylene sails and ropes are made (Dacron in the USA), and which is used in the building of 'fibreglass' hulls. When used in fibre form it is a 'saturated' resin. In fluid form, as it comes to the boatbuilder for hull moulding, it is known as 'unsaturated', and is commonly in the form of a solution of polyester in styrene. When a catalyst is added the styrene cross-links the molecular chains of the polyester to form a polymer, which is a network of linked molecules. (In a monomer the molecules live separate lives.) This crosslinking is known as curing, and it is a non-reversible process.

Polymers Broadly speaking, and as we meet them, polymers are 'plastics'. They are compounds whose molecules are linked together in chains, and never go about singly and unattached like the molecules of monomers, such as water or sodium chloride. When a resin sets, or gels, the molecules 'polymerise', linking into chains or even to more complex three-dimensional structures.

Polypropylene A plastics or polymer material which can take many forms. In boats it is used, for example, to make moulded hoods for outboard motors, or the cases of some radios. For a boat-owner its more significant use is in fibrous form to make rope which is strong in relation to its cost – though not so strong as nylon or polyester in relation to diameter. Polypropylene ropes have the advantage that they float, whereas nylon and polyester do not. This makes them good for dinghy painters and ski-tows, but not for anchor rodes. However, it tends to become brittle and unreliable if exposed to sunlight since ultraviolet radiation from the sun seriously weakens it.

Polystyrene Like other polymers, this one can take a variety of forms. It makes strong cheap rope, and it can be moulded into chairs. 'Expanded', it is also used to make the lightweight 'artificial cork' which is used in packaging and for buoyancy. Polyester resin dissolves polystyrene, and so can petrol. Some lightweight boat hulls have been made from expanded polystyrene, but with limited success and only among 'fun' boats at that.

Polyurethane Another polymer that can be used as varnish in one form, as expanded rigid cellular foam in another, and as a waterproofing for textiles in another. The ordinary boat-owner knows it best as a quick-drying varnish of great durability.

Pontoon A floating box, designed to act as a walk-way to give access to boats, or to support the spans of a floating bridge. Often called a Float in the USA.

Pooped, to be In ships of the past the poop was the raised after deck at the stern. We don't have poops nowadays, but if a sea breaks over the stern of your boat and into your cockpit she is pooped – and you become wet and perturbed. Fortunately it is a rarity, but if you ever find yourself in conditions where pooping seems likely or possible, clip yourself firmly to the boat so as not to be washed overboard.

Pop rivet A rivet which can be closed from one side with a special tool. The rivet is hollow and has a mandrel up its centre. The tool pulls the mandrel into the rivet so as to expand the inner end of the tube, and then snaps the mandrel off short. Just the thing for fixing attachments to an aluminium mast, for example, and not at all expensive.

Port (1) The vessel's own left-hand side.

Port (2) A commercial harbour.

Port establishment   The time of High water at a given port in relation to the phase of the moon, or in relation to some other port. (Please see Full and change.)

Porthole   Please see Scuttle.

Port-hand buoy   A buoy to be left on your port hand when approaching from seaward or in the direction of the Main Flood tide. Where the flood tide flows in a variety of directions, a conventional direction may be decreed and will be shown on the chart. Beware of the fact that you can rely on this information only where *IALA System A* applies, so if you are travelling far and you arrive in *System B* waters you can either make your approach astern or reverse the information. Anyway, if you are straying that far afield you'll know what to expect.

Port tack   Sailing with the wind on the port side. If you then meet a boat on starboard tack (wind on her starboard side) it is your duty to keep clear. Colloquially people speak of being 'on port' or 'on starboard'. Racing fiends who think you are blind, stupid or ignorant will often scream 'starboard' at you as if you were deaf as well. Tolerate them as best you can; they would probably beat their wives if they could not vent their emotions in this vulgar but harmless manner

Portsmouth Numbering System *(or Yardstick)*   This is a handicapping system based on recorded results of many races. It is used for mixed classes of boats, and attempts to average the relative performance of various types in many clubs over a long period. The numbers are published by the Royal Yachting Association in Britain.

Position line, Line of Position (LOP)   A line drawn on a chart to pass through the position of your boat. If you take a bearing of a fixed object ashore and draw the corresponding line seaward from that object, it is assumed to pass through the observation point – your vessel. A position line may be obtained by a visual bearing, a radio bearing, by a Transit or Range, by Soundings, or by a sextant sight of a star or planet.

Pot life The time interval, after the catalyst has been added, during which a resin remains sufficiently fluid to be used. Pot life depends mainly on the type and quantity of accelerator added to the resin, but as most amateur resins have the accelerator already added when we buy them, there's not much we can do about it. Once you add the catalyst you probably have between ten and fifteen minutes before the stuff gets too sticky for use.

Pound A small pool (or pond) in which dinghies may be kept afloat. Oddly enough exactly the same word is used for an enclosed area ashore where dinghies maybe kept high and dry. Take your choice..

Pram, praam A dinghy with a Transom at both ends. The other kind, with tapering bows, is called a 'stem dinghy' to differentiate.

Pratique Quarantine clearance on arrival in port. Primarily a medical clearance, it is nowadays just as often used for customs clearance. The actual official meaning of the signal letter Q, flown as the yellow Q flag when we go foreign, is 'My vessel is healthy and I request free pratique'. Neither goods nor people maybe put ashore until you have clearance.

Preventer Please see Backstay.

Prime meridian The Meridian which passes through Greenwich (England), Longitude zero.

Proa Whereas a catamaran has two hulls of equal size and the same proportions, a proa has one hull and a small outrigger. The latter serves partly as a float (to hold up) and partly as a weight (to hold down). But a proa is normally sailed with the wind on the outrigger side, and instead of tacking through the wind she swings her sail round to sheet at the other end, and what was the stem becomes the stern and vice versa. That may involve shifting the rudder (or steering oar) from one end of the craft to the other. Proas can sail fast.

Prohibited area An area marked on the chart where anchoring, fishing, or even passage may be forbidden for one reason or another.

Prolonged blast A sound signal consisting of a single hoot lasting from four to six seconds. A short blast lasts about one second.

Propeller Known also as a 'screw' or a 'wheel' it is the familiar two-or three-bladed device which propels a boat by screwing its way though the water. Water not being a solid, there is a certain amount of 'slip', defined as the difference between the actual movement of a water-screw and the theoretical movement of a similar screw working in the solid. A propeller is right-handed if it turns clockwise when viewed from astern: left-handed if it turns the other way. Most propeller blades are at a fixed Pitch, but some have Variable pitch (VP) blades, and some have reversible pitch for going astern. With reversible pitch, the shaft turns always in the same direction, and there is no need for a reversing gear. It is often possible to Feather the blades of a VP prop, so that they stand edge-on to the water flow and have minimum Drag when the boat is under sail. Some propellers fold to reduce drag – that's to say the blades hinge backward and come together like the palms of the hands in prayer and so present a form somewhat like a fish's tail. (Please see Pitch.)

Prow   An obsolescent word for the sharp end of a boat which might be revived with advantage. It embraces the head of the boat, including the Stem and Cutwater as far back as the Bows. That leaves the word 'bows' free for the actual shoulders.

Pudding, puddening   A pad or mattress of rope, coir matting or whatever you have handy to serve as a fender or anti-chafing gear.

Pulpit   A curved rail above the prow of a boat, running from bow to bow via the stem, wherein you may stand without fear of toppling overboard. (See also Push-pit.)

Punt   A flat-bottomed boat, whose bottom fore and aft slopes up to square ends. Mostly associated with quiet rivers on Sunday afternoons, but there are fast sailing punts in some parts of the world.

Purchase   The mechanical advantage gained by a Tackle or a lever, i.e. three-to-one, two-to-one, etc. It may also refer to the tackle itself.

Pushpit   A protective rail around the after end of a boat, so named by analogy with the pulpit. Some people get cross when they hear this word, but that is probably because they did not think of it themselves. Somebody has to invent new words for new things or we should have no language at all. A pushpit, of course, is a plain tubular structure and has none of the elegance of a Taffrail.

Put about, to   Or to 'put the boat about', is to change from one Tack to the other.

Put the helm down, or up   Please see Up.

Put off   To leave the shore in a boat, or to leave another boat in a lesser boat. 'We anchored off Cowes, where we saw a milkman on his round, and put off in the dinghy to see if he could spare us a couple of pints.'

Putty   The mud on which we all run aground sooner or later. One might just as well call it mud, but putty is the word that many yachtsmen seem to prefer.

Pyrotechnic   A firework used as a signal. May be a Flare (2)   , red or white, some kind of rocket signal or star shell, or an orange smoke generator for daylight use. Red pyrotechnics (and orange smoke) are used only to indicate distress.

Q

Q   The single-letter signal means, *'My vessel is healthy and I request a free pratique'*. The practical import of that strange expression is well-enough known as the Q flag which one flies on entering a foreign port, or returning home from foreign. The 'pratique' that is requested is 'permission' or 'licence' to hold intercourse with the shore. It may relate to health, customs or immigration rules. Hence the association of Q and quarantine, though in many countries hygienic considerations hardly enter into it nowadays. In the phonetic alphabet the word is Quebec, pronounced in the French manner as if spelled Kebek. Morse code, — —•—.

Quadrant (1)   A quadrant-or fan-shaped metal fitting at the rudder head which receives the steering cables. It ensures that the point of contact of each cable is tangential to a circular arc centred on the axis of the rudder.

Quadrant (2)   A now-outdated instrument for measuring angles, similar to and superseded by the Sextant.

Quadrantal error   In radio-direction finding, a displacement of the apparent direction of the transmitting station resulting from interference (reflection and re-radiation) caused by metal aboard the boat herself. Wire rigging and guard rails are the most likely causes of quadrantal error, especially when the wire forms a closed ring. A guard rail with 'breaks' in it is less likely to cause trouble.

Quant   A long, and often heavy, pole with a fork at one end and a wooden 'truck' or pad against which you can shove with your shoulder to drive the boat along in shallow water. Most seen nowadays on the traditional types of Dutch boat. The word is also used as a verb, with tenses formed in the regular manner.

Quarter   The after end of the side of a vessel. The starboard quarter is the 'back right-hand corner'. The quarters complement the Bows, and like bows they indicate no precise point, but rather a region and a direction. Thus a ship may be seen 'coming up on the port quarter' which is equivalent to an approach from over your left shoulder.

145

Quarter badge A protective piece of timber fitted at the extreme after end of the ship's side where it meets the Transom. Usually given a pleasing shape, and often designed to run in with a Rubbing strake. (See Badge, bow.)

Quarter knee The Knee joining the Gunwale to the Transom. One each side, of course.

Quick flashing light A light which flashes at a rate of sixty times a minutes or more.

R

R Romeo in the phonetic and •—• in Morse. A useless letter for most of us since it has no meaning in the International Code.

Race A fast-running stream or current, usually caused by the tide and occurring where the stream is constricted, either because a channel narrows or because it shoals. Eddies and Overfalls are commonly found in a race.

Racing flag A small rectangular flag or burgee, formerly flown at the masthead to indicate that the boat was actually participating in a race, though some owners seemed to think its meaning was, 'I was in a race last week', or 'I may be in a race some day soon'... It was largely because of that abuse that in 1976 the Royal Yachting Association decided to discontinue its use.

Racking seizing A way of binding two ropes together (or Seizing them) by winding the line between and round so as to make a number of figure-eight turns.

Racon A radar beacon with a transponder, which detects a ship's radar emission and responds to it by transmitting its own signal. (Please see Radar reflector and Ramark.)

Radar reflector A passive reflector of radar emissions, usually made of three plane surfaces meeting at right angles to each other. The result forms eight three-sided funnels. Such reflectors are mounted on buoys and beacons so that ships equipped with radar can locate them. Any private craft, of whatever material of construction, should carry a radar reflector if she moves in waters where she may encounter ships. The reflector should be as large as feasible, and certainly not less than 15 inches, and preferably at least 18 inches, across the diagonal. The reflector should be hung from three of its corners, so that one 'funnel' faces up to the sky as if to collect rain. That will leave six funnels to face outward around the horizon.

Radar reflector

Radio beacon   A fixed radio transmitter, usually identifying itself by a Morse code signal, on which a bearing can be taken with a Radio direction-finder. Marine radio beacons are sited specifically to assist sea vessels, but a small-boat skipper can also make use of aero beacons if they are sited near the coast. (But some aero beacons transmit on VHF, whereas marine beacons are usually in the low frequency band.)

Radio direction-finding   Commonly known as RDF, and even more commonly as DF, this is a most useful navigational aid. Lighthouse authorities maintain transmitting beacons at well-chosen locations, any one of which can be identified by its own call sign in Morse code. The receiver's aerial (to take a typical example) is rotated until the reception reaches a minimum – the null point. When the signal is at a null, the aerial is pointing towards the station, and though the other end of the aerial is pointing away from it, there is usually little difficulty in deciding which end is which. At first sight it might seem better to turn the aerial for the maximum signal, but a null gives a clearer indication of direction, as you could judge by picturing a flashlight shining across a room on to a postcard: only when the card is edge on to the lamp will it be almost entirely unlit. Rotate even slightly and one side or the other will be seen. (I must stop – this is not meant to be a handbook of navigation.)

Radio telephone   Just what its name implies. Speech-communication radios work on medium frequency (MF), high frequency (HF), or very high frequency (VHF). VHF is most commonly used by private boat owners because it is cheaper and more compact than the other kinds- but its range is much less. In what is called simplex working both parties speak over the same channel, and you cannot receive while your 'transmit' button is pressed. Hence each party must say 'over' to signal to the other that he has finished speaking and is ready to listen. Duplex operation works on two channels, and permits ordinary conversation without need for the 'over' drill.

Raffee   A useful word, and worth reviving. Could be used for any spare sail set flying high from the masthead in light weather. Was formerly a small triangular or square sail set flying from the masthead in clippers and other big sailing craft. But they are dead and gone alas, and have no more need of this useful word.

Raft, to   To moor several boats side by side, all lying to the single anchor or mooring of one of them. This is great fun, if you are that sort of person, and hell if you're not.

Rail Very often called a Toe-rail nowadays, the rail is the piece that forms the deck edge. Not as high as a Bulwark, it may nonetheless have a capping piece. In the past it was made of timber, but nowadays it may be of angle-section aluminium alloy, with close-spaced holes which provide useful attachments for this and that. An undecked boat does not have a rail, but has a Gunwale. The railing that stops you falling off some decks is best called the Guard rail.

Raise, to To raise the land, or a light, is to approach sufficiently near that it appears above the horizon.

Rake Of a mast, is forward or aft inclination. If not specified, it will generally be aft. Used also as a verb, and of other parts of a boat too, notably the Transom.
Ramark A radar beacon that transmits a signal without need of being triggered by a ship's emissions. (Please see Racon.)

Range (1) The alignment of two objects to give a Position line. Better known in England as a Transit.

Range (2) The difference in level between successive High and Low waters – in other words the amount the tide rises or falls on a particular day. The Rise of the tide is the amount that High water is above Chart datum, though rise is now yielding place to Height, under which heading I have perversely said more about range. Please check. (And see illustration under Tide.)

Range, to To lay out an anchor cable or the like on deck or some such convenient place.

Rate (1) The speed of a tidal stream or current is its rate. Usually given in knots.

Rate (2) The daily amount by which a ship's chronometer gains or loses. If the rate is consistent it is easy enough to make allowance.

Rating The 'handicapping' of a racing yacht based on extensive measurements and the application of more than a few formulae to see 'how she rates'.

Ratline A step formed between a pair of shrouds, and made of timber or rope. Ratlines form rungs and offer a way to the masthead, or at least to the Hounds. A fine seaman-like term which may come in handy one day is to 'rattle down' the rigging. It means either that you fitted ratlines, or that you adjusted them for neatness and tautness.

Rat tail Or *rat's tail*, is a pointed end to a rope, made by removing strands. Seen at the termination of a Bolt rope on a sail, for example.

RCC Royal Cruising Club.

Reach, to To sail with the wind abeam or forward of the beam. You may sail a close reach, but that is not so close to the wind as close-hauled. There is a noun from this word, as in, 'We crossed the bay in a single reach', meaning that the boat was on the wind the whole way, but did not have to tack. (Please see Beat and Board.)

Reaching strut In effect a spreader to give a spinnaker guy a more effective angle when reaching. The inboard end of the strut is housed on the mast, the outboard bears on the guy. The same device is more often known as a jockey pole in the UK.

Ready about A helmsman's warning to sheet-hands (and to the cook below) that he is going to tack, so headsail sheets must be trimmed, and the cook must brace both herself and the saucepan. After giving a few seconds' warning the helmsman puts the helm down with the cry of 'lee-oh'. The essential point about this rigmarole is the interval between warning and action.

Reckon, to To make navigational calculations. The reckoning may be the task itself, but is more commonly the result, expressed as a position or perhaps a distance.

Rectilinear stream, or current A tidal stream that runs in more or less a straight line, on flood and ebb. The other kind is Rotary.

Reduction Of soundings you have made (or observed if you have an electronic gadget to save getting your hands wet), is to correct them to what they would have been if taken at Low water, the chart depths being those which obtain at that state of the tide.

Reedhorn A kind of Foghorn which uses a vibrating reed to make the sound. (Well, what did you expect?)

Reef, to To reduce sail area by rolling or folding part of the cloth – usually along the foot in mainsails and along the luff in headsails, though either form is found in either sail. The process of making a reef is commonly called 'tucking-in a reef', even where roller-reefing is used and there is no actual tucking. The reverse procedure is 'shaking out a reef', an expression that suits a condition where cloth has been bundled and crumpled up. A reef is in fact that area of a sail between the foot and a set of reef points, or between two sets of reef points. Hence the expression to 'take in a reef'. In times past the lowest reef was sometimes called the 'slab' and this term has been revived for the folding type of reef, where a pre-determined area of cloth is taken in (i.e. jiffy and points). The *Slab reef* contrasts with the rolled reef where the amount of cloth accommodated on the boom is continuously variable and not in discreet steps. All types of slab reef make use of Cringles (eyes) on the luff and leech of the sail, and these are first hauled down to form the new tack and clew of the sail. It is then necessary to tidy up the excess cloth along the foot of the sail, which is known as the Bunt. Whether or not there is a boom, the bunt can be firmly held by short lengths of cord, called Pennants or Points, which pass through eyelets in the sail cloth. Alternatively, but no so conveniently a continuous length of line may be threaded through the eyelets and around the bunt. The modern jiffy reefing for boomed mainsails makes use of elastic cord, a length of which is permanently threaded through the reef eyelets from luff to leech. After the tack and clew cringles have been hauled down to the boom, bights of the shock cord are stretched down and tucked under hooks on each side of the boom.

Reef knot   Pull the opposite ends of either rope to undo it, as shown here.

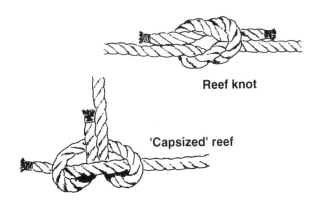

Reef knot

'Capsized' reef

Reef points   Please see *Reef, to*.

Reefing gear   Mechanical apparatus for roller reefing, either of a mainsail around its boom or of a headsail around its luff-spar or rod.

Reeve, to   To pass a rope through a block or an eye in the same sense as 'to thread' a needle. Rove is the past tense, and participles.

Register tonnage   The notional carrying capacity of a vessel used for port dues, taxation and so forth. National authorities calculate the figure by subtracting from the hull volume various allowances for crew's quarters, navigation room, engine rooms, and so forth. Even small private yachts may have a register tonnage, which may be a bit of fun and may be written on forms by petty officials who 'welcome' you in this port or that. But for private craft the whole thing is a nonsense. The one thing you can say for sure about Register Tonnage, is that it is not a matter of weight.

Registration   A commercial ship is registered with her appropriate national authority (for example the Registrar of British Ships). The process takes note of her Register tonnage which is a basis for the calculation of harbour dues. Private craft maybe registered with national authorities (and in some countries they must be).

Relative wind   Please see Apparent wind.

Release agent   A non-stick coating applied to the inside of a mould so that the gel coat of a moulding (for example, a hull) will not stick to it. An owner is not normally concerned, but carelessness in preparing the mould may result in a need for force to extract the moulding, with the loss of some areas of gel coat. These scars must then be patched in, and if detectable may be an indication of the working standards of the builder.

Render, to   To ease a rope through a Block or round a Samson post. The rope itself renders if it runs freely through a block, dead-eye or the like. Ashore one might say 'runs freely' where one would say 'renders' afloat.

Reserve buoyancy   The buoyancy provided by that part of the hull which is above the normal waterline and which can be immersed without flooding. An open boat with little Freeboard has less reserve buoyancy than a decked boat with cabin and watertight portholes.

Resin   There are innumerable artificial resins known to chemists, and thank Heaven we are concerned with only two or three of them. Polyester resin is the stuff many boats are built of. It is reinforced with glass fibres (Resinglass). An amateur can use polyester resin for repairs and odd jobs – just buy it and follow the instructions diligently. Epoxy resin is a first-class adhesive which is available to us in the shops, and no boat should be without a supply on board. Epoxy resin also forms the basis of good paints and surface treatments, as does Polyurethane, another synthetic resin. And that's really as much space as we can afford on this truly vast subject. (And see Fibreglass.)

Rhumb line   This is what you get when you draw a straight line between two points on a Mercator (i.e. ordinary) chart. Unfortunately it is not in fact the shortest distance between two points because the chart shows a distorted picture of the face of the earth. The shortest distance would be a 'Great circle', and it would be a curved line on your chart. But never mind – for most of the likes of us who sail only a hundred or so miles at a time, the difference is negligible.

Rhythmic rolling   A form of rolling motion which is induced by the interaction of sail and sea forces acting in harmony. For example, when running, a sea-induced roll may cause the spinnaker to start swinging, and that may in turn augment the roll. Another cause is the shedding of air vortices from the trailing edges of a sail.

Ribs   The ribs of a wooden boat are sometimes called Frames, usually if cut to shape, and sometimes called Timbers, usually if steamed to shape. You will appreciate that only wood of small scantlings is likely to be bent, so timbers are small and frames large.

Ride, to (1)   A boat rides to her anchor. When anchored by night she must show an all-round white light (two in some cases) known as a Riding light. In ordinary English a boat will 'ride out' a storm, but that has nothing to do with being anchored, she can do it while hove-to, or with bare poles, and the implication is one of riding the seas.

Ride, to (2)   A rope is said to ride on another when it crosses over and jams it. The most common use of the word is in connection with the sheet winches of modern sailing boats, when the loaded part rides over the hauling part and nips it tight, a situation known as a Riding turn.

Riding turn   Please see Ride, to (2).

Rig, to   To assemble and fit the rigging and sails up to, but not including, the point when sails are raised.

Rig   The general term for the arrangement of spars and sails on a boat, as in 'cutter rig'. One also says of a boat that 'she's cutter-rigged'. But the spars, stays and sails themselves are not collectively 'the rig' in the sense that one might want to say, 'We removed the rig and stored it under cover'. In fact that case you would have to say that you have 'removed the spars, sails and rigging . . .', the later being the wire stays and shrouds and their associated rigging screws. Various common rigs are discussed under their own entries: Bermudan, Cat, Cutter, Gunter, Ketch, Lug, Schooner, Sloop and Yawl.

Rigging   The actual wires and ropes comprising the rig. They fall into two sets, the Standing rigging which sustains and steadies the mast, and the Running rigging which raises and controls the sails and movable spars.

Rigging screw   A tensioning device of shrouds and the like. It has two eye-bolts threaded into opposite ends of a central body. One bolt is threaded left-handed and the other right-handed, so that when the body is turned the ends move simultaneously either in or out. (That's to say they move in opposite directions.) Rigging screws are the norm on modern boats for tensioning the rigging. They are commonly called bottle screws, though small ones may be called turnbuckles.

Right bank   Please see Left bank.

Right-handed propeller   One which, when viewed from astern, rotates clockwise. (Please see Wheel effect.)

Right of way   Not a very good term in relation to sea rules. The Collision Regulations are phrased in terms of duty to 'keep clear' or to 'give way', rather than in terms of any rights.

Rigol   A dying word, pronounced 'wriggle' (with a bit more of the o at the end though), and perhaps worth salvaging. It means a small waterway or water channel, of which there may be several on a boat. In particular it describes the Eyebrow or miniature eave which arcs above a Scuttle to keep drips of water out.

RINA   Royal Institute of Naval Architects.

Rise   Of the tide, is the amount by which High water on that day is above Chart datum. But the word is going out of use, and Height has to serve. Technically 'height' may refer to any hour, whereas in the past 'rise' was the height just at High water.

Rising, or riser   A light fore-and-aft member in a wooden boat providing support for a Thwart or some other fitting. It is like a Stringer, fitted inside the timbers.

RNLI   Royal National Lifeboat Institution.

Common rigs

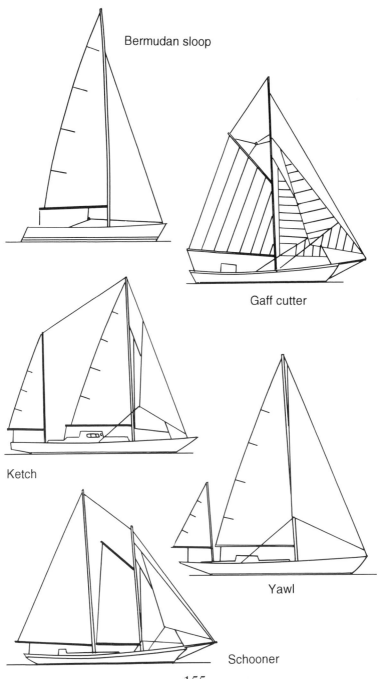

Bermudan sloop

Gaff cutter

Ketch

Yawl

Schooner

Roach The outward and rearward curve of the leech of a mainsail, an unnatural shape which is maintained by Battens. Roach makes a pretty shape, and gives untaxed area to the racing man whose sail area is calculated on straight corner-to-corner measurements. Little aerodynamic advantage can be expected, except in fully-battened sails of high Aspect ratio where the sail can be given a markedly elliptical profile. In that case the resulting aerofoil can be very efficient for fast close-hauled sailing. Otherwise, one is better off without roach or battens.

Road, roadstead Both or either mean the same thing – a sheltered place where boats can lie at anchor. 'Roads' is an alternative to road.

Roband A rope-band or short length of rope for tying around a sail or the like. Sailor's speech and sailors' spelling have resulted in variants such as roban and robbin.

Rocker The fore-and-aft curve to the keel or bottom of a boat. A punt has no rocker, for example, her bottom being a straight line. (Just to make it clear, rocker is not a thing, it is a quality.)

Rocket apparatus Not the signal rocket you may use in distress, but the line-carrying rocket which is fired from shore to ship, or ship to ship, usually as a preliminary to sending over a heavier stay for breeches-buoy rescue.

Rode (1) Noun. An anchor-cable, especially one of rope rather than chain. It is also the rope that drags a trawl.

Rode (2) As a verb (present or past participle) it describes the behaviour of a moored vessel under the influence of wind or tide. If she is lying head to wind, she is 'wind-rode'. If she went aground when lying head to tide, she was 'tide-rode' at the time.

Rogues yarn You may think you have heard many such from salesmen at boat shows, but it's not that sort of yarn. It is a coloured yarn embodied in the lay of a rope to identify either its composition or its ownership. Like the devices embodied in bank-notes, it was originally a deterrent to those rogues who sought to earn a little extra by selling government property from the dockyards.

Roll Both verb and noun, describes the lateral movement of a vessel. You don't need me to tell you that, but the word is included for the sake of completeness. The other principal motions of a boat are Pitch, Yaw, Heave, and Scend. (See Rhythmic rolling.)

156

Roller jib A general term for headsails which can be rolled around their own Luffs, whether for reefing or just for furling. The first, using a wooden Luff spare turning on a wire threaded through its length, was introduced by Captain du Boulay in 1887. Modern versions of the same idea use an aluminium alloy spar. Both these kinds may be used for reefing – that's to say with the sail partially deployed. The all-or-nothing furling gears have wire at the luff, as in the Wykeham Martin gear.

Rolling hitch One of the few useful knots. It is used when the pull is to be along a spar or a rope.

Load or pull

Rolling hitch

Rond anchor Please see Anchor for an illustration of this river-bank anchor. Its single fluke must be pressed home by the weight of your foot, and once in the ground it presents no danger to passing people or cattle. But such an anchor will not penetrate of its own accord, so it cannot be used for bottom anchoring.

Root Of a pier or jetty, the shoreward end. The seaward extremity is the Head.

Root berth A sleeping berth made of canvas or the like. One edge of the canvas is attached to the ship's side, and the other to a bar of wood or metal. In the daytime the whole is rolled up against the ship's side, but for sleeping it is extended and the bar lodges in suitable supports in bulkheads or ports. (Pipe cot is relevant.)

Roove *(rove)* A saucer-shaped copper washer which fits over a copper boatnail before it is riveted up tight. Also known as a rove or a ruff, though in the USA it is known as a Burr.

157

Rope We all know what that is, but remember that it can be of fibre or of wire. Rope is of various 'constructions', plaited, braided, or the ordinary laid (which means twisted). Furthermore, laid rope may be Hawser-laid, which means three strands twisted together in the usual manner, or Cable-laid, which consists of hawser-laid ropes twisted together. Cable-laid ropes are most commonly used for big hawsers, by the way, while hawser-laid ropes are used for sheets, halyards and the mooring lines of small craft.

RORC Royal Ocean Racing Club.

Rotary stream, or current A tidal stream that changes direction during the ebb or flood, or both, so as to swirl round in a large eddy. Such streams are found near promorttories. Its contrary is called a Rectilinear stream.

Rotating mast This is a mast which is free to turn about its own axis, not in complete circles but from port to starboard. This means that a mast of stream-lined section can turn to present its best aspect to the wind on either tack, and when close-hauled or on a broad reach. The Finn dinghy is an obvious example.

Rotator The spinner of a Walker or patent Log. It has a torpedo-shaped body and three angled fins.

Round to, or round up To bring a boat's head up on the wind.

Round bilge The conventional form of boat hull where the sides turn into the bottom in a curve. (Please see Bilge.)

Round the buoys Colloquial term for racing round a buoyed course. But to 'Go round the buoy' is to have a second helping. Hence a round boy.

Round turn and two half hitches One of the most widely used and useful of hitches. A double turn is even better.

Round turn and two half-hitches

Rove   This is either the past tense of to Reeve, or an alternative spelling for Roove.

Rovings   Filaments of glassfibre, bundled loosely together to make a thicker string. These strings may be woven into a cloth which is known as Woven rovings, which can be used as reinforcement for polyester resin in hull construction. Although woven rovings is a very strong material, Chopped strand mat is often preferred because it is difficult to get woven rovings to absorb sufficient resin. A mixture of the two types of reinforcement can be very effective in certain cases.

Row, to   What you do when the wind drops or the outboard stops.

Rowlock   In fact the rowlock is the hole into which the rowlock crutch drops. The word I use when I ought to say Crutch.

RT   Radio-Telephony

Rubbing strake   A Wale, usually of timber fitted along the outside or bottom of a hull to protect it from wear. A rubbing strake should be fitted in a way that allows easy replacement when it is sufficiently battered.

Rudder   A rudder has a Blade, the part which acts on the water, and a Stock above it to transmit torque from Tiller or steering gear. The lower extremity of the blade is the Heel, and the upper extremity of the stock is the Head. A Lifting rudder has a pivoted blade that swings up to reduce its Draught. The blade is then fitted between Cheeks, which are in turn fitted to the stock. A rudder may be of several kinds, notably outboard or inboard. The transom-hung rudder is outboard and easily accessible: its hangings are the simple Pintle and Gudgeon. The inboard rudder's stock passes through a trunk or tube, at the bottom of which there may be a watertight gland similar to that used with a propeller shaft. A Spade rudder stands in clear water, away from Keel or Skeg, an arrangement which may minimise drag but which leaves the rudder exposed to stray ropes, painters or plastic bags. A Balanced rudder is one which has some of its area ahead of the pivotal axis, thus reducing loads on the tiller. Something between ten and fifteen percent of the total blade area is enough to have ahead of the hinge line.

Rule of the road   The colloquial term for that section of the Collision Regulations which is headed 'Steering and Sailing Rules'.

Rule of twelfths   A means of estimating the rise or fall of tide for each hour of the six. In the first hour the change is assumed to equal one-twelfth of the range: in the second hour two-twelfths; in the third and fourth hours three-twelfths each;

in the fifth two, and in the sixth one. Quite a good system when the range is stated in feet, but not so convenient now that we have metres and decimetres.

Run (1) The distance covered in a stated time. The 'day's run' implies a 24-hour day, noon to noon.

Run (2) The after part of the underwater part of a hull. A pretty Buttock-line is always noticed by a sailing man.

Run, to To sail before the wind. To 'run under bare poles' is a heavy-weather tactic, all sails being furled and lashed down.

Runabout This is a small open motor boat capable of a fairly high speed – say 10-15 knots. If she were slower she would be a dinghy, if slower and a little bigger a launch, and if faster a sports boat. Anybody who wishes to take exception to what I have said is free to do so, for there is no firm definition of a word like this.

Runner Short for 'runner backstay', or should it be 'running backstay'? If you will turn to Backstay it will save me the trouble, and the publisher the paper, of saying the same thing twice.

Running bowline A noose made in a rope by making a bowline round the standing part. The noose is what a sailor would call a Bight, but a 'bowline on a bight' is not a slipknot like this – it is a bowline formed in a doubled rope. That's to say the bight itself is formed into a bowline.

Running by the lee Sailing downwind with mainsail out to the windward side. Evidently there is every chance of a gybe in such a situation, and it will usually be avoided. Conversationally one says 'she looks a bit by the lee' or some similarly diffident phrase so as not to hurt the helmsman's sensibilities.

Running fix A most useful navigational technique. Whereas the ordinary fix crosses Position lines taken from two or more objects as nearly simultaneously as possible, the running fix uses observations separated by an interval of time. One or more objects may be used to provide the position lines. The essential third item of knowledge is the distance and track made good between observations. For example, two position lines are obtained from a single wireless mast ashore at an interval of, say, ten minutes. If they are now drawn on the chart and the vessel's track is drawn to scale, there can be only one position where it will fit between those lines. (Indeed if you call the technique a 'running fit' it may become clearer.) For success the boat must be steered on a constant heading and distance must be assessed as carefully as possible with allowance for stream, current and leeway due to the wind. In poor visibility bearings from a radio beacon can be very helpful, perhaps mixed with a visual bearing. One uses all the information one can.

Running lights   Navigation lights as prescribed for a vessel making way in the International regulations for Preventing Collisions at Sea.

RYA   Royal Yachting Association.

S

S One to starboard, two to port, and three astern. Those are the sound signals, and the single letter S means, 'My engines are going astern', thus matching three hoots nearly (and intentionally) with the three dots Morse code for S. Sierra is the word in phonetic.

Saddle A wooden block on a spar, affording a rest for another spar, or for a stay. A Gaff saddle is similar in form to a riding saddle, the mast taking the role of the horse's back. It is made of metal, but covered with rawhide to lessen chafe.

Sag, to (1) A hull ashore, supported only at her ends, will sag in the middle. (And see Hogged.)

Sag, to (2) Usually in combination as in 'sag away to leeward', or 'sag off', it describes a boat making rather too much Leeway when sailing on the wind. Typical small family cruisers tend to sag away most badly when the sea is rough enough to slow their forward progress.

Sail Leaving aside the obvious meanings, both noun and verb, one need only comment that on a sailing boat you set a sail. Thereafter, you raise your anchor and 'set sail for paradise', or wherever your fancy takes you. Likewise, ugly great oil tankers 'sail' at 1500 hrs, and sometimes a steamship is said to 'set sail' in the meaning that she sets forth. Only when a boat has both sail and power as her means of propulsion does one take care to distinguish between the verbs 'to sail' and 'to motor'.

Sail area The sail area of a boat is variable, to accommodate to the wind strength. A common reference-point is the 'working sail area', which is not precisely defined, but may be taken to mean the total area of the sails that the boat would set in winds of Force 3 to 4.

Sail area/displacement ratio Like the Displacement/Length Ratio, this is a useful parameter in comparing one boat with another. The sail area is nominal, being that which is enclosed by two triangles, one representing the mainsail, and the other the area between mast, forestay and foredeck. One divides that area in square feet by the displacement to the power of 2/3. The formula looks like this:

$$\frac{\text{Sail area}}{\text{Displacement}^{2/3}}$$

and the displacement is in long tons of 2240 lb each. (Thanks heavens we have our pocket calculators to help us with powers of that sort)

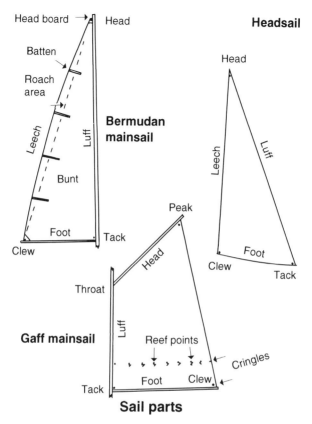

Sail parts

Sail cloth Any sort of textile used for making sails. But each sail is made up of several pieces, each of which is known as a cloth.

Sail coat A cloth cover such as protects a mainsail when stowed along the boom. With the cotton sails of the past the coat gave protection against damp: with man-made fibres it gives protection against the sun's ultra-violet radiation.

Sail on her ear, to To sail a boat at a large angle of heel, say with the lee rail awash.

Sail plan The drawing which shows the positions and sizes of sail, and of the spars and rigging, though there may be a separate and additional rigging plan.

Sail-stop, or sail-tie Just a length of rope, canvas or even an old pyjama-cord, which is used to tie a furled sail. But beware of those bungee-rubber cords with a hook at one or both ends: if you want to preserve your eyesight, ban them from your boat. Also called Gaskets, especially by square-rigged types.

Sailing directions Instructions as to pilotage – not to the handling of the boat herself. Sailing directions usually take the form of a book, and the term is almost synonymous with Pilot.

Saint Elmo's fire A corona discharge of static electricity from a boat's mast or her rigging. You may never see it, and when you do there's nothing you can do about it, so try to relax and enjoy the spectacle. It is silent, and not of itself dangerous. May be accompanied by a smell of 'ozone' or of 'sparks'.

Salting A low-lying area which is flooded at high tide. Ing was an old word for field or meadow.

Salvage In marine affairs has the same meaning as it does ashore – of things saved (such as members of the Salvation Army). But there is the specifically nautical usage (with legal implications) where a service of salvage is performed and, if proved in court, may merit an award of money. The amount of the award will relate to the value of property salvaged, the extent of the danger to that property, and the risks or difficulties overcome by the salvors.

Samson post A strong wooden post rooted in the keel and passing up through the deck where the top eight or twelve inches provide a strong attachment point for the anchor cable, or for mooring and towing warps.

Sandwich construction A form of construction used for hulls, decks and houses, in which two relatively dense skins are held apart and stabilised by a thicker core of lightweight material. The core may be of balsa wood, for example, or of foamed plastic. The idea is to save weight and achieve stiffness, for although a think skin of plastic material may be quite strong it will bend easily. Two such skins held apart and prevented from buckling by an inner core can be a hundred times stiffer than either alone. But it is essential to get a good bond between skins and core, and to be sure that there are no cavities into which water could penetrate.

SAR Search and Rescue (organisation or activity)

Satnav Satellite navigation system. May be used of any such system in a general way, but more often refers to the US Navy's Transit network which is widely used by yachts. A later and more accurate satellite navigation system is GPS.

Scandalise, to A gaff mainsail is scandalised by lowering the Peak, and by Tricing up the Tack so that the foot of the sail is raised. Result, a disgraceful-looking bag of floppy cloth. With so few gaffers around, this delightful word could well be salvaged and put to work for other inelegant antics with sails (some spinnakers perhaps?). So could that word 'trice', which can properly be used for the action of lifting anything upwards and out of the way by means of a rope. It's your word as much as anybody's; why not make free of it?

Scantlings   To a shipwright, speaking of timber, means no more than the dimensions to which it is to be cut or shaped. If you say, 'Let's look at her scantlings', you are going to assess the stoutness of her timbers, carlins, floors and so forth. (Please see Moulded and sided.)

Scend   This is the horizontal or fore-and-aft movement of a boat under the influence of waves – usually most noticeable in harbour. It is also the vertical movement (due to waves) of the water itself against a harbour wall, for example. Slightly confusing. . .

Schooner   A two masted fore-and-aft rigged sailing vessel with the taller mast aft (as sketched under Rig.) Naturally enough this mast is the mainmast and carries the mainsail. The foremast carries the foresail, usually with its foot on a boom like a smaller mainsail. Ahead of the foresail will be one or more Headsails.

Scope   The length of anchor cable or mooring rope. When anchoring it is always wise to give plenty of scope, by Veering plenty of cable.

Score   The groove made in the shell of a block to take the rope strop which surrounds it. A similar groove provided to locate a rope on a spar.

Scow   Just another of those words which has an infinite variety of meanings, of which the only thing in common is that they all refer to a small boat. In the USA a scow is long, lean, and of boxlike cross-section, with bilgeboards – that's to say centreboards port and starboard. But in Britain a scow is likely to be a clinker dinghy, eleven or twelve feet long, shallow in the body but beamy, and setting a lugsail.

Scow an anchor, to   To attach the anchor cable to the Crown of the anchor, and then seize it to the ring with a suitable twine or marling. While the pull is along the Shank no great load is put on the seizing, but if the anchor is foul the seizing will part when the cable is hauled up short and the strain comes at an angle to the shank. When the seizing parts the pull comes directly on the crown of the anchor, whose fluke should be pulled clear – you hope.

Screw   Propeller.

Scud, to To run off before the wind with a small amount to sail set. Foam, spray and low clouds driven by the wind are also all of them known as scud.

Scull, to To the river boatman it is to pull a boat with a pair of oars. To the seagoing boatman it is to propel a boat with a single oar over the stern by sweeping it from side to side while twisting it. A good dinghy will have a half-round sculling-notch in the transom to take the single oar. (And see Wangle, to.)

Scupper An opening in a Bulwark to allow water to run off the deck.

Scuttle More commonly called a porthole or portlight. A round opening window in a heavy metal frame.

Sea Yes, we all know what that is. But a sea is what a landsman would call a wave.

Sea anchor A drogue, or parachute-like construction, of timber, iron and heavy canvas, designed to resist being dragged through the water. In heavy weather a sea anchor may be streamed over the bow of a boat with the idea that it will hold her head to wind and seas as she drifts stern-first before the storm. Some people believe that sea anchors are effective, many others have been disappointed, and the whole business has provided much material for usually inconclusive argument ever since John Claus Voss commended sea anchors in *Venturesome Voyages*. The truth seems to be that some boats will lie to some sea anchors, others will not.

Sea breeze A wind flowing in from the sea to replace air over the land which rises due to the day-time heating by the sun. A land breeze blows the other way when, at night, the land cools more rapidly than the sea.

Seacock A valve on a Skin fitting to control the ingress or egress of water.

Sea kindly Describes a hull which rides comfortably at sea, whose motion is neither too lively nor too sluggish, and whose decks do not ship too much water. Like an amiable woman, a sea kindly boat defies precise definition, but is recognisable as soon as you take her out.

Sea mile A Nautical mile.

Sea room Sufficient space to manoeuvre and to do what you wish to do without obstruction by other ships, the land, shallows, or man-made constructions such as piers.

Seam   The gap between two planks of either the hull or the deck. Seams are Payed with caulking on a bed of cotton or oakum. In a sail or tarpaulin, 'seam' has its ordinary meaning.

Seamanship   The art and science of keeping out of trouble at sea, no matter whether your craft is a fully-rigged ship or a makeshift raft.

Seat   Please see Thwart.

Secondary port   Times of High and Low water are predicted for every day of the year for a few primary or Standard ports. The times for secondary ports are found by reference to the times at standard ports.

Sections   If you were to cut through a hull as if cutting a slice of bread from a loaf you would see the shape of the section at that point. Designers commonly draw ten sections for a modest-sized hull, of which the midship section, or midsection, is sometimes called the 'master section' since it sets the shape for all the others and does much to stamp a character on the hull as a whole. (Please see Lines, Bilge and Chine.)

Seiche   (pronounced saysh) A rise and fall of the water level in a marina or harbour occurring at an interval of a few minutes and unrelated to the ordinary tidal rise and fall or to regular swell running in from the sea. May be caused by changes in barometric pressure, or by waves of very long period which would not be noticeable in the open sea. In ordinary landsman's language you would probably say 'surge'.

Seize, to   To bind together two ropes, two spars, or almost anything to anything with several tight turns of small cord. The result is a Seizing. A Racking seizing goes over and between in a figure-eight pattern, instead of straight round the outside.

Self-bailer   A special type of drain for sailing dinghies in which water is drawn out either by the attitude of the hull which causes it to run aft, or by the lowered dynamic pressure on the outer skin resulting from the high forward speed. Either of those conditions is best satisfied when a dinghy is planing. A cruising boat whose cockpit sole is several inches above the waterline may have drains, and will usually be called 'self-draining', though some people might call it self-bailing. But such simple drains are never terms 'self-bailers'.

Self-steering   Please see Auto-pilot.

Self-tacking   A phrase that describes a sail whose sheet calls for no attention when passing from one tack to another. A conventional mainsail is self-tacking, but conventional jibs are not. A headsail can be made self-tacking either by bending a boom or club along its foot, or by leading its sheet to a traveller which is free to slide along a Horse across the foredeck.

Send down, to   A rather idiomatic expression, whereas a sail or a burgee is lowered at the end of the day, a halyard may be sent down at the end of the season. But a topmast or a yard would be sent down just for the afternoon. The phrase tends to be used of larger items or more permanent actions. (See strike, to.)

Senhouse slip   One form of slip hook for quick release. The Pelican hook is similar. The hinged tongue of the hook is held closed by a ring, and when the ring is knocked free the tongue flies open.

Sennit   Plaited or woven rope in more or less fanciful patterns.

Serve, to   To cover a rope or a splice by binding Marline or other Small stuff tightly around it. Where the end of a rope is served (to prevent fraying) the process (and the result) is commonly called (a) Whipping.

Servo rudder, servo tab   A small surface which, when acted upon by the water flow, moves a larger surface (e.g. the main rudder) by means of leverage. (And please see Vane gear.)

Set   Both verb and noun. A boat carried by the stream of a tide may be set to the west, or she may set towards the mouth of a river by the current. In either case one may say that there 'is a set' to the west, or towards the mouth.

Set up, to   To tighten up, as in 'setting up the shrouds'. Correct adjustment is implied, as well as tightening.

Sewed up   Rhymes with rude, not often used, but just in case you meet someone who likes to show he knows the words, it means aground or stranded. 'She' was sewed up about ten feet' means that she was high and dry at least several feet above Low water.

Sextant   An optical instrument for measuring angles, such as that between the sun and the horizon, between the top of a lighthouse and the sea at its base, or (with the sextant turned on its side) between two objects ashore.

Shackle (1) A metal link which can be opened or closed. The most common is U-shaped and is called a D-shackle, the open part of the U being closed by a threaded pin. There are many kinds of shackle, and I think the best way to acquaint yourself with them is in the pages of a chandler's catalogue.

Shackle (2) A measure of length – and rather variable from place to place. But for the likes of us it is usually fifteen fathoms, and relates only to chain cable.

Shaft log A strengthening member fitted on the Keel, Keelson or Deadwood where the Sterntube passes through the hull. Originally a shaped lump of timber, such logs may nowadays be made entirely of metal.

Shake out a reef A nice 'in' phrase for the process of un-reefing a sail. 'In the evening the wind fined away, so we shook out the reefs and brewed some tea. . .' And so the story winds on, while you do your best to look keenly interested.

Shank The central 'stalk' of an anchor.

Shape a course, to To decide a course, and set the ship's head on it. Commonly one shapes a course 'for' some specific point or place.

Sharpie A boat of simple hull form, with more or less flat bottom, and more or less flat sides, running together at the stem. Sharpies may be small pulling boats, small open dinghies, or decked cruising boats with cabins. The bigger sizes, fitted with leeboards, are relatively common on New England waters.

Sheathe, to To cover a hull or deck, usually a wooden one, with an impervious layer. The technique which appeals to many amateurs is to sheathe the boat with glass cloth (or chopped strand mat) and polyester resin. Unfortunately, polyester does not always bond very well to the timber – epoxy resin would better, but it is harder to work with and more expensive. There are proprietary types of sheathing, some based on rubbery compounds, others using reinforced plastics. All require that the wood beneath be sound, free from rot, and free from paint, oil, or large gaps and cracks. Copper sheathing was formerly much used to protect wooden hulls against Teredo in tropical waters. Although copper sheet is very expensive, the initial capital cost is offset by the saving of the annual anti-fouling paint which would otherwise be necessary, so in the long term sheathing may prove cheaper as well as more convenient.

Sheave The actual wheel of a pulley Block. Special types of sheave are made for rope, wire and chain, and it is important to get the right type. Moreover, the larger the diameter of the sheave the more easily the cable will run, and there is a definite minimum size for each size of cable. The makers, fortunately, know all about that, so the size of block is proportioned to size of rope, with sheave diameter, Score and Swallow all in harmony. The noticeably large sheaves used with small ropes in the multi-part mainsheet tackles on some racing dinghies are made that way for easier Rendering – in other words for maximum mechanical efficiency.

Sheer The curve of a boat's gunwale or top strake when viewed from the side. The Sheer plan is a drawing of the side elevation. (See Lines for illustration.) A conventional sheer runs down from a high point at the stem, reaches its lowest somewhere near amidships or a little aft of that, and then rises again towards the stern. A hogged sheer is the reverse – hump-backed and piglike.

Sheer, to To put the rudder over to one side. Sometimes done when a boat is at anchor, to make her lie to one side and more steadily: this is called 'giving her a sheer to port', for example. (And see Cast, to.)

Sheer legs, sheers or jeers Long poles, spars or struts, two or three in number, set up to lift and step a mast, say, or to lower an engine into a boat.

Sheer pole A rod or stick fixed between the lower ends of a pair of shrouds so that neither of them can twist.

Sheer strake The topmost plank in a boat's side.

Sheet A rope attached to the Clew of a sail, and used to pull it in or to ease it out.

Sheet bend For joining two ropes of unequal thickness. Please see sketch.

Sheet bend

Sheet-horse Please see Horse (1).

Shelf In timber construction the shelf is a component running fore and aft along the tops of the ribs, and providing support and attachment for the deck beams.

Shell The outer casing, or shell, of a block.

Ship Please see Boat.

Ship, to To set a component or part in its working position. Oars must be shipped in their rowlocks before you start rowing. Later they will be unshipped... and then 'boated'. Fortunately, it is only in 'boating oars' that the word boat is used as a verb, but to 'ship oars' means the opposite and is a common source of confusion. Otherwise you do such things as shipping winch-handles in their sockets, or oil lamps on their brackets. That is the specialised seaman's use of the verb. One also uses it in the ordinary landsman's sense of taking anything on board, from a cargo to a crew, from a sewing machine to a nasty great wet sea. Ugh!

Ship's papers Mainly the certificate of registry, but also any documents pertaining directly to that particular boat, such as receipts for harbour dues, customs clearances, and so forth.

Shipshape In good order, tidy and efficient.

Shipworm Please see Teredo.

Shoal A place where the water is relatively shallow. The word is noun, adjective and verb. 'There is a shoal over there.' 'The water is pretty shoal over there.' 'The water shoals quite quickly on the eastern bank.'

Shoal-draft (boat) One designed to float in less water than the average for her size. Usually tends to be beamy.

Shock cord Or bungee. Elastic cord made of rubber strands inside a textile sheath. Has many and valued uses on a boat, but eschew hooked end-fittings and save your eyes for another day.

Shore Apart from being the land where it meets the sea, it is also a strut used to prop up a boat on dry land. A boat is brought ashore for the winter and while on shore is shored up with shores. Simple!

Short boards Short tacks. (Please see Board.) But note that short planks are a way of building a wooden hull cheaply – a way that requires many joints between the short pieces. A conscientious builder will use the longest possible planks, and for boats up to about ten tons that should mean full-length planks throughout.

171

Shorten in   To shorten the scope of the anchor cable. By contrast, sheets are usually 'hardened in', though you would be perfectly well understood if you asked your crew to shorten them.

Shorten sail   To reduce the total sail area set, either by reefing, or by Handing or Furling one or more of those in use.

Shoulder of mutton   Please see Bermudan.

Shoulders   The shoulders of a boat are at the fore-part of the hull, just abaft her head. (Please see Bow.)

Shroud plate   The fitting on the hull to which a shroud or stay is secured. (Please see Chain plates.)

Shroud roller   A loose tubular sleeve encasing a shroud and intended to mini-mise friction and wear in either a headsail or a sheet which passes across it.

Shrouds   Stays, usually of wire rope, supporting the mast at each side. Cap shrouds go to the top of the mast, 'lowers' go to some intermediate point, often about two-thirds of the way up, where Spreaders are fitted.

Shy   A spinnaker set to receive a wind more or less on the beam, instead of over the stern, is said to be set shy.

Side-lights   The red (port) and green (starboard) navigation lights, normally fitted at the sides of a boat, though the modern Collision Regulations allow them to be combined in a single, centrally-mounted lamp on any vessel of less than twenty metres in length.

Sided   Please see Moulded and sided.

Simplex working   Please see Radio telephone.

Single up, to   To cast off all mooring lines, except one at each end of the boat, preparatory to getting under way.

Single whip   Technically, a rope passed through a fixed block so as to change its direction can be called a single whip. But the term is best used for a tackle in which there is one moving block. That gives a two-to-one mechanical advantage – less the loss due to friction, of course.

Sit out, to   To sit on the gunwale of a sailing dinghy, often with toes hooked under a strap fitted for the purpose, so as to use one's weight to the best advantage in opposing the heeling due to sail force. To Hike or Hike Out in the USA.

Skeg   A shallow keel at the after end of a boat, or a deeper fin giving support to the rudder. It may also have been put there to protect the rudder or propeller when the boat grounds.

Skin drag   The water resistance to a boat going through the water comes from several causes. Of these one is skin friction. This is minimised by maintaining a clean and smooth hull surface (though a highly polished one is not always the best). Weeds, barnacles and bumps of that sort make the skin drag very much greater. (Please see Drag.)

Skin fittings   This term embraces a variety of components associated with necessary holes in the hull. For the main part, such fittings take the form of metal or plastics pipes with flanges and backing plates. Sometimes an inlet fitting will have a coarse integral strainer to keep out the bigger particles of seaweed. A seacock itself may on occasions be termed a 'skin fitting', though in other contexts a distinction would be made between the seacock and the skin fitting to which it is screwed. It is good practice to reinforce the hull in the region of a skin fitting, usually with a backing pad. The fitting must be well bedded, and bolts or other fastenings must be of a material which will not corrode in sea water nor set up a galvanic action with the material of the fitting itself.

Skipper   Properly a qualified master – though in practice the title is justly given to all those who show themselves able to handle the boat of their choice in a seamanlike manner.

Skylight   A glazed frame, like a small greenhouse or garden frame, built on deck to admit light and air, and usually admitting water as well – even when closed.

Slab reef   Please see Reef, to.

Slack water   The time at High water, or Low, when the tide ceases to run.

Slant   A wind that allows you to fetch your course without being absolutely close-hauled.

Slatting   The rattling, shaking movement and noise of sails which are fluttering in the wind and are not filled and drawing. To a seaman this is an irritating sound, partly because the sails and gear are being worn out to no good purpose.

Slick   A smooth patch of water. The most notorious patches are the oil slicks which pollute our waters from time to time. But a slick may form in the lee of a hull, or by reason of some tidal current effect.

Slides   Small, specially shaped pieces of metal or plastic which are attached to the Luff or mainsail and hold it to the mast by sliding in the Track.

Slip, to   'To slip, haul out, strike over and shore up. . . £'. Thus the dreaded end-of-season account from the boatyard. A boat is slipped when she is brought to the slipway and there grounded or settled into a mobile cradle. (The 'striking over' is the process of moving her from the cradle to her winter resting spot.) Like so many other nautical words, 'to slip' has other meanings, notably to drop your mooring, or simply to cast off from a quayside: 'We slipped at 0400 and, once clear of the harbour wall, laid for the headland on port tack. . .' Less happy is the occasion when, with your anchor foul of some obstruction on the bottom and the water getting too rough to stay where you are, you have to slip your cable. Having first buoyed it, you free the Bitter end from the boat and drop it all overboard, hoping to return and retrieve it some sunnier day.

Slip hook   Please see Senhouse slip.

Slipway   A firm sloping roadway, of concrete, railroad sleepers, etc., running down into the water for the convenient launching and retrieval (slipping) of boats. Known as a 'slip' colloquially. (And see Ways.)

Sloop   No definition of this word is possible. Current usage, though tends to reserve it for fore-and-aft rigged yachts of moderate size, setting only a mainsail and one headsail (see sketch under Rig). A few hundred years ago a sloop, insofar as rig was concerned, would have had a short fixed bowsprit while a Cutter would have had a longer but reefable bowsprit. The cutter could thus carry more sail in light airs and tended to be the choice when speed was required – as in smuggling. Speed was also required by the revenue men to chase the smugglers, so they adopted the cutter rig too. Today, usage links 'cutter' with a two-headsail rig (staysail and jib), and that is not infrequently allied to a fixed bowsprit much shorter than those of the old-time cutters. At the same time, the modern sloop has lost her bowsprit completely and sets her single headsail to the stemhead. But note that her overhanging bow may carry the stemhead farther forward than that of the old-fashioned sloop with her straight-up stem – in effect many a modern sloop has integrated a short bowsprit into the hull structure itself. (Please see Cutter.)

Slot effect Here's a fruitful field for the talking of nonsense. The 'slot' is the gap formed between Headsail and Mainsail, and many people believe it has some magical property simply because some aeroplanes use leading-edge slots when flying at high angles of incidence. But the two cases are not comparable because an aeroplane's wing is so different from a mast with a cloth sail trailing from the back of it. The best way to sum it up is to say that if you have a sail behind a mast, you can improve the airflow over the lee side by careful adjustment of an overlapping headsail. The slot so formed will speed up the air flow over the lee side of the main and reduce the turbulence caused by the mast. But the slot is not a propulsive device of itself: if you were to make a single sail equal to the combined area of main and jib, and if you were to hank it on a forestay so that it was free of mast-turbulence, its propulsive effect would be greater than that of the two sails and their slot.

Slutter A word that is something of a rarity which was coined by John Illingworth for a rig which has something of the sloop and something of the cutter. Only one headsail is set at a time, but there is a choice of two, one of which is set to the masthead (light weather) and the other to some lower point on the mast (stronger winds).

Small stuff A rather vague term for cord, twin, marline, Hambro line and all the other stuff you might use to make whippings, servings or lashings

SNA Society of Naval Architects.

Snap shackle There are various kinds, but all avoid the screw-in pin of the common shackle by using some form of hinged closure which is supposed to lock itself securely in the closed position.

Snatch block A block whose shell can be hinged open at one side to allow the rapid insertion of a rope without reeving it all the way from the end.

Snatch a turn, to I can't make any distinction between the snatching and catching of turns. In each phrase the concept is one of getting a turn of rope quickly around a bollard or the like which will sustain the load while you have a think. It implies temporary holding without making fast.

Snub, to To check a rope or a chain sharply. The boat may do it herself, snubbing at her anchor cable in heavy weather – that's to say coming up short on the cable with a jerk. A Snubbing winch is a small winch consisting of a drum with no lever but with a ratchet mechanism so that when you shorten a rope turned around the drum it acts as a brake.

Snug down, to   To hand sails, or reef, and generally make everything fast on deck and below in preparation for heavy weather.

Soft eye   A plain eye in the end of a rope, without a Thimble.

SOLAS   Safety of Life at Sea Convention.

Soldier's wind   The kind I like. A fair or free wind that saves you having to sail Close-hauled.

Sole   The sailor's word for the floor. You stand on the cabin sole, or the cockpit sole. But dinghies usually have Bottom boards or Gratings, not soles. (Please see Floor.)

Solent rig   A jocular term for what is sometimes said to be the week-end yachtsman's preferred rig – that's to say no headsail, mainsail set but strapped down hard, while the boat proceeds under power.

Soon   Means that the forecast weather is expected to arrive within twelve hours. Please see Imminent.

Sound, to   To find the depth of the water, by means of an Echo sounder or a Lead line, or just a long pole. Hence a sounding.

Sound   As a noun it means a navigable passage between two sea areas, or an arm of the sea or large inlet, with good depths. As an adjective it means the same as ashore, in good condition, but is perhaps more favoured by seamen than landsmen.

Soundings, in   Approaching land from the ocean, a ship reaches the point where the water shallows sufficiently to permit soundings to be taken – say about 100 fathoms. She is then 'in soundings'.

South cone   A black cone hoisted by Coastguards, harbourmasters and other shoreside officials to indicate the expectation of a gale from a generally southerly direction. The point is downward. By night three (usually red) lamps are suspended in the form of a triangle, point down. A North cone is the other way up.

Span Usually a wire, but could be rope or chain, stretched between two points to spread the load. A dinghy to be lifted on deck could have a wire span from stem to transom, the lifting tackle being attached at roughly the mid point of the span. The yard of a gunter sail sometimes has a wire span along its length to which the peak halyard is attached.

Spanker Not much used now – and that's a pity. It corresponded to the sail which we should now call a Mizzen or a Jigger. (In old books you may also find the same sail called a 'driver'.) The sail which the Dutch sometimes set from masthead to stern, and which they call an *aap* (ape), could well be called spanker in English.

Spar Mast, boom, gaff, yard, spinnaker pole … all are spars. It is the general term for sticks or poles used as part of a boat's rig, whether made of wood, metal or any other material that may come along. (See Yard.)

Spar buoy A buoy with a vertical pole sticking up through its middle so that it looks like a toffee-apple dropped sticky end down.

Speak a ship, to To communicate with another ship at sea, by any means. . .may be by flags, Aldis lamp, or even by speaking to her.

Speed/length ratio This ratio is abbreviated as $V/\sqrt{L}$. It is the speed in knots divided by the square root of the waterline length in feet. For example, a boat with 25 foot WL gives a square root of 5. Then, when she is moving at 5 knots her speed/length ratio is exactly one. At a speed of 10 knots her ratio would be two. The ratio is of significance for Displacement hulls (i.e. those which don't plane on the water) because it is rarely that such hulls achieve better than a speed/length ratio of 1.5. In fact most don't do as well as that: a ballasted sailing boat of 25 foot waterline would do well to achieve a ratio of 1.3 and to sail at 6.5 knots, though she might easily do it with a 30 horsepower engine in calm water.

Spherical buoy Oddly enough a spherical buoy. According to the international buoyage system it has no port/starboard significance, but if painted orange is used as a 'special mark' to indicate such things as practice zones, sewer outfalls and such odds and ends. If painted in red and white vertical stripes it indicates safe water, and you may pass either side.

Spider band A metal band carrying a number of eyes, lugs or other pick-up points which is fitted around a spar for the attachment of stays, or simply to house Belaying pins.

Spike   Usually a Marline spike

Spile, to   To transfer the curvature of a solid object to a drawing by a variety of means. For example, a pair of dividers maintained at a constant separation can be used: one point will follow the curve and the other will scribe a line on a flat board held in a suitable position.

Spinnaker   A large parachute-like headsail of very light material used mainly for running downwind, but also carried in a beam wind when it is said to be set Shy. First introduced in 1865, the spinnaker was not always so balloon-shaped as it commonly is today, and even now a smaller and flatter type is used by some cruising owners. The sail is set with a pole to one lower corner, controlled by the Guy, and has a sheet to the other corner, though those who are not constrained by racing rules may use two poles, or none, or they may opt for a cruising chute.

Spinnaker chute   A tubular container lying along the underside of the deck with a bell-mouth emerging through the deck near the stem. The spinnaker can be housed in the chute with its halyard attached, ready for rapid hoisting when the boat turns on to the downwind leg of the race.

Spinnaker sleeve   *(or sock)* A long sleeve of light cloth in which the spinnaker is hauled aloft. The sail is then broken out by gathering the sleeve up at the head of the sail, for which purpose it has its own continuous halyard-cum-downhaul.

Spit   Either a narrow strip of land projecting into the seaway, or a submerged shoal of long and narrow shape, and by that I mean longer and narrower than a Horse.

Spitfire   A small Headsail (jib) of heavy canvas and stoutly roped, to be set in the heaviest weather. The term seems to be yielding to 'storm jib'.

Splice, to   To join two pieces of rope by interweaving the strands. The resulting joint is a splice. In the Eye-splice the rope's end is turned back and woven into itself to form a loop. In the *Back splice* (illustrated) the three strands are formed into a Crown knot and then immediately tucked back into the rope to make a thickened end which will not unravel. The *Cut splice* is made by splicing the two ends of a short piece of rope into the body of a longer piece, rather like the handle of a a basket. The short splice *and long splice* join two pieces of rope end-to-end. In the Short splice (also illustrated) the strands of each rope are unlaid, then the ropes are married together and the strands of each are tucked under the still-laid strands of the other, working against the lay. The splice is thicker than the body of the rope because it contains six strands instead of the normal three. The Long splice is quite different. Strands in each rope are unlaid for a greater length and the ropes are married. A strand of one rope is then unlaid for an even greater length, and a strand of the other is laid up in its place. The procedure is repeated for the other rope. The remaining two strands (one from each rope) are cut where they meet at the middle of the splice, allowing enough to tie them together with a reef knot. The other matching pairs of strands are similarly tied. The result is barely thicker than the original rope, but not very strong and consequently not much used.

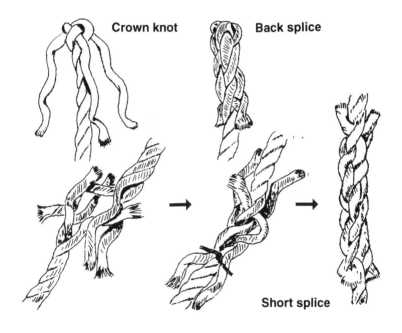

Crown knot

Back splice

Short splice

Spline   To the shipwright a spline is a thin strip of wood which is glued into a seam when the gap is too wide for ordinary caulking. Similarly a spline may be used to repair a cracked plank, after the crack has been opened with the saw to make a slot of regular shape. On the drawing board, too, a spline is a thin strip of wood (sometimes of other flexible material) which can be used to draw curved lines such as hull waterlines. In the engineering shop a spline is a raised ridge on a shaft which keys into a corresponding slot on a pinion or other female member. As a verb, you would spline a crack in a hull, and you would have a splined shaft ... but I have not heard draftsmen talk about 'splining lines'.

Split rig   The general term for a sailplan set on more than one mast, such as a ketch or a schooner. This allows the total sail area to be split into smaller, and more easily handled parts. Although a cutter splits her headsail area into two, people do not normally consider her to deserve the term 'split rig'.

Spoil ground *(also 'dumping ground')*   An area of sea bottom reserved for the dumping of waste of one kind or another. Usually clear of any likely anchorage, and in relatively deep water. Marked on the chart by a surrounding dashed line, and at sea (if at all) by yellow buoys.

Sponson   Broadly speaking a subsidiary structure extending from the side of the ship. The port and starboard floats of a trimaran would be called sponsons, and when used of small pleasure craft the word normally implies some sort of stabilising float. But in ships a sponson may be a gun platform jutting from the side, or the platforms forward and aft of the paddle-wheels on a steamer so equipped.

Spoon bows   These rise clear of the water and are rounded in their lower sections. They contrast with the wedge-like bows of the old straight-stemmed boats. See sketch under Bow.

Spreader(s)   Struts, normally used in pairs to hold the Shrouds away from the mast and so widen the angle at which each shroud meets the masthead. The term cross-tree may be applied to a pair of spreaders made in a single continuous unit, but on ships, cross-trees may be quite short arms or brackets whose purpose is simply to form attachment points for various blocks and eyes.

Spreader lights   Lights arranged to shine down and illuminate the deck, and especially the region of the foot of the mast, for night work. For convenience they are often mounted on the undersides of the spreaders – hence their name – though similar lights may be fitted directly to the mast itself.

Spring   A mooring rope used to restrain fore and aft movement of a boat. Normally, two springs are used, one leading from aft forward, and the other leading from forward aft. Except in the most sheltered waters, a pair of spring is essential when mooring alongside.

Spring, to When a plank or other structural component lifts, or springs away from its attachment point it is said to be 'sprung'. 'She had several sprung planks, among other damage. . .' Hence a boat will spring a leak, and here the word has an affinity with the next entry.

Spring tide These tides occur approximately every fortnight and have a greater range than Neaps. Both are covered under Tide. The word spring derives from a springing up, just as in a freshwater spring bursting forth from the earth, and just as living things burst out in spring time. A plank which springs is one which, having been bent into shape, breaks free and springs out of place . . . but I've already mention that.

Sprit A pole or spar, and most commonly the long spar that extends the peak of a four-sided Spritsail. The sprit runs diagonally from the foot of the mast where, in Thames barge jargon, its downward thrust is supported by a wire or chain called the 'stanliff'. Please see illustration.

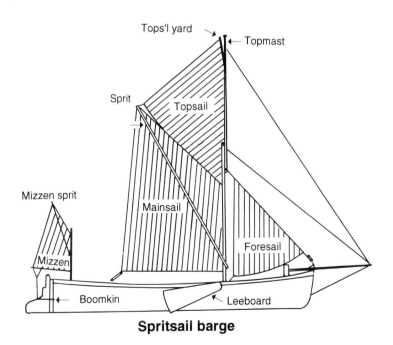

Spritsail barge

Spun yarn A small type of cord, similar to marline but rather coarser. Not much used nowadays but was formerly used for serving warps, and for odd lashings.

Squall A sudden, but relatively short-lived, increase in wind force, often with a change of wind direction, and with rain. A white squall comes with a clear sky; a black squall comes under ominous lowering clouds, and often with rain.

Square rig The type of rig which uses four-sided sails hanging beneath yards which are suspended from the mast at their midpoints. There is thus an equal area of sail each side of the mast, whereas the 'fore-and-aft' rig sets all, or nearly all, the sail to one side of the mast.

Squaresail An approximately rectangular sail which is set on a Yard so that its centreline coincides with the mast. Other four-sided sails such as the Gaff, Sprit-sail and various Lugs are set entirely or mainly to one side of the mast.

Squat *Verb:* a vessel is said to squat if she runs with her stern depressed. That commonly happens to an auxiliary yacht when driven at maximum engine power. *Noun:* a squat (in some parts of the country only) is a scissors type of boom Crutch.

SSB Single Side Band.

Stability The quality in a vessel that enables her to resist, and to recover from, a heeling force. Laymen (and laywomen even more so) tend to be apprehensive about 'tipping over', and insofar as small open boats are concerned, they are quite right to be cautious, for many accidents are caused by capsize. Larger, decked boats nearly always have ample stability. Although the subject is too extensive to treat fully in a mere dictionary, it is useful to know what is meant by the two terms, 'initial stability' and 'ultimate stability'. A wide-bottomed vase with a heavy base will have good Initial stability, but a narrow-bottomed vase which is rather top heavy will have low initial stability. But even though the beamy and well-ballasted one will resist being toppled, neither will right itself when once laid flat: neither has 'ultimate stability'. The toy clown with rounded and weighted base has all the Ultimate stability you could ask for – he always comes back up when knocked down. Yet the clown has low initial stability because it is quite easy to tilt him the first few degrees. He heels more easily than the broad, ballasted vase. Boats may have either kind of stability, or a mixture, depending on their beam, their shape, and their ballast. In ordinary speech a boat with high initial stability is said to be Stiff. The converse is Tender.

Staff A pole or stick used to support an ensign or a burgee. A bigger, stouter pole is a Stave and forms the main part of a Boathook.

Stanchion A vertical post, usually of metal tube, supporting the guard rail or lifelines which surround the decks. If your boat is big enough to have an awning she may have taller stanchions to support it.

Stand-on vessel Under Rule 17 of the Collision Regulations, when one of two vessels has to keep out of the way of the other, the other 'shall retain her course and speed'. In other words she stands on. This makes it easy for the give-way vessel to avoid her, whereas if both change course a collision could result. Nevertheless, no vessel is given right of way over other vessels in the Collision Regulations, and in the last resort the stand-on vessel has a responsibility to take avoiding action if that is the only way to avert a disaster.

Stand, to To head the boat in a specific direction. You can stand across a bay, or stand into it, and in each of those examples the implication is one of positive motion in a positive direction. But when a vessel Stands off she may lie hove-to or sail around aimlessly, waiting at some distance offshore. And when she Stands on and off, she first stands (i.e. sails) towards the shore, and then away from it, but only with the intention of killing time and not with the desire to get anywhere.

Standard port A port for which times and heights of tides have been specially and fully calculated. A Secondary port is one for which tide times are found by applying a 'difference' on a standard port.

Standing part The end of a tackle that is permanently made fast, by contrast with the hauling part.

Standing rigging The fixed rigging, such as Shrouds and Stays, which supports the mast, bowsprit and so forth. Halyards, sheets and so forth form the Running rigging. (Well, that's no surprise, is it?)

Standing wave A surface wave which does not move forward. Seen, for example, where a fast-running stream crosses a submerged ledge.

Star crazing A pattern of fine cracks in the gel coat of a laminated resinglass structure. The cracks usually radiate from a point where an excessive load has deformed the surface, and a sensible owner will clean them out and fill with resin, or perhaps lay on a good paint treatment. If star crazing results from normal loads you will know that the structure is too flexible and you will be wise to back it with extra stiffening.

Starboard The vessel's own right-hand side.

Starboard-hand buoy   Please see Port-hand buoy.

Starboard tack   Sailing with the wind on the starboard side and the mainsail out to port. When two sailing boats meet on crossing courses, the boat on starboard tack has right of way. The International Regulations for Preventing Collisions at Sea lay down that a vessel with her mainsail out to port is on the starboard tack, so the legal definition embraces running as well as reaching.

Start, to   To ease a rope slightly – for example a sheet. (Please see Check.)

Starve, to   To sail a boat so close to the wind that you starve her of that essential nourishment. She is then said to be 'starved'. Starving and Pinching are almost synonymous.

Station pointer   A pilotage instrument with three arms pivoted on a graduated disc. If the three arms can be aligned with three fixed and identifiable objects the pattern so formed can be transferred to the chart where the focal point of the arms must correspond with the position of the observer. I doubt if many private owners ever find a use for gadgets of this kind.

Stations   The yacht designer divides the hull length into a number of stations, each of which is in effect a plane or cross-section of the hull. From the owner's point of view, it is only necessary to get the point that when the designer refer to 'station number six', he simply means to draw your eye to the sixth station on the drawing aft of the stem. (Please see Lines for illustration.)

Stave   A stave is a stout pole, such as forms the main part of a boathook. A staff is somewhat less robust.

Stave in, to   To make a hole in a hull by knocking, or bursting, a plank inward. The past tense and participle is 'stove-in'.

Stave off, to   To fend off, as in normal speech.

Stay   Usually the forward and after mast supports (forestay, backstay), but not the lateral supports which are called the Shrouds. There is also the Bobstay, leading down from the bowsprit end to the cutwater. But the lateral stays are the 'bowsprit shrouds'.

Stay, to   To turn through the wind from one tack to the other. If a boat fails to stay she may get In irons.

Staysail   Please see Headsail.

Steaming light The white, forward-showing light carried by a powered vessel by night or in bad visibility. In the Collision Regulations this is called a 'Masthead Light' (though not required to be carried at the masthead) and it must show from dead ahead to 22.5 degrees abaft the beam on each side. A vessel of less than fifty metres length may show one such light: those longer must show another similar light farther aft and higher up. A boat under sail does not show a forward white light.

Steep-to A shore which slopes down steeply into and beneath the water is said to be 'steep-to'.

Steerage way A rudder has no effect in still water and no useful effect when a boat is moving very slowly. Steerage way is simply the speed at which any particular vessel becomes controllable in any particular circumstance. Steerage way will be a higher speed in rough water than in smooth, for example.

Steeve, to Some bowsprits are pivoted so that they can be cocked up to a more or less vertical angle. The sailor says 'steeved' or even 'steeved up', so take care not to cock it up.

Stem That lovely great hunk of oak that forms the forward extremity of the hull. In many modern boats of course, you don't get oak, you get a laminate of polyester resin and glass fibres, but it's still called the stem because there ain't no other word. (By the way, take care to distinguish between the stem and the Bows.) The lower part of the stem is the Cutwater, and the hull immediately adjacent to that is the Forefoot.

Stemhead *(fitting, roller, etc)* The stemhead is the top of the stem and is normally capped with a metal component which may serve more than one task, commonly to anchor the lower end of the Forestay, and to provide a Fairlead for the anchor cable. The fairlead may have two cheeks with a roller between, and it is more than likely that the cheeks will be too low, too flimsy, or sharp-edged, and that the roller will be about one-quarter the diameter it should be. (As you can see, I don;t think much of most stemhead fittings!)

Step (1) A fitting in which the heel of the mast is located. A mast is stepped when it is installed in the boat. Furthermore it may be stepped on deck (often in a Tabernacle) or it may pass through a hole in the deck to be stepped on the keel.

Step (2) A step-shaped break in the bottom line of a high-speed hull which allows the water flow to break away from the hull skin.

Step, to   Please see Step (1).

Stern   The extreme after part of a hull, embracing the Transom or Counter or, in a double-ender, the Stern post, which corresponds to the Stem at the other end. Please see the sketches.

Sterns

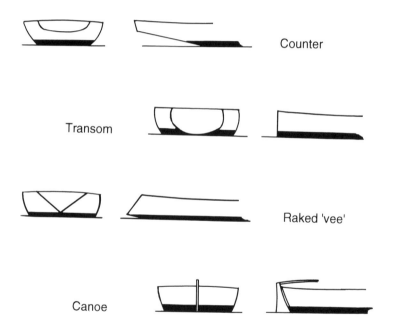

Stern board   When a sailing boat sails (or drifts) backward she makes a stern board. The manoeuvre is sometimes intentional, but whether intended or not, control can be maintained provided the helmsman appreciates that the rudder will now work in the opposite of its usual sense. (It will be worthwhile to see Board.)

Stern drive   A form of transmission between engine and propeller in which a horizontal shaft from the engine passes through the transom to bevel gears which turn a vertical shaft running down outside the hull to a point below the waterline. Here a further set of bevel gears achieves a second right-angle turn to rotate a more or less horizontal propeller shaft. This form of drive allows the engine to be sited well aft in the hull and (usually) allows the 'drive leg' with the lower gear housing and the propeller to swing clear out of the water for inspection or repair. Transom drive, and inboard-outboard are other names given to this arrangement but the commonly-used term 'Z-Drive' is the property of a single manufacturer.

Stern gland   A sleeve around the propeller shaft packed with compressible material so as to allow the shaft to turn without admitting water. The packing can be compressed by means of a large nut which also encompasses the shaft.

Stern light   A white light near the stern of a vessel showing from dead astern to 22.5 degrees abaft the beam on either side. Must be shown by both powered and sailing craft. The arc of the stern light is complementary to that of the Steaming light, the two together covering a complete circle.

Stern sheets   The volume in the extreme after part of an open boat – often the region beneath the tiller or beneath the after thwart.

Sterntube   A metal tube built into the deadwood at the stern of a hull (or embedded in a resinglass moulding) to form a duct through which the propeller shaft can run. The forward end of the sterntube usually embodies the watertight stern gland, and a bearing for the shaft may also be part of the assembly.

Stern way   Usage has it that a sailing boat makes a Stern board, which is usually a shortlived manoeuvre, whereas a powered vessel makes stern way, which usually implies a more deliberate and extended manoeuvre. Despite the foregoing, stern way is always the proper term for any movement astern. (See Stern board.)

Stiff A stiff boat is one which does not heel easily. (Please see Stability.)

Stock (1) The cross-bar of an anchor.

Stock (2) The upper part of a rudder to which the tiller is connected. The lower part is the Blade.

Stockless anchor Please see Anchor for a sketch, but don't bother to buy one unless you are buying a 500-ton millionaire's steam yacht. Such anchors are not effective at the sort of size that a private pleasure boat could carry, since they depend on great weight to make them hold. (And if you wonder why that should be, let me give you a clue: the area of an anchor increases as the square of its linear dimension, its weight as the cube. Small anchors have to apply their weight on the smallest possible area in order to penetrate – in a word they need to be sharply pointed.)

Stool Much the same as a low stool in shoreside life, its purpose is to support and steady a hull ashore. While a Shore is a strut from three to six feet long, say, a stool is usually not more than a couple of feet in height, and is made out of planks about two inches thick and a foot wide, forming an open box.

Stop, to (1) To set a sail 'In stops', it is furled up and tied around with stops of thin and feeble twine, rotten cotton, or rubber bands. The stops will break when the sheet is pulled and the wind begins to fill the sail. Such a sail is stopped.

Stop, to (2) To pack or pay a split or small hole with putty or some other form of Stopping.

Stopper (1) A rope bent on to (for example) an anchor chain to hold it temporarily. Might also be a rope bent on to another (Rolling Hitch) to take the load off it while you make some adjustment.

Stopper (2) A device that instantly holds a sheet fast. Known as lock-offs in the USA, these valuable gadgets usually take the form of a lever operated cam which squeezes and grips the rope. They are commonly used with sheets and halyards, allowing several different ropes to be hauled taut by just one winch.

Stopper knot Any bulky knot which serves the purpose of preventing the passage of a rope through a fairlead or a block, but a Figure-eight knot is the most common among Yachtsmen.

Stopping Putty-like compounds which are used to fill minor dents and cracks before painting.

Stopwater A wooden dowel inserted between mating pieces of timber to prevent the passage of water. Where two pieces mate, as in the scarf-joint between stempost and keel, a hole is bored across the joint so that half its diameter is in one of the parts and half its diameter in the other. If water enters, the dowel swells and so fills the bore tightly enough to prevent further penetration.

Storm In weather forecasting, implies weather worse than a gale. Let's not linger over such subjects. . .

Stormbound If you don't care to leave harbour because you are deterred by a Force 3 wind, you can tell your friends that you were 'stormbound', and hope that they think the conditions were simply impossible.

Storm cone Coastguard stations and some other authorities display black storm cones to warn that gale winds (not necessarily Storm winds) are expected. If the point of the cone is upward the gale is expected from the North: if the downward, then from the South.

Storm jib Please see Spitfire.

Stove in Part of a hull that is broken inward by a force from outside is said to have been stove in. (See Stave in.)

Stow, to In a boat things are stowed whereas at home they are 'put away'. If you want to compliment your wife in front of friends, tell them that she makes a 'jolly good stow'. Non-sailing friends might think you meant to say 'stew', but others will know the importance of a careful stow before setting forth on the rolling sea.

Strait A narrow sea passage between two lumps of land.

Strake The whole of one plank in a boat's hull. Even if it has been necessary to use more than one length of wood to stretch the length of the boat, the result is normally considered one strake.

Strand The ordinary rope that most of us use consists of three strands twisted together, and each strand consists of three yarns twisted together.

Stranded Run ashore, usually accidentally: 'strand' is no longer used for 'shore', except by poets.

Stream, to Usually of patent (Walker) log. You 'stream the log' when you put the rotator and line into the water. At the end of the passage you 'hand the log-line', which means that you pull them back on board. You could also stream a sea anchor, or any other object on a line astern.

Stream In British parlance the rise and fall of the tide gives rise to tidal streams. In the USA these are tidal currents. Take note that the British hydrographer reserves the word current for large-scale movements of oceanic water, such as the Gulf Stream . . . So what? The important thing is to take the stream (current) when it is favourable: it's the direction that counts, not the name.

Stretchers Transverse wooden battens in the bottom of a pulling boat against which the oarsmen can brace their feet.

Strike, to To lower some item or other – perhaps a burgee, a sail or a topmast. (See Send down.)

Stringers In wooden construction, fore-and-aft members running the length of the hull. Some may be quite light, others (e.g. bilge stringers), quite heavy. A moulded resinglass hull may have light wooden stringers bonded into the laminate for extra stiffness.

Strop A ring of rope, perhaps with an eye for a shackle, which is used to make an attachment to a spar, a barrel or some such.

Strum-box The strainer which any competent boat-builder fits over the intake end of the bilge pumping system. May actually be in the form of a metal box with perforated walls, but whatever its shape, its purpose is to keep shavings and other cloggers out of your bilge pump.

Styrene 'Fibreglass' boats are built of resin reinforced with glass, and the resin is commonly polyester dissolved in styrene. The styrene is a monomer which, with the help of a catalyst, links (polymerises) the chains of polyester molecules into a three-dimensional structure. This is the curing process. You need enough styrene but not too much, and any little that is left over gives rise to the typical smell of a 'fibreglass' boat. (At least, that's what I think.)

Suit of sails A boat is equipped with a suit of sails. All her sails may comprise more than one suit and collectively they are her 'sail wardrobe'. (But the place where the sails are stowed in their bags is the sail locker! And the owner keeps his shore-going suit in a 'hanging locker', not a wardrobe.)

Surface tissue A finely woven cloth of glass fibres which, when laminated with resin, will result in a relatively smooth finish.

Surge, to To pay out, or ease off, a rope a little at a time by letting it slip round a bollard or winch drum.

Survey A technical examination of a vessel's hull, rigging, or machinery to determine their condition and fitness for service. But a survey is not a valuation.

Swaged end The old way of making an eye in the end of a wire was to turn it back and splice it. A quicker and easier way is to swage the two parts of the wire together by clamping them in a sleeve of compressed metal. The die which forms and compresses the metal is itself a Swage.

Swallow The passage between the Shell of a block and its Sheave, through which the rope must render freely. (And see Breech.)

Swash *(or swatch)* A shallow area which does not uncover at low tide but whose presence makes itself known by disturbing the seas on the surface. Its presence may also be revealed by a swashmark, a line of bubbles, foam and debris on the surface of the sea that is roughly related to the area of the swash below.

Swashway *(or swatchway)* A navigable channel through a region of Swashes.

Sway, to Had a special meaning in the old sailing ships, but is used by yachtsmen for the lifting or lowering of stores, and so forth, with a rope. You may sway your kitbag from deck to quayside, for example. (See Fleet, to.)

Sweep A long oar, often of the kind used for steering or sculling over the stern.

Swell (1) A thickening of the Gunwale of a small boat (often by means of an extra bolster of wood) to provide strength for a Rowlock.

Swell (2) A long ponderous undulation of the sea, but whose waves do not break.

Swift, to To draw tight with a line or lanyard, usually with a transverse pull, as may be done with a line that holds a halyard away from the mast by hauling toward a shroud. If, for example, you have twin backstays you can tighten them both by swifting – that's to say by drawing them toward each other with a linking lanyard.

Swifter A noun, not an adjective. It is a rope used for swifting. I had thought the word obsolete till I came across it latterly in a piece of modern writing by the late Colonel H G Hasler relating to the junk rig. Long ago the word was particularly related to the rope linking each capstan bar to the next, so forming a complete ring. But the thing itself, the noun, and its associated verb, are useful for today's yachtsmen and seem worth preserving.

Swig, to   To swig on a rope is to make the end fast around a cleat, say, and gain slack by hauling laterally, then taking up what is gained.

Swing a compass, to   A compass which suffers deviation due to magnetic material in the boat can be checked by swinging. That means to hold the boat approximately at one point, but with her head at successive directions around the horizon. When the boat is brought to rest at each point the bearing of some fixed point ashore is read from the compass. Since any magnetic material in the boat will have been moved around the compass during this process the deviation it causes on each heading can be noted. These errors can be noted on a Deviation card or they may be plotted as a curve on graph paper.

Swing the lead, to   A slang term meaning to feign sickness so as to escape duty. A seaman who wants to take a sounding will Cast the lead, not swing it.

Swivel block   A block whose eye is free to swivel.

Swivel   *(or swivel link)*   A connector whose two parts can rotate in relation to each other. Would be inserted in a mooring chain, for example, to avoid an accumulation of twists over a period of months.

Syntactic foam   A lightweight filler consisting of resin mixed with microscopic glass bubbles. (see Microspheres.)

T

T (1) The single-letter signal means, *'Keep clear of me, I am engaged in pair trawling'*. This is an important signal for pleasure-craft skippers, and since the signal flag consists of red, white and blue in three vertical bands you might mistake it for the French ensign. The Morse code is one dash, but the above signal cannot be made by a single hoot because that means, 'I am altering my course to starboard'. Tango is the word for T in phonetic.

T (2) True. Please see North.

Tab (1)` Please see Servo rudder.

Tab (2) Please see sketch under Hank.

Tabernacle A metal or wooden structure, in the shape of an open box, which locates and supports a deck-stepped mast. A bolt passing through tabernacle and mast can provide a pivot point for lowering the stick. Although the tabernacle supports the downward thrust of the mast it should not suffer any of the wrenching or side loads, which are taken by Shrouds and Stays. (See Lutchet)

Tabling Those parts of a sail which are reinforced by doubling or trebling the thickness of the material and over sewing.

Tachometer An instrument for measuring the rate of revolution of the engine.

Tack (1) The lower, forward corner of a sail. May be hauled down tight by a Tackline or a Tack tackle. (See Clew and Head.)

Tack (2) Please see Tack, to

Tack, to When sailing close-hauled, to turn the boat's head through the wind so that the sails draw on the opposite side. When sailing with the wind coming from port, the boat is 'on the port tack', and, as you might guess, she is 'on starboard' when the wind comes from her starboard side. To make progress to windward by sailing first on one tack and then on the other is 'tacking' or 'Beating to windward'. Although tacking usually implies close-hauled sailing, it is sometimes desirable to 'tack down wind', turning slightly off the wind first to one side and then to the other. That may be faster than running directly down wind, and it may avert the risk of an accidental gybe. (please see Wear, to.)

Tackle   Naval types call it tay-ckle, perhaps to avoid confusion with fishing tackle. But however pronounced, it is an assembly of one or more blocks with one or more ropes to achieve a mechanical advantage. Tackles are rather fun and enjoy a variety of names for their many forms – the Spanish burton, the single whip, the gun tackle and the luff tackle, for example. Sadly, they are little used on modern craft and are to be seen mainly in mainsheets, kicking straps and tack downhauls.

Taffrail   The rail around the stern of a boat which may save you from falling overboard. Modern yachts do not have the elegant wooden rails of their forebears, but have tubular metal railings instead. These are quite sensibly called Pushpits.

Tail   A short rope attached to a block or anything else so that it can be bent on as convenient.

Take a turn, to   To pass a rope around a post or bollard. (See Snatch, to.)

Take off, to   Of tides. After the Spring tides the daily range diminishes and tides are said to be taking off. But note that unlike 'Making', one does not hear this term used of a single tide.

Take the ground, to   A boat takes the ground when the tide recedes and leaves here there. This is a gentler process than running aground which almost always implies and error, whereas taking the ground suggest that it was the skipper's intention – or at least his expectation.

Take up, to   A planked wooden boat may become so dry ashore that the planks shrink and allow water to leak between when she is put afloat. But as the wood swells she will 'take up', which simply means that her seams will close up.

Talurit   A patent form of Swaged splice for wire rope. Also the machine which enables you to tailor it . . .

Tang   A metal strip, bolted or riveted to a spar, to provide an attachment point for shrouds, stays and the like.

Telegraph buoy (beacon)   One that marks the position of a submarine cable. The point where a cable reaches the shore is marked by a 'telegraph cable landing beacon' which can be identified by its diamond-shaped, red and white topmark.

Tell-tales   Two kinds. One is the compass which the skipper mounts over his berth so that he can check what you are doing at the helm even when you think he is asleep. The other is a short length of cotton or tuft of wool which is attached to sail or shrouds to show the direction and steadiness of the air flow.

Tender (1)   Any small boat used to take people or stores out to a bigger one. Your inflatable dinghy, for example.

Tender (2)   An adjective this one, and it means the quality of heeling rather easily. It refers to a boat's initial Stability, rather than the ultimate. Nevertheless, excessive tenderness is the last thing you want in a tender.

Teredo   Or 'shipworm', is a mollusc that looks like a worm. At microscopic size it penetrates underwater timber and there spends the rest of its life, eating your boat away. Remaining within the thickness of the planking it can grow to a foot or more in length and as fat as your finger. The galleries made by teredo will destroy the structure of a wooden ship. . .but they do not abound in temperate waters. They can be held at bay by a sound coat of Anti-fouling paint, or by copper sheathing, and they die if the boat is removed from salt water for a fortnight or more.

Terminals   The fittings that form eyes or attachments in the ends of wire ropes. There is the swaged, or Talurit type of eye, and there are patent devices with screw-together bodies which clamp the end of the wire in some way. They ought to be called 'terminations', but even a bus station is called a terminal instead of a terminus nowadays. Standards are falling. . ..

Terylene™   Please see Polyester.

Thames measurement (or tonnage)   When an owner talks about his 'five tonner' he refers to a peculiar type of tonnage which has nothing to do with weight. More than a hundred years ago the Royal Thames Yacht Club adopted a formula for estimating the tonnage of yachts, and we still can't break free of it. The formula takes no account of weight, but relates entirely to length and beam, as follows:

$$\frac{(L-B)\times B\times \tfrac{1}{2}B}{94}$$

The measurements are taken in feet. Because beam acts twice as a multiplier, fat boats have disproportionately large tonnages. (Please see Displacement and Register tonnage.)

Thermal wind   A wind caused by differential heating, usually of sea and land. For example the sun heats the land more rapidly than the sea, the air rises over the land and a Sea breeze flows towards the shore to replace it. By night the land cools more quickly than the sea, and the result may be a Land breeze in the opposite direction.

Thimble   A metal or plastic eye that fits inside an eye formed in rope or wire rope to prevent chafe. A thimble may be round or pear-shaped.

Thixotropic   Thixotropic paints and resins are those which do not easily run when applied to a vertical surface, though they are quite easily brushed out or spread. Very convenient.

Thole pins   Wooden pegs or dowels shipped vertically in pairs in the gunwale so as to constrain an oar for rowing. Most people now use Rowlocks. (Sketched at Coble.)

Throat (1)   The space in a block where the rope passes through, but Swallow is the preferred term.

Throat (2)   The upper forward corner of a gaff sail.

Thumb cleat   A small cleat with only one horn. To some people it looks like half a cleat.

Thumb knot   The ordinary knot. You know, the one that you always called a knot from your earliest days.

Thumb knot

196

Thwart   The thwartships plank which forms a seat in an open boat. There may be several such, depending on the size of the boat, and in addition to their role as seats they may also be essential components of the boat's structure. Still, the main thing is to remember that the transverse seat in an open dinghy is called a thwart. Some dinghies also have seats to port and starboard for the helmsman and, sometimes, for the crew. These are called side benches, but I cannot think that is a specifically nautical term.

Tidal atlas   A handy little booklet compiled by hydrographers which shows the direction and speed of the tidal streams around the coast for each hour of the Flood and Ebb. There is a tidal atlas for each section of coast – see the Catalogue of Admiralty Charts. (See Tide tables.)

Tidal stream   The rise and fall of the water level in the great oceans naturally causes a flow out of or into narrower seas, such as the English channel, though some (like the Mediterranean) are so narrow and shallow at their entrances that the effect is very limited. The flow of a rising tide is called the Flood, and that of a falling tide is called the Ebb. If the tide starts to come in, one may say that it is 'Making', though the same term is used for the period of days between Neaps and Springs when tidal heights are growing greater. During the reverse process, after springs, tides are said to be 'Taking off'. Tidal streams are important to small craft because they commonly attain speeds of two or three knots, and in a four or five-knot boat there is a world of difference between two knots against you and two knots with you. Apart from its influence on one's speed of progress, the direction of the tidal stream is important in relation to the wind: 'wind against tide' tends to kick up a rough sea. (See Tidal atlas, and Height of tide.)

Tidal wave   The combined gravitational pulls of the sun and the moon draw up the earth's ocean into a hump, called a tidal wave. This wave moves across the water as the earth rotates, and though it is only a low lump (unnoticed by seafarers), its effect when it reaches the shallower waters near land is to create the to and fro surges which we call Tides. It may be worth mentioning that the expression 'tidal wave' is commonly mis-used for a phenomenon which should be called a 'Tsunami'.

Tide   Tides are one of the most important factors to be taken into account by the coasting skipper. It is the rise and fall of the level of the sea at regular intervals, corresponding to the phases of the moon. That is so because the moon's phases are an indication of her position in relation to the sun, and it is the combined gravitational attraction of those two bodies which raise the sea. The moon's monthly (28-day) cycle gives the tides a fortnightly cycle, the tides being greatest when the sun and moon are either on opposite sides of the earth or on the same side, and least when they are at a right angle. The greatest tidal Ranges are called

197

Spring tides, and arise at the new and full moon; the least are called Neaps and occur at the quarters. In between, tides are in between – obviously. The fortnightly cycle of tides is rather convenient to live with: if High tide is around midday this week-end then it will be around midday in a fortnight's time, but at morning and evening next week. The times of High and Low tides for each day of the year are shown in Tide tables, often free from chandler's shops, but also in Almanacs and suchlike, Also shown are the Heights. (Please see also Tidal stream.)

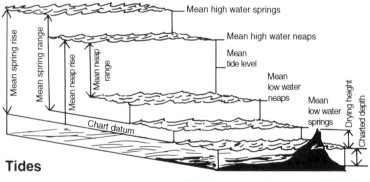

Tides

Chart datum = Lowest Astronomical Tide(LAT)

Tide gauge Usually takes the form of a post standing up in the water and marked in metres. It shows the current height of the water surface above chart datum, that is to say the depth which is at that time additional to soundings shown on your chart. To be absolutely correct, it shows the height of the tide. Be aware though, that it does not show directly the local depth of water; that is the function of the Depth gauge.

Tide rip A stretch of water where a fast-flowing Tidal stream creates turbulence, usually because the bottom shallows.

Tide-rode A boat lying at anchor is said to be tide-rode when her hull is laying primarily in the direction of the Tidal stream. Alternatively she may be Wind-rode.

Tide tables Tables showing times and heights of High water.

Tight Short for watertight. Used of a good hull which does not make water.

Tiller The lever or handle by which the rudder is turned. In some dinghies a tiller extension may be necessary for the helmsman who sits so far outboard that he cannot reach the tiller itself. In big heavy boats tiller lines rigged with tackles may be needed to augment the muscular power of the helmsman. Tiller lines without tackles may also be used to fix the helm in a chosen position.

Timbers The ribs of a hull are called Frames and timbers. Timbers are usually bent to shape, after steaming, while the heavier frames are usually sawn to shape or laminated.

Tingle A patch applied to a hull to stop a leak. Commonly a copper sheet nailed down over a piece of cloth which has been well coated with tallow, but the exact ingredients are likely to be a matter of improvisation.

TM Thames Measure (tonnage)

Toe-rail A low raised lip along the deck-edge. May be a Wale of wood, or a length of light alloy angle-section extrusion, or may be an integral part of the resinglass moulding.

Toe straps Lengths of webbing running fore and aft in a racing dinghy, and arranged so that the crew can hook their feet under them when Sitting the boat out. (And see Hiking straps)

Toggle An elongated wooden button. Found on the hoist of a signal flag or the front fastening of a duffle coat.

Tonnage The various kinds of tonnage are a great source of confusion. As far as private owners are concerned the three kinds that may matter are Displacement, Thames measurement, and Register tonnage. The matter is further confused, though by the racing classes who compete for Quarter, Half and One Ton Cups in craft whose design is closely controlled by lengthy and complex rating formulae which have nothing to do with tonnage in its ordinary sense.

Top hamper All the structure above the hull, notably deck-house, Dog-house, companion, rails, radar scanner and so forth. All such creates windage, tends against stability and generally hampers the boat in her efforts to cope with wind and sea.

Topmark A shape mounted on a beacon or a buoy to convey information. May be elaborate or primitive, and they vary from place to place and country to country, though important seaways conform to the conventions of the International Association of Lighthouse Authorities.

Topmast The true topmast, in the form of a separate spar which could be 'sent up' to extend the height of the lower mast, and struck and 'Housed' on the foreside of the lower when its weight and windage aloft would be an encumbrance, is now rare. There are still a good many gaffers around with longish pole masts, approximating to the total length of former mast-plus-topmast assemblies, and the upper part of such a long mast may by convention be called the 'topmast'.

Topsail As this is a practical dictionary, I don't think we need concern ourselves with square riggers, but on a Gaff-rigged boat such as any ordinary chap might own, the topsail sets above the mainsail and fills the triangle between gaff, mast and sky. It may do more if set on a Topsail-yard, a pole which extends higher than the mast and to which the luff of the topsail is laced. (See Jackyard.)

Topsides The sides of the hull between the waterline and the deck.

Topping lift A rope from the mast to the boom end which supports the boom and allows you to lift or lower it. (See Lift.)

Tosher A small open Cornish fishing boat noted for her good carrying capacity resulting from plenty of freeboard and firm bilges.

Track (1) The locus of the ship's progress over the face of the earth – the actual line along which she travels. Please see Course, as that will save space here.

Track (2) A channel or ridge, running from top to bottom on the after side of the mast, and in or on which the Slides on the luff of the sail can (you guessed it!) slide.

Trailboards   Carved decorative boards fitted to port and starboard of a hull, at Bows and Quarters (or both). Although a word not much used in day-to-day life, a trail is any design or pattern based upon trailing, intertwining tendrils, curlicues and the like. (See Quarter badge.)

Trailing board   A plank bearing rear lights, flashing indicators and the registration number of the towing vehicle, which is fitted to a dinghy being trailed on the road.

Trailing edge   The after edge of a sail, a keel or a rudder – or any other surface subject to fluid flow. Specifically used in relation to aerodynamics and hydrodynamics. Note that the trailing edge of a sail is at the Leech, while the leading edge is at the Luff.

Training wall   A sea wall or embankment built for the purpose of directing the current or stream in the required direction. For example at a river mouth where the water would naturally slow down and deposit silt, a training wall will constrain the water to move faster, and so carry its silt out towards the deep.

Trampoline   A net of rope or webbing filling the gap between the two hulls of a catamaran, usually forward.

Transferred position line   A fix is usually taken by crossing two Position lines observed within a few minutes of each other. But where a significant time must elapse between the observing of the two position lines, the first must be translated along the ship's track by the distance that she has travelled in the interval.

Transit   One takes a transit by sighting two objects in line. If the objects can be located on the chart, the observer is obviously somewhere on an extension of the line passing through them, and such knowledge is invaluable in pilotage. Furthermore, if the bearing of such a transit is observed with the compass, the reading can be compared with the magnetic bearing derived from the chart and any compass deviation can be deduced. A practical navigator will always be on the lookout for pairs of objects which provide good transits, and will frequently use them to check his compass.

Transom   In housebuilding and shipbuilding a transom may be simply a crossbeam, but in small craft the word refers specifically to the transverse after end of the hull, including any stiffening beams or structure. A hull may have a pointed stern, a cut-off transom stern, or an up-sloping and overhanging Counter which itself may end in a miniature 'transom' to which the name 'archboard' is properly given. There is an illustration under Stern.

Transom drive Another name for Stern drive.

Transom flap Rather like the cat-flap which lets the cat out through the kitchen door, a transom flap opens to allow water to escape from inside a planing dinghy.

Trapeze Used in sailing dinghies, is a length of wire attached to the mast near the head and ending in a sling-seat in which the devoted crew can support herself with legs braced against the gunwale, and with all weight out to windward.

Traveller A fitting which travels, literally but not far. For example one which attaches a sheet to a Horse. For another example, an iron ring which slides along a bowsprit so that you can attach the tack of the jib from the foredeck and then haul it outboard. A third example is a ring which travels up the mast of a lugger – the halyard is made fast to the ring and the yard of the lugsail is hooked beneath.

Traverse tables Not much used by the likes of me, these tables show the course and distance from point A, where you are, to point B, where you want to go. Points A & B are expressed in degrees of latitude and longitude. Alternatively, if you know where you started and how far and on what heading you have travelled, the tables will reveal where you are now. On the whole it's easier, more reliable and more satisfying to draw a line on your chart.

Treenail Please see Trunnel.

Triatic stay A fore-and-aft stay running between the heads of two masts.

Trice up, to Or to 'truss up', can be used in much the same way as a farmwife talks of trussing up a chicken. You can trice up almost anything with cord or rope, but in practice this old term lives on mainly in gaff-rigged boats which have loose-footed mainsails. Such craft will have a tricing line attached to the Tack of the sail, running through a block at the Gaff jaws, and down to the deck. The tack of the sail can thus be hauled up to reduce the sail area and spoil its shape so that the boat moves slowly. The sail is then half-way to being Scandalised.

Trick A period of duty at the helm or on watch. To 'take a trick at the helm' is altogether more U than 'steering for a bit'.

Tricolour lamp A lamp showing red in the proper port sector, green in the starboard sector, and white astern. The International Regulations for Preventing Collisions at Sea, 1972, permit sailing boats of less than 12 metres length to carry such a 'combined lantern' at the masthead.

Trim, to (1) To adjust the set of the sails to best advantage.

Trim, to (2) To adjust the sit of a boat in the water to the best advantage, usually so that she floats parallel to the designed waterline, though there may be times when it is desired to trim a boat by the head (bow down) or by the stern (bows up) for some special purpose. In a rowing boat, the request 'trim the boat' requires the passengers to shift their weight so that the boat will be level. The verb may also be intransitive, as they say at school, for the boat herself may be observed to 'trim by the head', for example.

Trim tab A small underwater plate fitted at the stern of a motor boat to act like the elevator of an aeroplane. Often mounted in pairs, trim tabs are usually required to lift the stern and so make the hull trim to a running angle which causes least drag in the water. Some trim tabs are at a fixed angle, others can be controlled by the helmsman.

Trimaran Although this word has been formed from catamaran, it is misleading if it suggests that because a catamaran is a two-hulled boat a trimaran is three-hulled. The trimaran, like the Proa, has a single hull which is too narrow to be stable without the assistance of a Sponson or an Outrigger. But whereas the proa has only one sponson, a trimaran has two. In most tris, only the leeward sponson is in contact with the water, the other being lifted clear by the slight heel of the boat.

Trimming ballast Please see Ballast.

Tripping line A line attached to the Crown of an anchor and leading up to the deck so that the anchor can be broken out of the ground. The tripping line may be seized to the Shank of the anchor by a flimsy bit of line to avoid accidental tripping, while a strong pull for intentional tripping will break the line and so apply the pull to the crown end of the anchor. A tripping line may lead to the deck, or to a freefloating anchor buoy. In the latter case a few feet of rope immediately beneath the buoy should be weighted so that it will hang straight down, clear of the propeller or rudder of any passing craft. If you have a fair idea of the relevantdepths, a simple scheme is to use a shorter tripping line, with its upper end seized to the anchor cable itself. The line should be short, but long enough to be above the water and at hand when the cable is hove short.

Trot A line of moorings, properly with riser-chains fixed to a common ground chain, though often used of any line of mooring buoys.

Truck   A circular wooden capping piece for the top of the mast. It keeps water from entering the end-grain, and its overhanging rim offers a suitable place for the fitting of a burgee-halyard sheave. Also an obsolescent name for a Parrel bead.

True wind   The wind with the direction and velocity as measured by a stationary observer (e.g. on an anchored vessel). By contrast, the Apparent wind is the wind observed from a moving vessel.

Trunk   A vertical passage open at top and bottom, such as the housing in which a dagger board slides up and down, or the broader passage which allows an outboard motor to do the same . An air duct to or from an engine compartment is likewise called a trunk, but only if it is relatively short and uncomplicated. Where it is long and tortuous the idiom will be to talk of 'trunking'.

Trunnel, treenail, or trenail   A nice rounded West-country man's way of saying treenail, which may also be pronounced as spelled, or as 'trennle'. Anyway, it is a wooden spike or nail, used for holding planks to timbers, and so forth. As a fastening it is not likely to be used in private pleasure craft, being better fitted to craft of bigger size where the Scantlings give sufficient thickness for a trunnel to get a grip.

Trysail   A small sail of heavy canvas, set on the mast in place of the mainsail and sheeted aft with powerful tackles. It is in fact a riding or steadying sail which dampens the rolling of the hull in gale or storm conditions.

TSDY   Twin Screw Diesel Yacht.

Tsunami   A series of extremely large waves caused by submarine earthquakes. They travel for thousands of miles and cause devastation when they reach an inhabited shore. Newspapers call them 'tidal waves', mistakenly. If tsunami does not roll off the tongue, you can quite correctly call them seismic sea waves.

Tuck in, to (1)   Where reef points, slab, or jiffy reefing are used, one speaks of 'tucking in a reef' or even 'taking a tuck'. 'It was blowing pretty hard, and we had a couple of tucks in', is the well-sounding way of saying that the first and second reefs had been made. Properly speaking, a reef is that actual area of canvas between two rows of reef points, and when that panel has been tucked in and tied down you have certainly 'taken in a reef'.

Tuck in, to (2)   A seaman also tucks in a splice, and uses that verb where 'make' would be the ordinary word.

Tuck The underwater part of the stern of a hull, corresponding to the Forefoot at the other end. At the tuck the sides, bottom and transom (if any) all merge neatly together.

Tumblehome An inward slope of the upper parts of a hull or cabin side. The opposite of Flare.

Turk's head An ornamental knot, used to make a stopper or handhold at a rope's end. Looks more like a turban or Turk's hat than his head.

Turnbuckle The same thing as a Rigging Screw, though the implication is of small size.

Turn end for end Please see End-for-end.

Turn in all standing, to A jolly expression for going to bed fully dressed and ready for all the pleasures of leaping out again at a moment's notice.

Turn of the bilge The part of the hull where the 'bottom' meets the 'side', and there is a general curving upwards. In fact it is that very part of the hull properly called the Bilge, a word which itself derives from 'bulge'.

Turn of the tide The period of slack water when the tide is about to flow the other way.

Turn to windward, to Turning to windward is what most people call tacking – but with the implication that the boat tacks repeatedly and makes progress to windward. Idiomatically, there is no such thing as one 'turn to windward' in the way one turns a boat's head to the wind. In short it is not the same as mere Luffing, but the process of getting to windward, first on one Board and then on the other. (Please see Beat, to.)

Turn turtle To turn completely upside down. Is used only of craft, whereas Capsize is used of a coil or rope, a fried egg or anything (or anyone) else.

TVO Tractor Vaporizing Oil. In former times was fuel used by some marine engines. Now extremely rare.

Tweaker A light line attached to a Sheet at some midpoint so that the lead or tension in the sheet may be adjusted more finely. The tweaker may be made of elastic cord in order to maintain a constant tension.

Twelfths rule Please see Rule of twelfths.

Twin keels This is a proper term to use for those (sailing) boats which have a pair of keels, but no central keel. Bilge keels are then reserved to those craft (sail or power) which have a main central keel and a subsidiary keel on either side of it. Usage does not in fact hold to this purist distinction.

Twisted shackle Deliberately so shaped, and not the result of straining, this type of shackle has the axis of the pin at a right angle to the plane of the bow. In most shackles they lie in the same plane.

Two blocks When two blocks of a tackle meet and no further movement is possible. (Same as Chock-a-block.)

Tyfon An acoustical beacon – all right then, a foghorn – operated by compressed air and emitting a medium pitched note rather similar to the Whistle of a steamer, so beware! (Compare with the Diaphone.)

U

U   The single-letter signal is one that every skipper should know because it may be of some importance to him. If U ••— is made to you by light, sound or flag, it means, 'You are running into danger'. But be careful not to confuse it with V, which is only one dot different. The phonetic for U is Uniform.

Una rig   The single-sailed type of rig used by the American cat-boat *Una* which aroused much enthusiasm (and copying) when she appeared at Cowes in 1854. Although that particular rig raised the Gaff by a single halyard and a complex system of blocks, the term Una rig is generally applied to the Cat-boat pattern, where the mast is stepped well forward and no jib is carried. (But not to the various kinds of lug which are used without a jib.)

Uncovered   In pilotage, a rock or other obstruction which is never covered by water at any state of the tide.

Under bare poles   With no sail set. (But understood to be making way due to the wind pressure on hull and rigging.)

Under command   Please see Not under command.

Underfoot   An anchor, a mooring buoy, or any other object is underfoot when it lies vertically beneath the vessel's Forefoot, whether it be at the surface, or on the bottom.

Under the lee   On the leeward side of . . . a headland, a harbour wall, a ship's hull or whatever.

Under-run, to   If you have a line out to a post and you work your boat along the line towards the post, then you under-run that line. The same expression applies even when the end of the line is being brought aboard and coiled on deck.

Under sail (power)   Too obvious to mention, you might think, but worth commenting that for the purpose of the Collision Regulations a vessel being propelled by both sail and power is regarded as under power, and subject to the relevant rules.

Undertow   The current which flows to seaward from a beach on which waves are breaking. The flow is below the water surface.

Under way Making way through the water. Often confused with Under weigh, which is a term specific to an anchor, meaning that the weight of the anchor is off the bottom and on the cable. The foredeck hand may call out that the anchor is 'under weigh', whereupon the helmsman may feel free to get the vessel under way (though slowly). The cause of confusion is pretty obvious.

Unwatched On charts, a light which is not continuously under human supervision, and could therefore be extinct for some time before being put to rights.

Up (Up-helm, etc.) A sailor's life is much influenced by wind and tide, and the terms Up and Down are much used in the sense of towards or away from wind or stream. Thus up-helm means that the tiller should be moved to the upwind side of the boat, which is usually topographically up as well, being towards the higher side of a heeled boat. Down-helm is evidently the opposite. To sail Higher, or to Point higher is to sail nearer to the wind, but 'Lower' is rarely used in this sense. (See Bear away, to.)

Up anchor An exhortation to get on and weigh the thing, or just a verb as in, 'We'll up anchor as soon as we've heard the early forecast'.

Up together, up port, up starboard Instruction to oarsmen, or by a wife to her husband, requiring oars to be pulled equally, or more strongly on one side than the other. When pulling out to the mooring, your wife in the sternsheets will earn more respect with such terms than such phrases as, 'Left a bit, Mortimer…'

V

V Signalled by any means, this one letter tells the world, 'I require assistance', Compare with W, and also note that this is not a signal of dire distress (as the letters NC would be). In Morse code V is ••• — and in phonetic, Victor.

Vane gear Automatic steering gear which holds the boat at a constant angle to the Apparent wind. The vane senses the wind direction and actuates the tiller so as to correct any deviation from the pre-set relationship between boat's head and wind direction. In some cases the vane acts directly on the tiller, in others it acts through a Servo rudder or tab. Both the latter are underwater surfaces which, when displaced to a small angle by the wind vane, apply the power of the water flow to the task of moving the tiller. There are many permutations of vane gear.

Vang A rope attached to the upper end of a Gaff or a Sprit so that it can be pulled towards the centreline of the boat to reduce twist in the sail. By analogy, a fore-guy which is rigged to prevent a boom swinging aft when running, with a danger of a gybe, may also be called a boom-vang.

Variable pitcher propeller A propeller the pitch of whose blades can be controlled while under way. That much is fairly obvious, but more careful observation reveals that most VP props are also reversible, with the range of pitch extending from coarse ahead to coarse astern. An extension of the idea is the VP prop which also feathers, in that the blade pitch goes beyond any usefully propulsive angle to the point where the blades are edge-on to the water flow and the drag while sailing is minimised. The conventional VP and reversing prop turns always in the same direction, requires no reverse gearbox, and should permit fine control of thrust by varying blade pitch without changing the throttle setting.

Variation (magnetic) Charts are drawn with North towards the earth's geographical north pole, but the Magnetic pole is not in the same place. Thus over most of the world's surface a compass needle will point to east or west of the true pole, and the angular difference between that heading and true north is called the variation. Furthermore, the magnetic poles (North and South) do not remain in the same spots, but move slowly at a predictable rate. Fortunately the variation, and the yearly rate of change, is shown on charts, and there is no more difficulty in allowing for the difference between 'magnetic' and 'true' than there is in allowing for a watch which reads fast or slow. So don't allow the 'experts' to frighten you, nor to obliterate common sense with mumbo-jumbo. Just look and see what it says on the chart. (See Deviation.)

Vector A vector is, for our purposes, a line drawn on a chart. Its length is proportionate to a distance travelled and its direction on the chart corresponds to the actual direction of movement. A vector diagram combines two such lines, for example the southward movement of a vessel over the sea, and the simultaneous eastward movement of the sea itself, to produce a resultant.

Vee-bottom A form of hull the two halves of whose bottom meet at the keel in a shallow V. Most such hulls are in fact what is more commonly called Hard chine, as in Sharpies.

Veer, to (1) To pay out a rope or cable – especially of anchor chain.

Veer, to (2) The wind veers when it shifts in a clockwise direction – for example it veers from south to west. Conversely, it Backs when it shifts anti-clockwise, from west to south, say.

Ventimeter Actually a trade name for a neat, effective and economical anemometer. But the word is so handy that, like 'Hoover', it tends to be used of any inexpensive instrument for measuring wind speed.

Very light Named after the inventor, Very, this is a flare which is projected to a goodly height from a special pistol.

Vessel It may matter to you to know that under the Collision Regulations a 'vessel' is defined as 'every description of water craft, including non-displacement craft and seaplanes, used, or capable of being used as a means of transportation on water'. It therefore includes a water-ski, the dinghy you tow astern, a surf-board, and presumably an inflated rubber ring. Whether that should be borne in mind or ignored as nonsensical when interpreting other rules about the conduct of 'vessels' and the lights or shapes they are supposed to exhibit, I leave to you.

VHF Very high frequency radio transmissions, used mainly for radiotelephony, and effective over moderate ranges only – up to about 50 miles.

Vigia A warning on a chart to be vigilant for a possible danger, not exactly specified nor even certain to exist. Reported potential dangers, which may or may not exist and whose position is doubtful, are themselves called vigia.

Vmg Velocity made good to windward. In trying to make to windward the helmsman must achieve the best balance between speed through the water and direction of motion. He may point higher, but at the cost of some loss in speed. He may sail faster, but farther off the wind. The best compromise results in the best Vmg.

V over root L For an explanation of this arcane expression please see Drag.

W

W   As a single-letter the signal means, *'I require medical assistance'*, and could therefore be one worth committing to memory. The Morse code •— — may be made by any means, which in practice implies either light or sound. In the phonetic alphabet the word is whiskey, which is one of the better kinds of medical assistance.

Waist   The middle part of a boat, and oddly enough the region where (like mine) her beam is greatest. (But old ships often had high forecastles and high poop decks, so the middle looked waisted when viewed from the side.)

Wake   The turbulent or smooth water left astern of a moving boat. The wake reveals the actual track of the vessel through the water, and if the line of the wake makes an angle with the centreline of the hull, then that is the angle of Leeway.

Wale   A strake, strip or plank which stands proud of the rest of the hull. The gunwale is properly a finishing strake above all the others in a hull, but the term is used for the upper edge of any hull, whether planked or not. An Inwale is a separate stringer running fore and aft on the inside of the upper edge of the hull. (Incidentally, the word itself is of the same origin as 'weal', a raised ridge on the flesh. Also incidentally, notice how often gunwale is mis-spelled 'whale'.)

Wall knot   A knot which makes a useful 'knob' on a rope. It has the advantage that it can be made at the end of a rope (as a handhold, say) or in the middle of a length of rope. But for that latter, the rope must first be unlaid as far as the knot, and then laid up again after the knot is made. It is in the same family of knots as the Matthew Walker.

Wangle, to   A verb which I (and other people of discernment) like to use for the process of sculling over the stern with a single oar or a Yuloh. Most people call it 'sculling', but that term is equally used of two oars used abeam.

Wardrobe   The complete tally of a boat's sails are called her wardrobe, in the manner of clothes in 'my lady's wardrobe.' (See Suit.)

Warp, to   To move a vessel by hauling on ropes.

Warp A rope normally used for mooring the vessel to a quayside or other fixed point, and stout enough for that purpose. Some people talk of an 'anchor warp', but the idiom is more commonly 'Cable' when an anchor is concerned, even though the rope could be of the same kind and size (even the very same rope itself) as would be used on another occasion to moor to the shore.

Wash The turbulent Wake left by a moving hull. Wake causes no appreciable disturbance, but wash upsets teacups.

Washboard A removable board which can be fitted across any opening to keep water out. Commonly a companionway or cabin entrance is closed by several washboards, fitted one above the other, and lodging in vertical channels in the portals.

Watch Either a period on duty, or a detachment of rew members acting as a unit for watchkeeping purposes. Thus one watch (detachment) may take the first watch (first tour of duty), while another watch is off duty and enjoying the 'watch below'. Although ships normally keep watches of four hours (though with two two-hour dog watches in each 24 to break the diurnal repetition of the same watches!) family crews on small craft usually make their own special routines. (See Dog watches.)

Watch tackle Another name for a Luff tackle.

Watching Used almost always of buoys, it means that it is visible above the water – that's to say doing the job for which it exists. A waterlogged buoy, only just visible, is said to be 'only just watching'.

Waterline The line traced by the water level around the sides of a floating hull, or a drawing of the same outline. The length on the waterline (LWL) is the straight line length from stem to stern in the plane of the waterline, also called the Waterplane. The actual waterline of a vessel may be higher or lower than the designed waterline (DWL) to the extent that she is heavier or lighter than the designer intended. For the purpose of design, the hull is deemed to be sliced fore and aft in planes parallel to the real waterplane, but above and below, and the outlines of these sections are also known as 'waterlines' to naval architects. They are in effect the waterlines that would occur if the boat were loaded much above or below the normal – assuming she did not sink or capsize. There is a diagram under Lines.

Watermanship The art and practice of handling small open craft, such as a rowing boat, in relatively sheltered water.

Watersail   An extra sail set low down – for example beneath the main boom when running in very light wind.

Waterways   Channels or grooves around a cockpit, say, or under the lid of a cockpit locker, whose purpose is to drain water off in the same manner that the gutters of a house carry rain water away.

Wave   Whereas a landsman would say that a big 'wave' struck the ship, a seaman would commonly call it a 'sea'. On the other hand, a seaman speaking or writing technically about the length, height and periodicity of these surface disturbances will use the word 'wave'. 'Sea' and 'seas' are the words used for direct personal experiences when the speaker might actually have got wet.

Way   Movement through the water. A boat 'makes way' when she moves, either ahead or astern. She is 'under way' when actually moving, and then she is said to 'have way on'. If she has a lot of way on, the implication is one of considerable momentum and potential danger. (Incidentally, an anchor is often Weighed when a vessel is about to get under way, but the vessel herself is never 'under weigh'.)

Way enough (way 'nough)   Mainly used as an order to cease rowing and let the boat carry on under her own way, the expression is also used with the same meaning as 'that's enough' in ordinary parlance, whether the listener is hauling a halyard, or pouring Scotch into your glass.

Waypoint   A position which a navigator postulates to suit his own convenience. It may be an actual geographical feature, or just an arbitrary point on the surface of the sea, for which a course may be laid. The recourse to waypoints has become more general since the introduction of Decca and GPS, since you have to give the things an objective, such as one mile off your intended harbour, for example.

Ways   Rails or tracks of wood or metal down which a vessel is launched. Note that a slipway, or slip, is more like a road sloping down into the water. Such a slip could have ways recessed in its surface, like tramlines in a city street.

Wear, to (1)   To turn a sailing craft from one tack to the other by turning down-wind – or to Gybe if the craft is rigged fore and aft. Pronounced 'ware', so that you may say, 'ware heads, I'm going to wear ship', instead of the shorter 'gybe-oh!'.

Wear, to (2)   Craft wear their flags and burgees. People, on the other hand, 'fly' their club burgees and house flags. In other words, when you are flying your burgee your ship is wearing it.

Weather, to   To pass on the windward side of any obstacle, object or craft. As far as I know there is no verb for passing to leeward of an object. One covers such events by a negative statement, as 'She won't be able to weather it', or 'We failed to weather the buoy, and a few minutes later we were on the putty'. Such statements imply an unaccomplished desire to weather the mark. Where the intention was to pass to leeward one might say 'We left the buoy to weather', or, 'We passed to leeward of the buoy'.

Weather   As an adjective, as in 'weather side', 'weather shore', it is to the side (or shore) from which the wind is blowing. 'Going to weather' is going to windward, perhaps of the tide or of a boat herself. (See Lee.)

Weather cloth   A canvas (or similar) screen erected to protect the crew from wind and spray. The 'dodgers' fitted at each side of a cockpit are the most common form of weather cloth.

Weathercock, to   The tendency of a boat to turn head-to-wind. Mainly used of a boat at anchor, or moving under power, and not used of the Griping or Luffing tendency of a sailing boat on the wind.

Weather helm   A sailing boat which requires the tiller to be held Up towards the weather side of the boat is said to 'carry weather helm'. The weather helm is required to resist the yacht's natural tendency to luff, or turn into the wind. This tendency is common to most single-hulled sailing craft and results from the fact that when the boat is heeled, the thrust of the sails acts well to leeward of the drag of the hull, resulting in a rotating couple. Some boats carry Lee helm in light winds, when they are sailing almost upright – that's to say the helm has to be held Down towards the leeward side to prevent the boat's turning away from the wind. Although quite acceptable in light winds, lee helm is undesirable if it persists in fresher breezes. Weather helm then has the benefit that the boat's natural tendency in a gust is to turn head to wind, and so relieve the heeling (and possibly capsizing) pressure of the wind on her sails. (Please see Balance.)

Weatherly   Describes a boat which can sail close to the wind – i.e. which makes good progress 'to Weather'.

Weep, to   To leak slightly or slowly, in a mere trickle or a drop at a time. The result is 'a weep'. A weep may flow inward, as through a Stern gland, or outward when rain water from the deck finds its way out through a topsides seam. Rust marks may result, and will be termed Weeps.

Weigh anchor, to   To break out the anchor from the sea bed and lift it clear of the bottom. (Might be as well to see Way.)

Well (1) A small cockpit set in an area of deck. Most modern yachts have broad cockpits and relatively small side decks – or even none at all. The other extreme is a large area of deck and a small well – perhaps only big enough to accommodate the legs and feet of the crew who actually sit on the deck itself.

Well (2) A hollow trunk in the after end of a small boat through which an outboard motor may be shipped. The sides of the well rise well above the waterline, and the lower end is open. When the boat is stationary exhaust fumes from the running motor may rise up in the well and suffocate the engine by displacing air it needs. Sea water may also slop up the well in bumpy weather. For both those reasons it is a good idea to fit a baffle plate around the outboard leg so as to blank off most of the opening when the engine is in place.

Well (3) Or 'well, that', in naval parlance means 'enough'. In other words stop hauling, or winching...

Westing Distance made good to westward. 'Easting, northing and southing' correspond.

Wet and dry 'Sandpaper' whose abrasive particles are bonded with waterproof glue, so that it can be used for rubbing down surfaces which are kept wet, so as to wash away grit and dust.

Wet exhaust Unlike that of a motor car, the exhaust from a boat's engine is rarely exposed to a flow of air, and is best cooled. The common way of doing that is to inject into the stream of gases some, or all, of the water which has already circulated through the cooling galleries of the cylinder block. The presence, or absence, of water at the exhaust outlet provides a primary check on the working of the whole engine-cooling system.

Wetsuit Clothing which fits the body like a second skin, and which absorbs water. Held immobile, the water provides a degree of thermal insulation for the wearer.

Wetted surface The total underwater area of a boat. Part of the Drag of a hull results from the friction of the water ('skin friction'), and the greater the wetted surface the greater that component of the total drag. Aerodynamicists also use the term of surfaces exposed to air friction, and it may be used in that sense in yacht design too, though Windage is the nautical term for the totality of air drag.

Whaler A clinker-built pulling or sailing boat, with relatively narrow double-ended hull and centreboard. Usually about 27 feet long.

Wheel effect   The sideways push of a rotating propeller, especially noticeable when it first begins to turn or when its speed increases. If the propeller is 'right-handed' (turning clockwise when viewed from astern) it will tend to take the stern to the right (starboard). The same propeller when running in reverse will tend to take the stern to port. The effect is as if the propeller were a wheel, though with a very poor grip, and it is easy to picture the direction in which the wheel would run.

Wheelhouse   A permanent and fully enclosed steering position with windows above deck level. A wheelshelter is either less permanent – of canvas, for example – or not fully enclosed – like a locomotive cab, say. A sort of half-way house … and see House, by the bye.

Whelps   Raised ribs on the barrel of a winch or capstan, or raised strips along the after end of a boom. On a winch barrel their function is to grip, but on a boom their function is to increase the diameter locally for better roll-reefing. The greater diameter takes up more cloth in the after part of the sail and so prevents boom-droop.

Whip, to   To bind the yarns of a rope's end so that they will not fray. Hence Whipping.

Whip (or single whip)   A tackle using one moving block, and given a two-to-one purchase.

Whipstaff   A type of tiller which stands more or less vertically, turning about a more or less horizontal axis. Whereas the conventional tiller sweeps a large area of the cockpit, a whipstaff springing from the region of the cockpit sole is much less obtrusive. But there are mechanical complications in transmitting the motion to a vertically-pivoted rudder.

Whisker   A strut or spreader extending from the stem to widen the angle of a bowsprit shroud. Usually in pairs, of course.

Whisker pole   A light spar used to hold the clew of a headsail outboard when running.

Whistle   The technical name for a ship's hooter or siren, which gives forth a deep resonant note.

Whistle-buoy   A navigational buoy which hoots or honks or booms, or groans, or moans. Actuated either by a gas bottle or by the pumping action as the buoy rises and falls with the seas.

216

White ensign   The white flag with a red cross and the Union Flag in the upper corner by the Hoist which is worn by ships of the Royal Navy, and by members of a club called the Royal Yacht Squadron.

White horses   The gleaming white crests of just-breaking waves in the open sea

White squall   Please see Squall

Wimple   A long masthead pennant, or streamer, of the kind that is flown by Dutch flat-bottoms.

Winch   A difficult one, this, because it is not possible to make absolutely precise distinctions between a Capstan, a Windlass and a winch. But capstans are normally big, and are found on ships' decks or on quays. Their barrels normally turn about vertical axis. A windlass may turn on either a vertical or a horizontal axes, but on yachts and pleasure craft the axis is usually horizontal, and a windlass has a chain Gipsy because its purpose is to bring home the anchor cable. A winch, though, does not have a Gipsy and its drum is used only for ropes such as halyards, sheets and mooring warps. The axis of a winch may be vertical or horizontal. In practical terms, a yacht could commonly have one anchor windlass, one or more halyard winches, and a couple of sheet winches. If she has a centreboard or leeboards, she may lift them with winches.

Wind gradient   The difference in wind speed close to the sea surface and at some height above it. The gradient is most noticeable on rivers, where the nearness of the land with all its slowing objects such as bushes and trees has maximum effect. Note that this is not the same as a Gradient wind.

Wind-rode   A boat is wind-rode when she lies at anchor with head to wind. If the effect of the tidal stream is stronger, she will lie Tide-rode. In the same anchorage and at the same time some craft will be wind-rode and others tide-rode, depending on their relative proportions of Wetted area and Windage.

Windsail   A canvas chute or funnel which is rigged above decks in hot weather so as to catch any available breeze and deliver it down through a hatch to the accommodation below.

Wind shadow   Will be the wind shadow of a sail, a building, or a cliff, and is the region to leeward where the wind speed is sensibly diminished because of the interference of that object. (See also Dirty wind.)

Windage Either the wind drag itself, or the extent of the drag-creating parts of a craft which are exposed to the wind, as in, 'She's got a lot of windage', meaning that she has a high superstructure (See Top hamper.)

Windlass Please see Winch.

Windward Toward the point from which the wind is coming. The opposite of Leeward.

Wing-and-wing Running downwind with two sails extending on opposite sides of the boat. Also Goose-winged.

Wishbone A double spar in the form of a flattened ellipse with a sail lying between the two parts. As each part has an aerofoil curve, and the canvas lies against each in turn as the boat tacks, the sail can adapt to a better shape than is possible with a straight gaff or boom. The one thing to be noted about a wishbone spar is that its shape is in no way reminiscent of a chicken's wishbone.

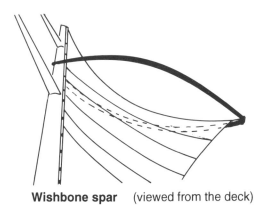

Wishbone spar   (viewed from the deck)

Work, to A hull 'works' when parts move in relation to each other. Leaks commonly result.

Work the tide, to To plan a passage so as to get the best advantage of any tidal stream towards the desired destination.

218

Working sails The sails that are carried in winds of about Force 3 to 4. There's nothing very precise about this term, but it excludes heavy-weather sails on the one hand, and light-weather sails on the other.

Worm, to To fill the spiral grooves between the yarns of a rope by winding twine around. This levels the surface, which may then be Parcelled with canvas before Serving, or may be served directly.

Worm For Shipworm please see Teredo.

Woven rovings Please see Rovings

Wrecks Abandoned craft, either adrift or cast up on the shore are technically wrecks. In the United Kingdom any person recovering such craft or parts of them or their gear or cargo, must declare his salvage to the Receiver of Wrecks who may be contacted through the nearest harbourmaster.

Wring, to If you have wrung out a wet pair of socks by twisting them, you will get the point. Of hulls in particular, mariners saying 'wring' where a landsman would say 'twist'. Thus the heeling moment of a mast when sailing closehauled can impose a high wringing stress on the hull. A hull which has been distorted by twisting is said to be 'wrung'. (See also Hogged.)

Wung-out A sail which is freed off until it is effectively at a right angle to the line of the boat is said to wung-out. (It should, grammatically, be 'winged-out', but long ago someone found it easier and jollier to say 'wung' presumably by association with fling, flung.)

WT Wireless Telegraphy.

Wykeham Martin gear A simple roller furling device for jibs which was introduced in about 1907. The jib has a wire luff which is shackled to a ball-bearing swivel on the halyard. The tack is shackled to a drum rotating on ball bearings, and the drum is turned by a length of line which leads to the cockpit. Because the wire luff cannot transmit any useful degree of torque, the system cannot be used for reefing.

X

X The single letter, which may be signalled by any means, conveys the message, *'Stop carrying out your intentions and watch for my signals'*. In phonetic it is called X-ray, and in Morse it is —••—.

Xebec At this point the author of a nautical dictionary is expected to drag in an obsolescent Mediterranean lateen-rigged craft called the xebec. He may have overlooked the umiak, the caique, the tjalk, the sambuk, and yole and even the schokker. Yet, though his readers have no concern with xebecs, the word has to go in under X, or reviewers will quickly pound on such a glaring omission.

Y

Y Means *'I am dragging my anchor'*, and that could be very significant if you yourself should be lying astern of a large vessel making Y. The phonetic is Yankee and the Morse —•— —.

Yacht, yachtsman, and so forth Here we have the most difficult word of all. It is broadly correct to call almost any pleasure or sporting craft a 'yacht', but convention expects a certain status or size of any craft so named. A sailing dinghy is not a yacht because she is too light and flighty, yet an open ballasted-keel boat of no greater size earns the title of yacht by her sobriety. A small fast motor cruiser is not a yacht, but a big fast motor cruiser probably is, and a big slow motor cruiser certainly is. Sailing boats with cabins are all yachts, provided they are used for what we call pleasure, hell though it often is. People who own, skipper or crew on pleasure craft propelled by sail are all called 'yachtsmen', even though they may sail dinghies which are not yachts. The people concerned with power craft, however, become yachtsmen only when the craft themselves are staid enough to become motor yachts. Boats propelled by oars or paddles ain't yachts, nor are the people in them known as yachtsmen. To make even more confusion, there are local and regional usages: in some places yacht is any boat with a sail, a 'cruiser' is any powered craft with a cabin, and a motor boat is a powered craft which is open. Probably none of this matters very much. The only really important thing is never to call your own boat a yacht. An owner who talks about 'my yacht' marks himself as a bounder, a braggart, a parvenu or just a pedant . . . but certainly not as a yachtsman. A yachtsman always owns a boat.

Yankee A big jib with a high Clew – that's to say with the foot running upward and not holding low down to the rail.

Yard (1) A spar setting across a mast and normally used to support a sail. A Gaff, which terminates at the mast, is not called a yard, but the spar which forms the head of a Gunter sail is more often called a yard than a gaff, even though no part of it should cross the mast.

Yard (2) The ordinary term for a boatyard – that's to say a place where boats are built, repaired or stored . . . provided that it stands by the water. Inland boatbuilding factories are never called 'yards'.

Yarn Threads or filaments become yarn when twisted or spun together. The yarn may then be used in that state, or several yarns may be twisted together to make a Strand.

Yaw, to A boat yaws whenever she turns to left or right. A hull may have an inbuilt tendency to yaw one way or the other, and a towed dinghy may yaw repeatedly, first to one side and then to the other.

Yaw A hull in the water has six principal degrees of freedom – i.e. six main ways in which it can move. It can Roll from side to side. It can Pitch, see-saw fashion. It can Yaw, turning left to right. And it can Heave, rise or fall vertically. It can also make leeway or drift sideways, and it can Scend, accelerate or decelerate in the fore-and-aft line. Furthermore, it can do several of these things at once.

Yawl A two-masted vessel whose after mast (mizzen) is stepped well aft (as sketched under Rig.). It used to be said that a yawl's mizzen must be stepped aft of the rudder post, but that no longer applies, as you may see if you will kindly turn to Ketch. The main merit of the yawl is that in heavy weather it permits the setting of a riding sail right aft, helping to keep the boat head to wind and sea. This is especially valuable if you want to ride to a sea anchor.

YBDSA Yacht Brokers, Designers and Surveyors Association.

Yoke A cross-member on the head of a rudder, from the ends of which lines may be taken for steering. This device is used on rowing boats and on some motor boats.

Yuloh The Chinese name for a long oar specially designed for sculling over the stern. It is not the same as the long oar which is called a Sweep in English, since its shaft is either curved or cranked, and may also be slightly flexible. These special features allow the blade of the Yuloh to twist on each stroke so as to bite the water. The inboard end of a Yuloh is held down by a rope strop which supports both the weight of the long outboard part and also the thrust of the blade.

Z

Z As signal it means, *'I require a tug'*. But when shown by a fishing vessel (which you will recognise by her lights or shapes), it means, *'I am shooting my nets'*. In Morse code the signal is – –•• and in phonetic the word is Zulu.

Z-drive Trade name of a particular brand of Stern drive.

Zenith In navigation, the point in the celestial sphere which is directly above the observer – i.e. the extension of a line joining yourself to the centre of the earth.

Zulu One last indulgence, dear reader, before we say farewell, for there's nothing practical for you or me in those handsome old Scottish fishing luggers called Zulus. Double-ended, two-masted, with a long bowsprit and an equally long Bumkin (to sheet the after lugsail). The Zulu design originated in 1879, and the name is said to have been inspired by the Zulu war which was then in the news. The only Zulu you are likely to see nowadays will be a model in a museum – more's the pity.

Adieu

Books from Waterline

Hand, Reef and Steer by Tom Cunliffe
Traditional seamanship for classic boats.
Publication January '92
ISBN 1 85310 309 8

Going About Cruising by Andrew Simpson
An introduction to cruising for consenting adults.
Publication January '92
ISBN 1 85310 293 8

The *Tips from the Top* series

Quarrie on Racing by Stuart Quarrie
Tactics, navigation, sail-trim and crew work explained by one of Britain's top
international racing yachtsmen.
ISBN 1 85310 300 4

Chisnell on Instrument Techniques by Mark Chisnell
How to put all the instruments on a modern boat to their best use.
Publication January '92
ISBN 1 85310 311 X

Cunliffe on Cruising by Tom Cunliffe
Really practical tips to help the cruising yachtsman.
ISBN 1 85310 301 2

Write for a complete catalogue of Waterline Books to
101 Longden Road, Shrewsbury, SY3 9EB, England